THE ARCHAEOLOGY OF THE DEAD

Lectures in Archaeothanatology

STUDIES IN FUNERARY ARCHAEOLOGY

Vol. 1 *Social Archaeology of Funerary Remains*
Edited by Rebecca Gowland and Christopher Knüsel

Vol. 2 *Deviant Burial in the Archaeological Record*
Edited by Eileen M. Murphy

Vol. 3 *The Archaeology of the Dead*
Henri Duday

Vol. 4 *Burial in Later Anglo-Saxon England c. 650–1100 AD*
Edited by Jo Buckberry and Annia Cherryson

Vol. 5 *Living through the Dead: Burial and Commemoration in the Classical World*
Edited by Maureen Carroll and Jane Rempel

Vol. 6 *Living with the Dead: Ancestor Worship and Mortuary Ritual in Ancient Egypt*
Nicola Harrington

Vol. 7 *Death and Changing Rituals*
Edited by J. Rasmus Brandt, Marina Prusac and Håkon Roland

Vol. 8 *The Archaeology of Cremation*
Edited by Tim Thompson

Vol. 9 *Death Embodied*
Edited by Zoë L. Devlin and Emma-Jayne Graham

Vol. 10 *Life and Death in Asia Minor in Hellenistic, Roman and Byzantine Times*
Edited by J. Rasmus Brandt, Erika Hagelberg, Gro Bjørnstad and Sven Ahrens

Vol. 11 *Burial and Social Change in First Millennium BC Italy*
Edited by Annia Cherryson and Jo Buckberry

Vol. 12 *Death as a Process*
Edited by Jake Weekes and John Pearce

Vol. 13 *Engaging with the Dead*
Edited by Jennie Bradbury and Chris Scarre

Vol. 14 *Grave Disturbances*
Edited by Edeltraud Aspöck, Alison Klevnäs & Nils Müller-Scheeße

THE ARCHAEOLOGY OF THE DEAD

Lectures in Archaeothanatology

Henri Duday

Translated by Anna Maria Cipriani and John Pearce

OXBOW | books
Oxford & Philadelphia

First published in 2009. Reprinted in 2011, 2014 and 2020 in the United Kingdom by
OXBOW BOOKS
The Old Music Hall, 106–108 Cowley Road, Oxford OX4 1JE

and in the United States by
OXBOW BOOKS
1950 Lawrence Road, Havertown, PA 19083

© Henri Duday, Anna Maria Cipriani and John Pearce, 2009

Paperback Edition: ISBN 978-1-84217-356-5
Digital Edition: ISBN 978-1-78297-340-9

A CIP record for this book is available from the British Library

Library of Congress Cataloging-in-Publication Data

Duday, H.
  [Lezioni di archeotanatologia. English]
  The archaeology of the dead : lectures in archaeolthanatology / Henri Duday ; translated by Anna Maria Cipriani.
     p. cm.
  Based on an intensive specialist course in burial archaeology given by the author in Rome Oct. 18 to Nov. 6, 2004.
  Includes bibliographical references.
  ISBN 978-1-84217-356-5
  1. Funeral rites and ceremonies--Rome. 2. Human remains (Archaeology) 3. Human skeleton--Analysis. 4. Rome--Social life and customs. 5. Thanatology. I. Title.
  DG103.D7813 2009
  393.0937--dc22
                              2009040889

All rights reserved. No part of this book may be reproduced or transmitted in any form or by any means, electronic or mechanical including photocopying, recording or by any information storage and retrieval system, without permission from the publisher in writing.

For a complete list of Oxbow titles, please contact:

UNITED KINGDOM	UNITED STATES OF AMERICA
Oxbow Books	Oxbow Books
Telephone (01865) 241249	Telephone (610) 853-9131, Fax (610) 853-9146
Email: oxbow@oxbowbooks.com	Email: queries@casemateacademic.com
www.oxbowbooks.com	www.casemateacademic.com/oxbow

Oxbow Books is part of the Casemate Group

Front cover: La Caouna de Moux (Aude, France), collective burial in a cave, Eneolithic.

Back cover: Tomas Mondragón, The mirror which does not deceive, Pinacoteca of the church of La Profesa, Mexico City. Photograph by Oscar Ramirez Otero.

Contents

Preface *Paola Catalano and Stéphane Verger* vii
Note on the Author and the Text x

Introduction 1

1. Preliminary discussion 3
   1.1. Funerary archaeology and corpse taphonomy 7
   1.2. Different types of funerary deposits 13
   1.3. Primary and secondary burials 14

2. Individual primary burial: the pre-Neolithic burial at Bonifacio (Corsica) 15
   2.1. Anatomical terminology 16
   2.2. Differences between the original burial and the form of the deposit observed at excavation 16
      2.2.1. Flattening of the rib cage 16
      2.2.2. Rotation of the head 17
   2.3. The ritual dimension of excavation observations 19

3. Individual primary burials: additional aspects 21
   3.1. The arrangement of offerings and elements of ornament and dress 21
   3.2. The archaeology of funerary behaviour or the archaeology of rites? 24
   3.3. Identifying a primary burial through the analysis of anatomical connections 25

4. Relationships between the internal and external environments of the corpse (I): the analysis of environmental conditions within the burial 32
   4.1. Decomposition in a void 32
   4.2. Decomposition in a filled space 38
   4.3. The Grotte de Foissac: some observations on taphonomy in an underground environment 40

5. Relationships between the internal and external environments of the corpse (II) 45
   5.1. 'Verticalization' of the clavicles 45
   5.2. Voids that form around the corpse 46
   5.3. The filling of the internal volume of the corpse 52
      5.3.1. *The chronology of filling the volume freed by the decay of soft tissue* 52
         5.3.1.1. Delayed filling 52
         5.3.1.2. Progressive filling 54

Contents

	5.3.2. The mechanisms of filling the volume freed by the decay of soft tissue	54
6.	Burials of babies who die within the first six months of life	58
7.	Double burials and 'reductions'. Reflections on the notion of burial. Palaeopathology and archaeology	72
	7.1. Burials containing the remains of two individuals	72
	7.1.1. Asynchronous deposits: 'reductions' and related acts	72
	7.1.2. Double burials	73
	7.2. Reflections on the notion of burial	76
	7.3. Palaeopathology and archaeology	78
	7.3.1. Documenting a physical handicap	79
	7.3.2. Determining the cause of death	82
	7.3.3. Biological calcifications and ossifications	85
8.	Secondary burials	89
9.	Funerary complexes (I)	93
	9.1. Cemeteries and necropolises	93
	9.2. Multiple burials	98
10.	Funerary complexes (II): collective burials, the karst shaft of La Boucle at Corconne (I)	104
11.	Funerary complexes (III): collective burials, the karst shaft of La Boucle at Corconne (II)	118
12.	Funerary complexes (IV): collective burials, the dolmen of Les Peirières at Villedubert	131
13.	Cremation	145
	13.1. Secondary cremation deposits	145
	13.2. Anthropological parameters in cremation burials	146
	13.3. Quantifying the human remains in the tomb	150
	13.4. Primary cremation deposits	152
Conclusions and perspectives		154
Appendix: Anatomical terminology		156
Bibliography		157

Preface

This book was conceived of and created within the EU Culture 2000 programme *Living and Dying in the Roman Empire: New Perspectives in Funerary Archaeology. Cultural Influences from the Centre to the Periphery* (Culture 2000, Framework Programme CLT 2004/A1/IT-350). Based on our common interest and activity in funerary archaeology we initiated and developed this programme, which was coordinated by the Soprintendenza Archeologica di Roma and organised in collaboration with the École Française de Rome, the Collège de France, the University of Cambridge (UK), the Universities of Ferrara, Lecce and Pisa, the University of Picardy, the University of Bordeaux 1, the École Pratique des Hautes Études, King's College London and the Soprintendenza Archeologica for Emilia Romagna.

The primary aim of the project was to contribute to the development of common procedures for excavation, data collection and study of Roman cemeteries of the imperial period, through collaboration between archaeologists, anthropologists, historians and the heritage management sector. It is also aimed at building a lasting network of European scientific institutions, in order to promote a different way of working together both in the field and in the laboratory. To this end, centres of university research and teaching, institutions with responsibility for preserving and enhancing cultural heritage, the Italian Soprintendenze Archeologiche and archaeological contractors and museums have co-ordinated their actions around common issues and problems.

This collaboration took place over the year 2004–2005 and we hope that it will expand to other countries and institutions in the near future. It is mainly based on three principle areas of experience in research and archaeological preservation. The first of these concerns the area covered by the Soprintendenza Archeologica di Roma, which undertakes the excavation and study of numerous Roman cemeteries, in particular those identified during a recent period of intensive operation in the *Suburbium* of ancient Rome. The second concerns the excavation of the cemeteries at Classe, near Ravenna, conducted by a large group of archaeologists from Italy, France, Germany, and Luxembourg, directed by Maria Grazia Maioli, Jacopo Ortalli and John Scheid. The third concerns the specialized excavation of the Porta Nocera cemetery at Pompeii, which has been carried out in collaboration between the École Française de Rome and the Soprintendenza Archeologica for Pompei under the direction of William van Andringa and Sébastien Lepetz.

The first discussions of the results took place in meetings organized by John Scheid at the Collège de France in Paris (14th–16th February 2005) and by Martin Millett at the Department of Classics in Cambridge (4th–6th April 2005). Those have been turned into a book edited by John Scheid (*Pour une archéologie du rituel. Nouvelles perspectives de l'archéologie funéraire pour l'époque romaine impériale*) which is forthcoming in the *Collections de l'École Française de Rome*. A web site on funerary archaeology has also been set up, housed by the University of Cambridge with the collaboration of the Soprintendenza Archeologica di Roma and Metafora (a private sector company) (http://www.classics.

cam.ac.uk/museum/archaeological_research/burials/). On it can be found information related to the project programme, such as the presentation of project activities and the research teams involved, address lists *etc*.

Another aim of the project was to develop working procedures and means of communication and scientific dissemination adapted to the issues of funerary archaeology. For that purpose, different systems for the digital processing of information from cemetery excavations have been compared and standardised – in particular those used by the Institut de Recherche en Archéologie Préventive (as adapted for its Pompeii excavation), by the Soprintendenza Archeologica di Roma and by the team at Classe, Ravenna. This has led the Soprintendenza Archeologica di Roma and the University of Pisa to develop a common database that will soon be at the disposal of the interested scientific community.

A project to put on an international exhibition on the funerary world of ancient Rome, Italy and the north-west provinces of the empire was also discussed. In recent decades, research in this field has achieved very important insights which are of interest to a broader public, since they concern issues that are fundamental for both ancient Romans and modern Europeans. Archaeology and the history of religion and law allow us to focus on a very broad spectrum of cultural phenomena, including the adaptation and transformation of funerary rites everywhere after the Roman conquest and the ways in which grave goods, monuments and their decorations represent communities and individuals. As Peter Fasold reminds us, funerary archaeology, epigraphy and anthropology also enable us to assemble the fragments of individual lives: the anonymous biographies of a Roman slave, an Adriatic shipper, a soldier on the Rhine *limes* and an Insular prince. The new perspectives of funerary archaeology are clearly situated between two extremes of historical reconstruction. Their presentation to the public can do no less than show the wide range of disciplines and technologies used by scholars to document both broad cultural changes which emanated from Rome to influence the peoples of the empire, and the small events of anonymous lives on the margins of that empire.

Finally, this project aimed to develop specific intensive training for those specialising in funerary archaeology, doctoral students and young scholars, as well as for those working for institutions responsible for the protection, management and enhancement of archaeological heritage. An experimental Franco-Italian version of this course was organized by the Ecole Française de Rome, the Soprintendenza Archeologica di Roma and the Ecole Pratique des Hautes Etudes in Rome (18th October–6th November 2004). It was modelled on the courses that Henri Duday has organized annually since 1984 at the University of Bordeaux 1 in collaboration with Patrice Courtaud.

Many scholars contributed to the Rome course, including Paola Catalano, Dominique Castex, Patrice Courtaud, Ida Anna Rapinesi and Olimpia Colacicchi, but most of the teaching was done by Henri Duday within the educational programme of the Ecole Pratique des Hautes Etudes. Further sessions of that course have subsequently taken place. The EU Culture 2000 programme also represented a good opportunity to turn the lectures into a book, which was first published in Italian, then in French and now in English. The book will serve not only as a reference text for university students (it is not, however, a manual) but also as a guide which mirrors the aims, spirit and methodological principles shared by the participants in the *Living and Dying in the Roman Empire* project. We hope it will contribute to promoting international dialogue on funerary archaeology and, more generally, to reflection on the transformations needed in archaeological practice and argument.

Paola Catalano
Servizio di Antropologia, Soprintendenza Archeologica di Roma
Stéphane Verger
Ecole Pratique des Hautes Etudes, Paris

Note on the Author and Translation

Henri Duday is Directeur de Recherches for the Centre National de la Recherche Scientifique, UMR 5199, Laboratoire d'Anthropologie des Populations du Passé de l'Université Bordeaux 1, and Directeur d'Etudes at the Ecole Pratique des Hautes Etudes, with responsibility for the Palaeoanthropology laboratory. His academic training is in both medicine and archaeology.

This text is based on an intensive specialist course in burial archaeology given by him in Rome from 18th October to 6th November 2004. The course took place under the auspices of the Ecole Française de Rome, the Ecole Pratique des Hautes Etudes and the Soprintendenza Archeologica di Roma, within the context of the EU Culture 2000 Progamme which was initiated and organized by Paola Catalano (Servizio di Antropologia, Soprintendenza Archeologica di Roma) and Stéphane Verger (Ecole Pratique des Hautes Etudes, Paris), *Vivere e morire nell'Impero Romano. Nuove prospettive dell'archeologia funeraria. Influenze culturali dal centro alla periferia* (Programma Quadro CLT 2004/A1/IT-350).

A text was transcribed by Enrica Monzeglio, corrected and completed by the author and then translated and revised by Rossella Pace, Stéphane Verger and Paola Catalano. The Italian version was published as *Lezioni di archeotanatologia: archeologia funeraria e antropologia di campo* (Soprintendenza archeologica di Roma and Ecole Française de Rome, 2005). The terms 'archeotanatologia / archéothanatologie' and 'antropologia di campo / anthropologie de terrain' are unfamiliar and potentially misleading in English, but important for the approach taken in the book, as the author explains in chapter 1. For the English version an alternative title of 'The Archaeology of the Dead' has therefore been preferred, with the subtitle referring to the original title. This book was directly translated into English by Anna Maria Cipriani from printed transcripts of oral lectures given in Rome by the author Henri Duday. John Pearce revised the English text. Anna Maria Cipriani is a professional translator who has translated books, articles and papers into and from English, French and Italian and currently works in the UK. John Pearce is Lecturer in Archaeology in the Department of Classics, King's College London.

Introduction

'The mirror which does not deceive' is the title of the Mexican painting which I have chosen for the back cover of this book, since it seems to me that it summarises many of our pre-occupations when we discuss the archaeology of death. The left side of the painting shows a beautiful young woman, with the hand of one of the Fates poised above her head to cut the thread of life that runs through her body. On the right side of the picture, in contrast, the space for death is twice as wide as that for life and, with its outstretched hand, the skeleton seems to invite us to follow it. That space, at first sight indistinct, little by little becomes clearer and encourages us to reflect on the fundamental questions of our discipline. The cemetery is delimited by an enclosing wall which isolates it from the town, visible in the middle distance. There is a spatial connection between the worlds of the living and the dead and also a more or less real boundary between the two. A wide variety of trees is recognizable, in particular a pine and two cypresses, underlining the symbolic value of these species.

In the foreground an open pit seems ready to receive the deceased. This is the element of the tomb which archaeologists are more used to seeing, the underground element which is often the only part preserved. Beyond, a field is sown with crosses, markers which signal religious affiliation (the Christian cross) and identify the person. The plaques which are visible on some crosses serve as epitaphs. If the cemetery in the first place contains the bodies of the dead, it also represents a 'theatre' for commemorative cults. But memory is short and soon fades and dies: many crosses lean as if about to fall, pulling the dead into oblivion. The period for which the tomb is cared for, and with it the memory of the dead, undergoes considerable changes and this is clearly one of the important elements of the so-called 'life' of cemeteries. This also raises the problem of what happens to those human remains that are occasionally exhumed when older, forgotten burials are disturbed or when, more simply, lack of space makes their re-use necessary. The picture shows a skull at the foot of a cross and immediately behind it two further skulls and long bones at the foot of a cypress. The cemetery wall is also long-lasting but is beginning to crumble… and then, in the foreground, is the main character of this scene, the skeleton. A student of human osteology should not consider this picture as an anatomical reference image. There are no fewer than fourteen left ribs, the carpals are represented by one massive bone, the positions of the fibula and tibia are reversed and none of us has a patella like a figure of eight! However what strikes us first is the artist's concern with documenting the decay of organic tissue, putrefaction and the eating away of flesh. Worms and larvae emerge from the skull and mouth, while bunches of them mill on the little flesh left. This is pure fiction, since it is unlikely to find parts of the digestive system preserved when the ligaments have mainly disappeared. Nevertheless, the process by which a corpse is transformed into a skeleton is one of the key questions when excavating burials. The remains we find in excavation are skeletons, which once were corpses, and these in turn were once human beings. Bones record the significant events, the repeated behaviours which have marked our life. An internal mirror with many facets, the analysis of skeletons will allow us to re-discover the lives of people who came before us and will give us information on their view of death. 'The mirror which does not deceive'..., true, but unfortunately the mirror shows us only some aspects of the scene, leaving in the shadows entire areas which we would like to know better. This book is intended to examine the means at our disposal to allow the dead to speak, and, if possible, to identify the pitfalls which may deceive us. To achieve this purpose, it is compiled as a set of commentaries on the many images, some of which require further elaboration and, occasionally, digression. These elaborations and digressions may sometimes interrupt the linear structure of the book and for this reason it is not a manual as such. There are not systematic bibliographic references for each of the sites considered. It would have been tedious to refer to excavation reports which are difficult to find or secondary publications that touch only superficially on the burials on which I shall comment. For this reason I refer only to some theoretical and methodological publications.

Before beginning, I would like to thank all the people who allowed the lecture course on which this book is based to be made possible. First, my archaeologist and anthropologist colleagues, with whom I have the pleasure of working on excavation. Some have been my teachers and some my students. We have shared the same passion which, I hope, has allowed me to give back to them as much as I received from them. It was through my contact with them that I could both envisage and develop this research. Many of the images on which I shall comment are the result of this collaboration. My thanks are due also to Grégory Péreira, who introduced me to the amazing work by the Mexican painter Tomás Mondragón (1856) used as the cover image, which is kept in the church of La Profesa in Mexico City. More directly related to this EU *Cultura 2000* project, I also thank Stéphane Verger and Paola Catalano. This book also owes much to Enrica Monzeglio and Rossella Pace. It is to the latter that I owe the idea of shaping the text as a series of lectures that match the course on which it is based, the three-week *stage* in Rome from October to November 2004. During that time I also had the opportunity to strengthen my connections with the Ecole Française de Rome and to make new friends among Italian colleagues whose patience was demonstrated by following these lectures in French, which I very much appreciated. I will be happy if this work is the first step in a continuing collaboration.

Finally, this book is dedicated to Jean Guilaine, my teacher, with whom this adventure began in 1963 in the Grotte Gazel at Sallèles-Cabardès.

Lecture 1

Preliminary discussion

Although this is a course in archaeology, it also deals with many problems which derive from biology, including the study of bones, the decomposition of the corpse and the products of decomposition. Our task is to use these studies in order to understand cultural phenomena, which bring us back to the sphere of archaeology and, more specifically, funerary archaeology. This approach was developed in France twenty-five years ago in the early 1980s when rescue archaeology was being established. Initially this new subject was called 'l'anthropologie du terrain'. This formulation was very successful due to its apparent clarity for French archaeologists, 'l'anthropologie du terrain' being the discipline in which the person studying human bones, the anthropologist, whilst being a biologist does not only work in the laboratory but also in the field, *i.e.* on archaeological excavations, in order to participate directly in the collecting and recording of data.

Today however this expression should be abandoned, in order to prevent confusion with other disciplines. In France and other neo-Latin countries, following the definition that has long prevailed along the lines established by Paul Broca, anthropology is the discipline that studies the human being in his/her biological dimension. In Anglo-Saxon and northern European countries however, anthropology takes into account both biological and cultural dimensions of human behaviour. In the U.S.A., for example, the term 'anthropology' has the same meaning that we give to 'ethnology' and the adjective 'physical' must be added to distinguish the area of the discipline which primarily concerns biological parameters. This meaning is gaining increasing international acceptance. Archaeology therefore, in its 'ethnological' approach to the study of ancient populations, is called 'Palaeoethnology'. If we consider the time dimension, archaeology is then an anthropological discipline like history or linguistics. Moreover from the archaeological point of view, 'field' refers to 'excavation'. But an anthropologist-biologist who goes for example to Africa to study the demographic consequences of rubella vaccination also carries out 'fieldwork' which is different from excavation. To avoid confusion Bruno Boulestin and I (2005) therefore suggested the use of the term 'archaeothanatology', since 'thanatology' studies the biological and social components of death.

The simplest and most direct way to understand the nature of a discipline is to sample its bibliography. The first step naturally is to identify the authors of works published in this area. Generally however articles on burials are written by the archaeologists who excavated them and are rich in information of an archaeological type which relates to their specific training. This may differ from country to country and, even within a single country, between universities. Archaeological education is generally based both on learning to read stratification (the point of departure for all archaeological activity),

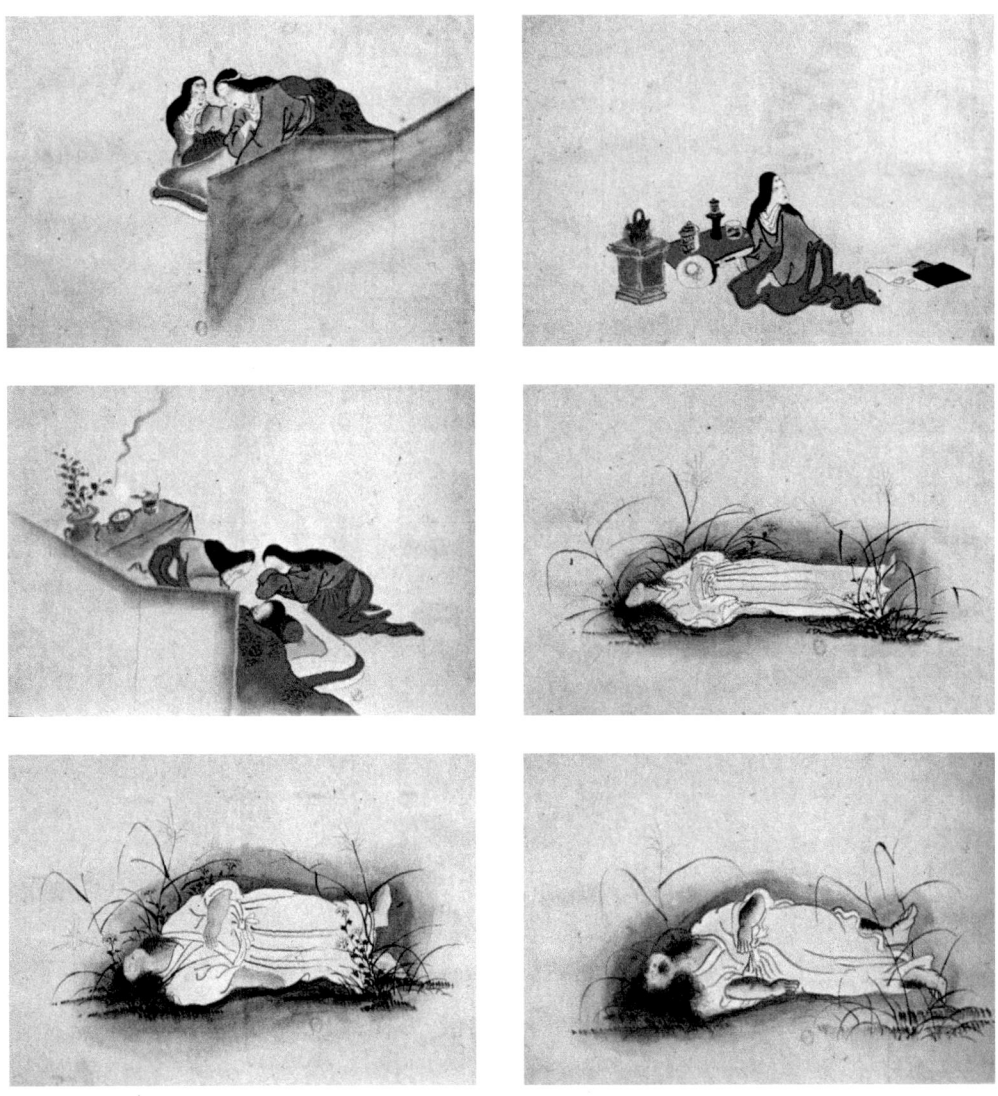

Figure 1. Japanese watercolour of the early 19th century (from E. Georges (1982) Voyages de la Mort. 265, Paris, Berger-Levrault). Photograph by J. L. Charmet.

1 Preliminary discussion

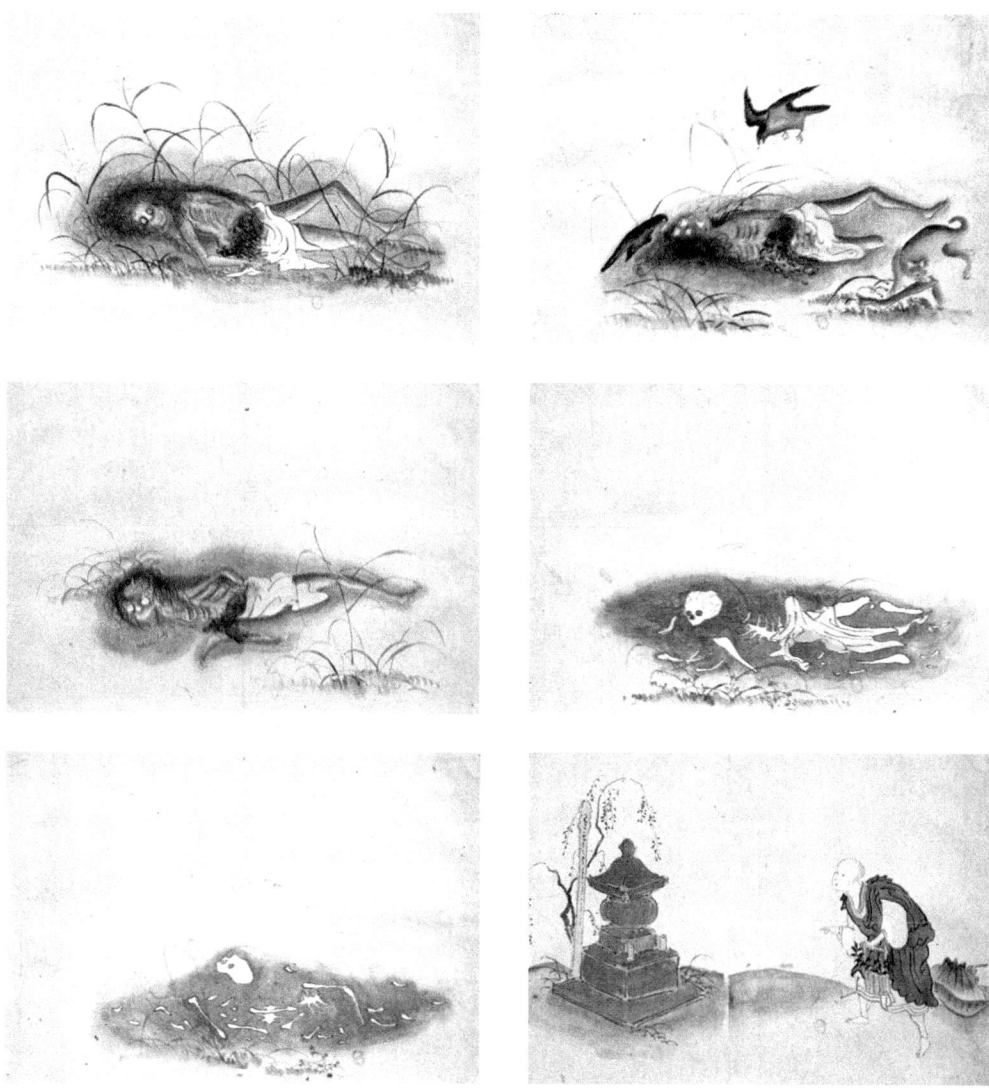

to recognise layers, stratigraphic units, fills and so on. Another area concerns the analysis of material culture such as grave goods (e.g. weapons, pottery) and architectural structures. Training which includes the study of human bones is rare. There are not many university courses in osteology for archaeologists, in France at least. This subject is more specifically taught in biology and, above all, in medicine.

When reading specialist publications we often then face a clear inversion in the hierarchy of importance of the different elements of the burial. The impression is often given that a corpse accompanies the brooch or the vessel, but the most important element of the burial is not the furnishing but the deceased: the brooch is not buried, but the deceased with the brooch.

The objective of 'archaeothanatology' is to reconstruct the attitudes of ancient populations towards death by focusing on the study of the human skeleton and analysing the acts linked to the management and treatment of the corpse. These are intended to enable the survivors to overcome the pain of this final parting and the unbearable anxiety that the bodies of relatives or friends are doomed to decompose. For that reason, funerary archaeologists should have a training to be applied in the field which is not limited to collecting human bones and taking them to laboratories. The responsibility for this disfunction should not be laid at the doors of archaeologists alone. In the past (and often still today), many anthropologists conceived of their work as being restricted to the laboratory and their dialogue with archaeologists was limited to asking where the bones came from and their date. Having obtained this information, the anthropologist applied the methodology of his/her own discipline, beginning what s/he considered to be his/her work, measuring morphological, morphometric and, if necessary, pathological characteristics of the bones. We should not forget that morphological anthropology is also a historical discipline, in that (like archaeology) it aims to understand the history of populations. Yet this approach to historical knowledge is situated at the very general level of population dynamics. It contributes in only an incomplete way to the understanding of the individual funerary complex.

While on the one hand archaeologists often lack sufficient training in anatomy to record the data related to the arrangement of human remains, on the other anthropologists/biologists do not have a real insight into archaeological issues, and the deceased is therefore excluded from overall assessment of the tomb. The bones are treated as extraneous elements, often published in appendices and therefore totally dissociated from the archaeological analysis. This is an epistemological aberration: the dead body is the *raison d'être* for the tomb and the central element around which, and in function of which, the acts were performed which funerary archaeology aims to reconstruct. The methodological choice for 'l'anthropologie du terrain' or 'archaeothanatology' consists simply of placing the deceased at the centre of interest in the tomb. This does not mean an undervaluing of the importance of grave goods, the social dimension of which is linked directly to funerary ideology and which often provides information for dating the grave. The fact that individual burials comprise perfect examples of closed contexts has given grave goods an essential role in reconstructing the relative chronology of different types of artefacts. But to use the grave goods found in the tomb to study, for example, the geographical distribution of an object (such as vessels from a particular production centre), belongs to economic rather than funerary archaeology.

1.1. Funerary archaeology and corpse taphonomy

To understand a burial is to bear in mind, above all, that skeletons were once corpses. To illustrate this point, we shall examine an early nineteenth century Japanese watercolour (Figure 1) comprising 12 vignettes showing the decomposition of a corpse which the artist must have carefully observed to represent so faithfully. Figure 1a represents the phase before death, with a woman lying on her bed protected by a screen. In Figure 1b, a servant or a relative seems concerned and alert. The following image (Figure 1c) shows the woman, now dead, and people beside her intent on the pre-burial treatment

Figure 1a. Detail of Figure 1, first scene.

Figure 1b. Detail of Figure 1, second scene.

Figure 1c. Detail of Figure 1, third scene.

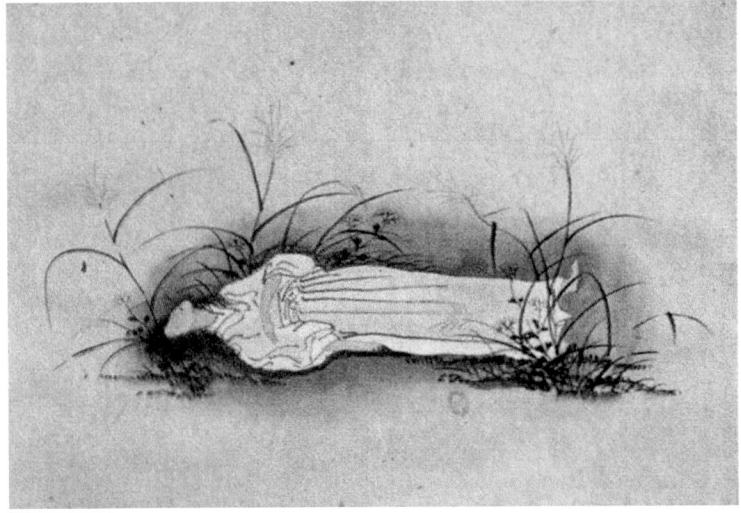

Figure 1d. Detail of Figure 1, fourth scene.

of the corpse, while an incense burner smokes on a table. This phase will interest the archaeologist who investigates the society in which the woman died and the causes of her death.

The following image represents the funerary deposit proper (Figure 1d): the corpse has been placed in an open space, a garden. The woman is laid on her back, dressed in a white tunic. Her left forearm is folded on her chest. Decomposition starts at the very moment of death, but sometimes may begin while the subject is still alive, when necrosis of tissue that is no longer supplied with blood takes place. The decomposition of the corpse takes place because of the action of two general factors, endogenous factors operating inside the corpse and exogenous factors working outside it. The endogenous

Figure 1e. Detail of Figure 1, fifth scene.

Figure 1f. Detail of Figure 1, sixth scene.

factors are primarily bacteria, as well as fungi, mostly found along the digestive tract of the deceased. While we are alive our body keeps their proliferation under control but after death these micro-organisms multiply rapidly and attack the body of the individual. There are two immediate consequences, temperature increase and the production of gas. The corpse swells, increasing in volume (Figure 1e) and some parts become coloured brown and grey by *post mortem* lividity (Figure 1f). In an open space the swollen abdomen can even burst if the temperature is high enough (Figure 1g). This phenomenon does not occur if the corpse is buried in the ground. In the image we see that the upper left limb, initially laid on the chest, has fallen to one side. Therefore, the position of the skeleton in excavation may be different from the one which it assumed when deposited. Organic

Figure 1g. Detail of Figure 1, seventh scene.

Figure 1h. Detail of Figure 1, eighth scene.

elements, such as clothing, generally decay together with the corpse. Figure 1h shows the intervention of exogenous elements. For example birds, like *corvidae*, may alight on a dead body to eat what remains of the eyes. A dog also carries off part of the lower right limb in its mouth. Figure 1i shows a corpse, partially defleshed, without its left leg and right foot. The exogenous elements are directly conditioned by the tomb architecture. In the burials of contemporary Christian Europe, animals able to disturb the deposit are usually very small, since the dead body is placed in a coffin underground or protected by a tomb. The identification of these exogenous animals will provide us indirectly with information on the tomb architecture and on the protection, if any, of the corpse.

At the end of the process dry bones are represented, with a small element of the

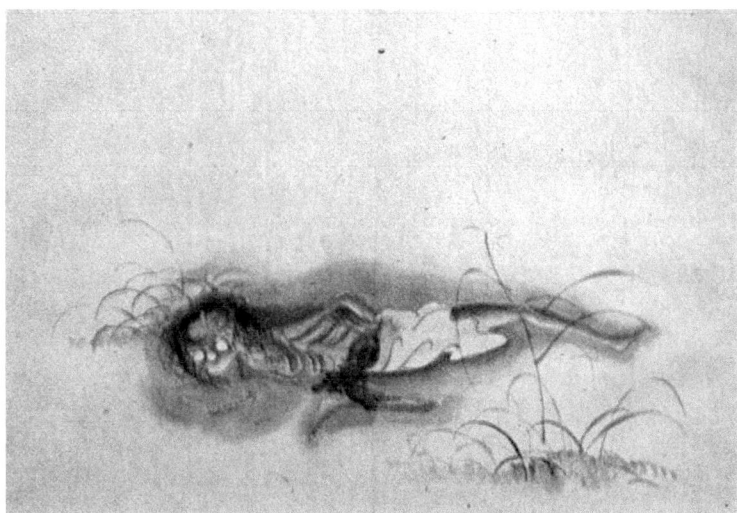

Figure 1i. Detail of Figure 1, ninth scene.

Figure 1j. Detail of Figure 1, tenth scene.

thorax still retaining its anatomical connections and some strips of tissue (Figure 1j). The surface of the ground has changed, soaked with decomposition liquids from the corpse and revealing traces of the action of earthworms that are often found near burials because the ground is rich in organic materials. In the end nothing remains except some disconnected bones (Figure 1k).

The final image (Figure 1l) relates to the marking of the tomb and to the cult of memory: a commemorative monument, a vertical stele with an inscription and a tree associated with the symbolism of death (here a weeping willow). People can gather around the burial to perform rituals, libations or funerary feasts, or to place flowers, for example chrysanthemums in contemporary Christian tradition.

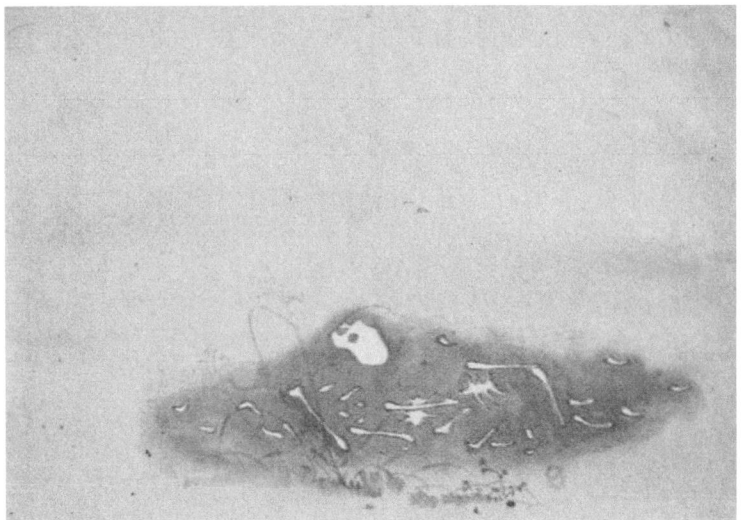

Figure 1k. Detail of Figure 1, eleventh scene.

Figure 1l. Detail of Figure 1, twelfth scene.

From the archaeological point of view, the most interesting elements in this process are those that provide information on the history of culture and attitudes. First we must examine the causes of death, their frequency among ancient populations, and the pre-burial treatment of corpses (Figure 1c). For these laboratory analyses are the primary source of information. Our knowledge of tomb markers and commemorative cults (Figure 1l) is chiefly based on direct evidence, such as bases of monuments, inscriptions, pottery, animal bones, and plant remains, whether burnt macro-fossils or pollen. Funerary archaeology is however aimed above all at reconstructing the initial burial deposit (Figure 1d), starting from the excavated remains (Figure 1k) and working backward through the transformations undergone by the corpse. It is important therefore that the archaeologist should not only know the bones, but also the various stages of decomposition, since these may significantly modify the original situation, *i.e.* as desired by those who created the burial.

Here then can be seen the importance of corpse taphonomy, *i.e.* the passage of the body from the biosphere, the sphere of living things, to the lithosphere, the mineral world. The term 'taphonomy' (from the Greek τάφοσ, burial, and νόμος, law) is commonly used in archaeological literature. It usually refers to the modes of preservation – or alteration – of organic elements after burial, but sometimes also refers to the phases before burial (for example traces of butchery in archaeozoology) or to the objects transformed by humans (flint, ceramics, metals *etc.*) or to archaeological sites. Funerary archaeology tends to give the term a meaning closer to its etymology: it refers to all the processes that affect human remains after their deposition, the preservation or non-preservation of every skeletal element and its arrangement in relation to others. The taphonomy of the body – rather than that of the skeleton – is one of the fundamental elements of funerary archaeology today. To work following the methodological pointers of forensic medicine may not only help to explain some anomalies and to create a body of reference knowledge on which to base comparisons but also help to reconstruct the original arrangement of the burial.

1.2. Different types of funerary deposits

There are different types of funerary deposits. A primary distinction can be drawn between individual burials, containing the remains of a single individual, and funerary complexes containing a number of corpses. Within these categories further distinctions can be made. When the complex comprises many burials (usually individual), each with its own structure, it may be called a 'necropolis' or cemetery. The term 'necropolis' derives from Greek, but its usage is not ancient. Strabo used it only for the cemetery of Alexandria, for its buildings resembled those of the town and only after Napoleon's campaigns in Egypt did historians and archaeologists popularise this term. In the cemetery each burial has its own structure and these individual structures are associated in a more or less organized complex.

Another category is a single architectonic container, such as a natural or artificial cave, hypogeum or shrine, which houses the remains of several individuals. In this connection, Jean Leclerc (1988; 1990) refers to multiple burials, which can be grouped in two types. A multiple burial comprises dead bodies which have been deposited in the same place simultaneously. This generally represents evidence for catastrophic events, massacres, plagues, floods *etc*, which have caused a mortality crisis. The minimum form of multiple burial, containing only two individuals deposited at the same time, is double (or 'bisomus'); if there are three bodies it is triple (or 'trisomus') and so on. Burials are collective where the corpses have been deposited at different times and where the structure has been built to allow for reopening for further depositions. While the term 'individual burial' is commonly accepted, the other types of burials do not benefit from a commonly accepted definition by archaeologists and historians, so these terms are clearly defined here as they are used in this publication.

1.3. Primary and secondary burials

A primary burial corresponds to what anthropologists and sociologists of death call the 'simple funeral'. It consists of a single ceremony during which the manipulation of the remains takes place. The body, still in a state of anatomical integrity, is then placed in its final tomb. Decomposition happens almost entirely at the place of burial. The most obvious examples are inhumations, but we will see later that primary cremation burials also exist: in this case fire rather than putrefaction destroys the organic elements.

A secondary burial corresponds instead to what anthropologists call the 'double funeral'. The human remains are manipulated at two different stages. First the corpse is put in a temporary burial where decomposition takes place. Such structures in medieval France were called *pourrissoirs*, in which the corpse was placed to decompose. After sufficient time had elapsed they were opened and the skeleton, or only part of it, was collected. For this reason, the archaeology of *pourrissoirs* is interesting because the bones that were deliberately left behind or forgotten relate to the behaviour of the population to which the deceased belongs. Afterwards the bones were transferred to a tomb. The final burial happens away from the place of decomposition. It is not therefore possible to observe the diagenesis of the corpse in the place of final deposition since the decomposition products were not created there. There are naturally both secondary inhumation and cremation deposits.

From a practical point of view it is not always easy to distinguish primary from secondary burials. Here we need to distinguish two levels of analysis. The first concerns the demonstration of the primary or secondary character of the deposit ('deposit' is a neutral term here that does not necessary imply human action, as in the case of a sedimentary or alluvial deposit, for example). It is an issue of distinguishing whether the subject was a corpse (primary deposit) or loose bones (secondary deposit) when it arrived at the place in which its remains were found. The second level of analysis concerns the demonstration that we are considering a burial proper, whether primary or secondary. If it is secondary, it is necessary to prove that the manipulation of dry bones had been planned from the start. This notion of pre-planning is indispensable for defining a secondary burial, since it distinguishes it from other later handling of dry bones, for example in the case of 'reduction' (see chapter 7). Finally, we have to understand whether the place of decomposition was of no importance for the population under study, or whether funerary rites took place there as well as at the final tomb.

Lecture 2

Individual primary burial: the pre-Neolithic burial at Bonifacio (Corsica)

In the case of the individual primary burial, the undecayed body is laid soon after death in the final tomb where it decomposes. If the remains are not disturbed, during excavation a skeleton will be found more or less in its original position. The Mesolithic burial at Bonifacio, in Corsica, excavated thirty years ago (Figure 2) is the first example ('La Dame de Bonifacio'). It is of a woman laid on her back, with her head turned to the right and her upper and lower limbs both extended parallel to the longitudinal axis of her torso. If excavation methods are precise enough, it will generally be possible to reconstruct the position in which the corpse was laid in the tomb.

Figure 2. Rock shelter at Araguina Sennola, Bonifacio (Corsica), Mesolithic. Excavation by F. de Lanfranchi, M. C. Weiss, and H. Duday.

2.1. Anatomical terminology

Appropriate terminology is needed for a rigorous description of the human remains found in burials. In order to describe the position of osteo-articular structures, it is necessary to use international anatomical nomenclature that has the advantage of having been translated into every language. To facilitate understanding of these terms, the table given at the end of the volume gives the current names for most skeletal elements.

It is important to employ accurate terminology in order to avoid confusion and misinterpretation in anatomical description. For example, in everyday language one might say 'the arms are parallel to the body', but for the anatomist 'arm' indicates the part of the upper limb between the shoulder and the elbow, excluding the forearm and hand. 'Leg' for the anatomist means what comes between knee and the ankle, but it is often wrongly used to indicate the entire lower limb. So the phrase 'the leg is bent' is incorrect, since it is obviously impossible to bend the tibia (it is more appropriate to say that a leg is bent at the thigh, *i.e.* that the knee is bent, since body movements are organized around the joints). Furthermore the body is described in relation to its normal anatomical position, *i.e.* upright and looking towards the horizon, with heels together, arms along the trunk, elbows turned outwards, the upper limbs parallel to the axis of the body, the palms of the hands turned forwards and the thumbs pointing outwards. In relation to the horizontal plane, what is above is 'upper', while what is below is 'lower'. In relation to the frontal plane, *i.e.* a vertical plane from right to left, what is in front is 'anterior', while what is behind is 'posterior'. In relation to the sagittal plane, *i.e.* a vertical plane going from front to back, what looks outward is 'lateral' while what looks inward is 'medial'.

In describing the layout of grave goods, the buried individual should always be taken as the reference point. Therefore 'to the right' does not mean to the observer's right but to the right of the deceased. However, the placing of the objects can always be described with reference to the cardinal points.

2.2. Differences between the original burial and the form of the deposit observed at excavation

If we return to the Bonifacio burial, the skeleton, although still in anatomical connection, does not give a faithful image of the original position in which the body was buried.

2.2.1. Flattening of the rib cage

First of all, since the ribs have collapsed to the floor of the pit the thoracic volume is practically nonexistent. Obviously the deceased has been buried with all its thoracic (heart, lungs) and abdominal organs (liver, spleen, bowels), but these elements soon leave a void as they decompose. At the front the ribs are joined to the sternum and at the back to the vertebrae. When those connections lose their functionality the ribs, which hang above the void created inside the rib cage, will inevitably fall. If the body is laid on its back, the hemithoraces fall symmetrically, as can be seen in the case of the Bonifacio skeleton. If the body lies on one side, the ribs at the bottom of the tomb do not change position, and only those on the opposite side will fall inside the thoracic space. The ribs that have been displaced are fixed in position again when their movement is blocked by the sediment which fills the internal volume of the corpse. This equilibrium disappears during excavation when this fill is removed to lift the bones. In this case, there is a major difference between the original situation and that pertaining when the body is found. However this is not the effect of reworking but a natural phenomenon, the force of gravity, and is a natural change, not a disturbance. Only in two cases can the body maintain its thoracic volume: if soil little by little replaces the flesh as it rots (this seldom happens, as will be described below) or if it has been buried in a pit with a narrow central grave in so-called 'gutter' form, with the two sides raised on which the upper limbs rest. During decomposition the corpse always interacts with its container and in this case the ribs are laid against the sides of the central narrow cut which support them and keep them in equilibrium during the decomposition of their ligaments. By observing and recording the depth of each element, we can see that the thoracic volume has been maintained. In these cases, we can see how important it is to understand taphonomic processes: the information relating to the structure of the tomb (in this case the particular form of the pit) does not derive from the displacement of bones during decomposition of the corpse, but rather from the fact that the usual displacement has not taken place.

2.2.2. Rotation of the head

In the Bonifacio burial the head of the deceased is well preserved and has rotated to the right (Figure 3). We need first to question whether this was its original position or whether this was caused by taphonomic processes. This observation is important, since for many religions the eyes of the dead may be turned symbolically towards a sacred place.

To understand how the rotation of a living head takes place, we must refer to functional anatomy and, more precisely, to biomechanics (Kapandji 1975). When we turn our head, seven cervical vertebrae are usually involved. Between the axis (C2) and the seventh cervical vertebra (C7) only a 20° movement is anatomically possible, corresponding to a mere two to three degrees on average between two consecutive vertebrae. Therefore a wide rotation is not possible. By contrast, a rotation of 60° may be possible between the axis (C2) and the atlas (C1), because of the nature of the articulation of the atlas with the odontoid process of the axis.

Anatomists do not agree on the exact degree of rotation between the atlas and the occipital, but it seems that this joint allows a slight rotation (since the occipital condyles do not stay parallel, but seem to follow the same circle). These displacements characterize the movements of a living body but also apply to a corpse since all the anatomical structures (ligaments, cartilage *etc*) are still present.

Let us imagine a corpse lying on its back on a flat surface, for example inside a sarcophagus, from an anatomical point of view looking forward (so that once deposited the gaze will be upwards). While the ligaments that link the head to the torso (*i.e.* those related to the cervical vertebrae) survive, the head will maintain its original position, but as soon as they break down it will fall to one side or the other because of the near

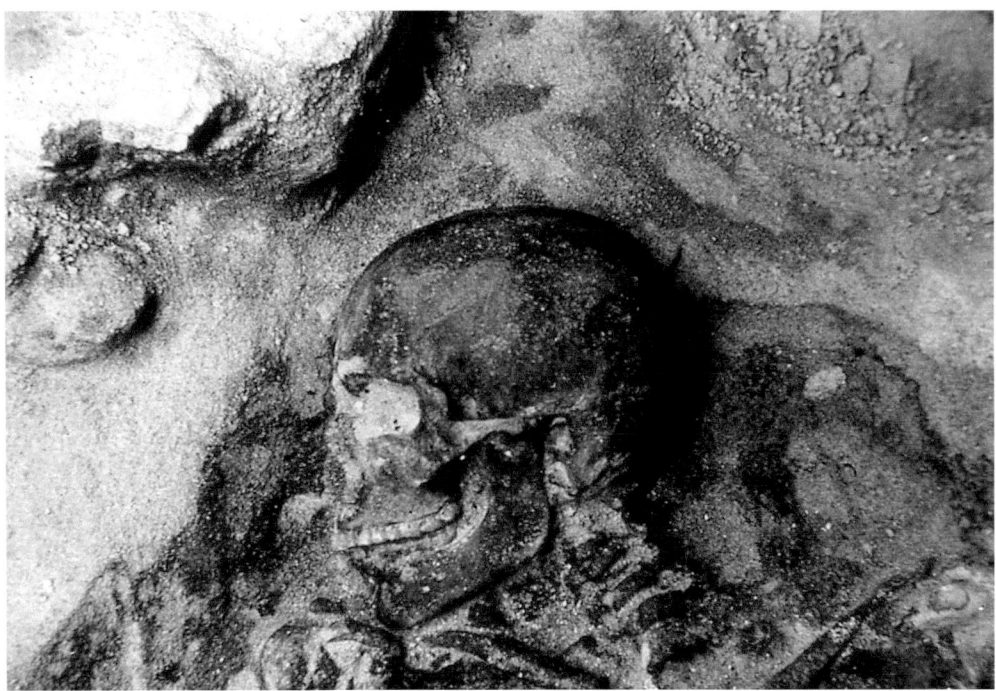

Figure 3. Rock shelter at Araguina Sennola, Bonifacio (Corsica), Mesolithic. Detail of the cephalic region. Excavation by F. de Lanfranchi, M. C. Weiss, and H. Duday.

spherical shape of the cranium in the occipital region. Ligaments do not however all break down at the same time and one intervertebral space therefore separates first whilst the others are still connected. For example the atlas remains connected with the occipital for a long time, often for one year and sometimes for three or four. Ligament detachment happens first either between C1 and C2 (this is, however, rather infrequent) or between C2 and C3, or between C3 and C4, while it occurs rarely between C4 and C5. It is only when this detachment happens that full head rotation takes place. If the deceased has been laid with its head turned, this remains on the floor of the tomb and does not move under the pressure of weight, even when the ligaments have disappeared: the cervical vertebrae maintain their original arrangement with a rotation which mostly involves the C1–C2 articulation.

If this is a taphonomic phenomenon, then a more obvious dissociation of the cervical vertebrae (of *c.* 90°) can be observed, either between the atlas and the axis or between the joints beneath. Therefore we must first observe the arrangement of the upper and the middle cervical vertebrae. When taking photographs of the burial as a whole (or drawing a plan of the skeleton), the area to be observed is at the upper end of the vertebral column, covered by the mandible and cranio-facial region. Once these are removed, it is necessary to take further pictures in order to complete the documentation.

2.3. The ritual dimension of excavation observations

Sometimes the reciprocal disposition of mandible and cranio-facial region is useful for discussing whether head rotation is an original or a taphonomic effect. If a corpse is lying on its back, often the mandible falls and the head slips in the opposite direction because the temporo-mandibular joints, *i.e.* those that join the mandible to the base of the cranium usually decay before those of the cervical vertebrae. Nevertheless, in some cases the order of the disassociation may be inverted: when the cranium falls it drags the mandible which is still linked to the maxillary bones. Therefore if there is a disassociation between the mandible and the cranium which has rolled, then we may infer that the rotation is taphonomic. If it is not detached then we cannot draw any conclusion, since the mandible sometimes remains with the cranium when it falls.

2.3. The ritual dimension of excavation observations

The 'Dame de Bonifacio' was found with her right hand in a peculiar position: her thumb, index finger and middle finger were extended, whereas the other two were bent (Figure 4). To reveal and record this detail a meticulous excavation method is needed. The trowel is to be avoided in favour of dentist's tools, so as not to displace the metacarpals and phalanges. Does the particular position of the woman's right hand, reminiscent of the gesture of blessing, have a ritual character? Very often an unusual

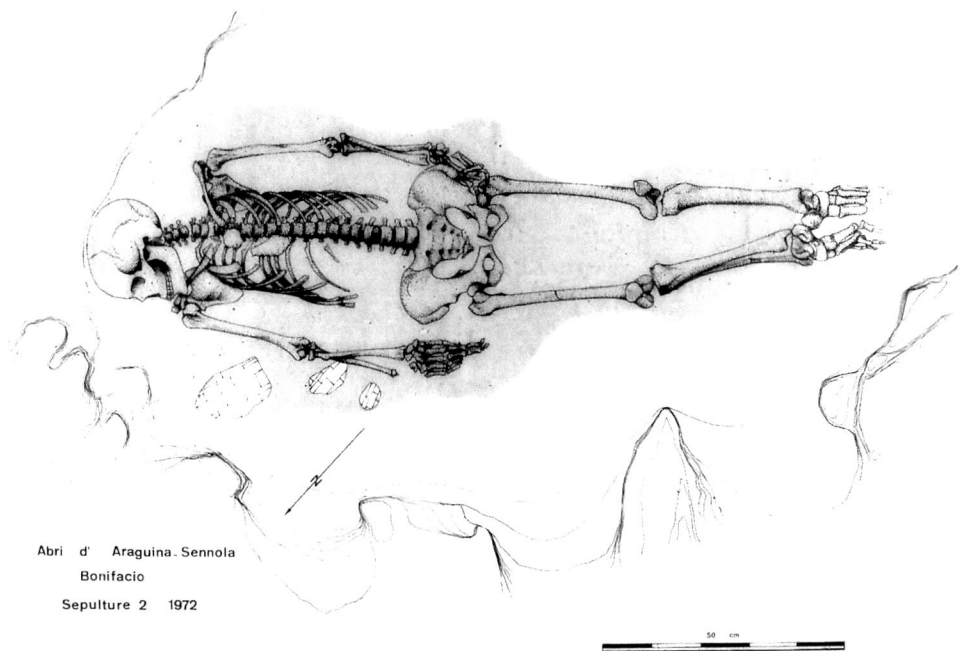

Figure 4. Rock shelter at Araguina Sennola, Bonifacio (Corsica), Mesolithic. General plan. Excavation by F. de Lanfranchi, M. C. Weiss, and H. Duday, plan by H. Duday.

or peculiar detail is considered as ritual in the archaeological literature, especially in funerary archaeology, since authors feel that their observations allow us to access the beliefs of past populations.

In order to establish a relationship between an observation made during excavation and a ritual action, we must first show that this action was intentionally performed during the original deposition. In this case the position of the woman's hand could be considered a chance occurrence, caused by an obstacle met by the hand at the moment of burial, such as small stones. In such a case a distinction between an intentional action and an accident is not possible from the internal evidence of the burial. It is necessary to verify whether the same observation is repeated in other burials from the same chronological and cultural context. The probability that such a case would be identically repeated by pure chance is obviously very low and we could then move to a ritual interpretation. However if this observation is not made in other burials, we cannot draw definitive conclusions since it may be caused either by chance or by a rare ritual, of which it is unlikely that further finds will provide us with many analogous examples. In this case it is rare to find comparisons with hand positions in other Mesolithic burials because the bones have generally been lost or have been destroyed because excavated in an inappropriate way. If the action is not repeated, we cannot proceed to any conclusion but it is nevertheless important to present this case precisely since in ten years time, and with the availability of a larger corpus, it may be possible to explain the phenomenon.

In the case of the Bonifacio burial, the bones and the entire surface occupied by the skeleton (except its feet) were dark red-brown in colour (Figure 4). This colour comes from a primary metamorphic rock (granite or similar), extremely altered by erosion. The deposit, similar in colour to red ochre or haematite, is foreign to the geology of the site and is only found at a spot several kilometres from Bonifacio, both *in situ* and in alluvial deposits. This is undoubtedly a deliberately addition to the deposit.

In studying burials, we are faced with two principal categories of observations. Some may be explained in ritual terms through the internal analysis of the tomb alone, others by contrast can only assume a ritual significance if they can be found in other burials of the same period.

Lecture 3

Individual primary burials: additional aspects

3.1. The arrangement of offerings and elements of ornament and dress

To address the question of offerings, we take as an example an early Neolithic burial from the Grotte Gazel (Aude, France), excavated in 1963 (Figure 5). The subject is an adult male laid on one side in a contracted position. Half of the grave was paved with great blocks of limestone. His feet and the ischiatic tuberosity of his pelvis rested on

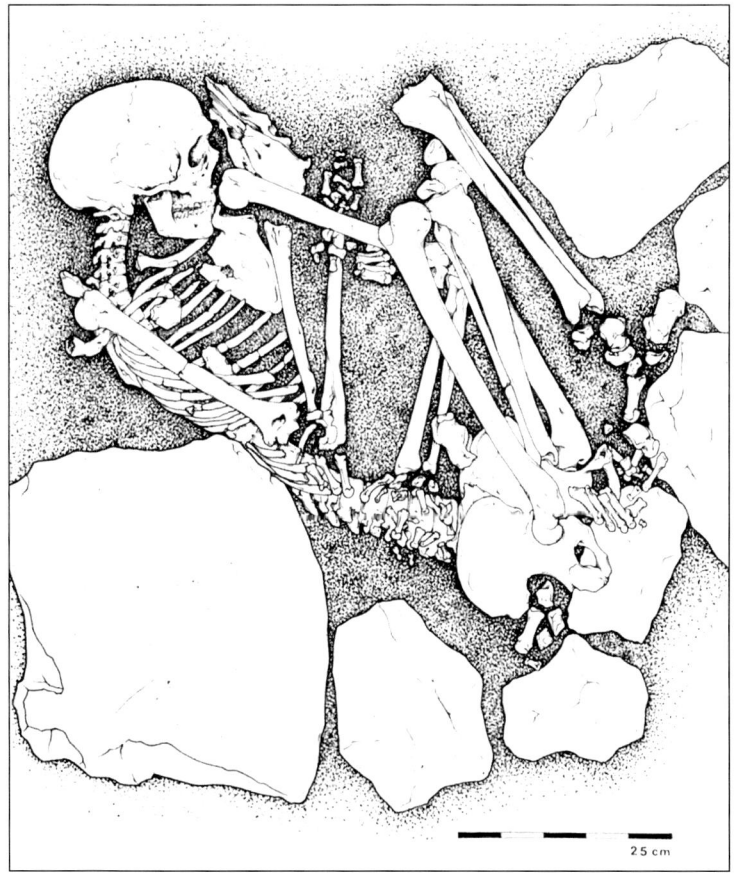

Figure 5. Grotte Gazel, Sallèles-Cabardès (Aude, France), early Neolithic. Excavation by J. Guilaine, plan by H. Duday.

the blocks forming the edge of the tomb. The skull of a small piglet was laid in front of his head as an offering. The meaning of the offering derives from its own properties but also sometimes from its position inside the tomb in relation to the corpse. The choice of preferred position can only be demonstrated when it is observed in several tombs. For example during the Middle Ages in the south of France, ceramic or glass vessels, probably containing holy water, were frequently placed in the tombs of monks and priests. They were systematically placed above the right or the left shoulder of the corpse, on one side or other of the neck.

Elements of grave furniture or dress could be used as offerings but this is not always the case. The deceased may have been buried with their clothes and their own jewels (for example, the wedding ring that we leave on the fingers of the dead because for us it is an integral part of them). This difference can be identified only through the study of the 'life' of these objects before deposition, for example through traces of wear. Whatever the case, their original position can be known only through a detailed examination of their position in relation to the bones. The first example considered is a fourth – third century BC burial in the necropolis of Aleria on the eastern coast of Corsica (Figure 6). Aleria was an *emporium,* a large thriving trading centre and the necropolis reflects the different degrees of wealth among the local population. It is situated on a hill that is deeply cut by a road that crosses it. On its slopes, at right-angles to the road, corridors cut into the rock lead to small funerary chambers. Once a funerary deposit had taken place, the passage connecting the chamber with the corridor was walled up with bricks of unfired clay and eventually filled with earth. In antiquity, when tomb 174 was robbed, part of the wall collapsed protecting some of the bones, including two rib fragments in contact with a bronze brooch. This position is surprising, since in ancient iconography, including statuary and painting, brooches are usually portrayed at the upper shoulder. The different position of brooches found in several burials in the same necropolis may show evidence of an evolution in dress, but we might ask ourselves whether this change concerns the living or only the dead.

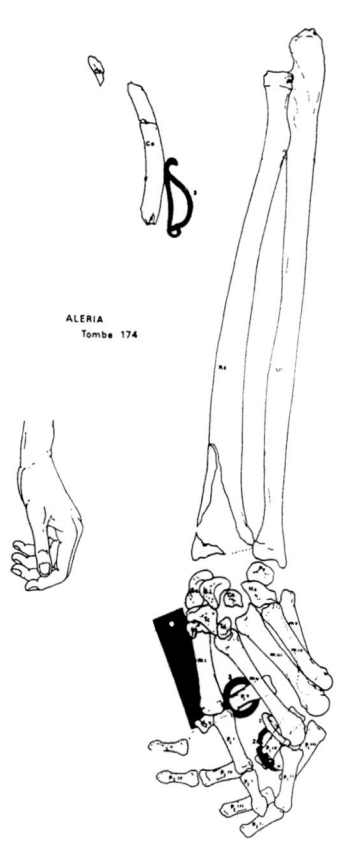

Figure 6. The pre-Roman necropolis of Aleria (Corsica), 4th–3rd century BC. Excavation by J. Jehasse and H. Duday, plan by H. Duday.

Moreover inside tomb 174 a left forearm and hand were also excavated, with a bronze rectangular plaque with two holes in it by the hand and rings on the fingers. It would generally be interesting to know which fingers usually bore rings (for example on some pictures of the Fontainebleau school, women are very often painted with rings on the intermediate phalanges). With this in mind archaeologists sometimes take the precaution of keeping the ring with the phalanx on which it was found. Except for the thumb and the little finger, it is very difficult to identify and to 'side' (*i.e.* attribute to the left or right side) isolated phalanges. This is possible only for the proximal phalanges, provided they are perfectly preserved, especially in their proximal area, and is generally impossible for the middle phalanges. The best method is to make *in situ* a proper anatomical dissection of the hand by following the order of the finger, starting from the metacarpal and proceeding to the proximal, middle, and distal phalanges for each ray (*i.e.* finger). In this case the deceased has a bronze ring on the proximal phalanx of the left little finger, a bronze spiral ring and a gold Etruscan ring on the proximal phalanx of the left ring finger.

During decomposition, elements of grave furniture and dress may be displaced, like anatomical structures. The Vix tomb (Burgundy), in which a woman was found with a sixth century BC large bronze crater, provides a suitable example. A finely worked golden ring weighing 400 grams was also found. The body was placed on a structure (the body of a cart from which the wheels were removed), which caused the head to fall to the ground when it collapsed. In the excavation photographs this ring can be seen near the cranium. The archaeologist who published it interpreted the ring as a diadem placed on the head which followed it when it fell. Today however it is interpreted as a necklace (torc) which fell by accident near the cranium, with which it had no initial connection (Eleure *et al.* 1989).

A more representative example is a double burial of early Neolithic date, found at La Chapelle-Saint-Mesmin near Orléans in France (Fig. 7). In a grave were laid a young woman, *c*. 20 years old, and an 18 month old baby with rich grave furniture. The baby wears a one-loop necklace made of dentalia, shells like small white tubes, while the

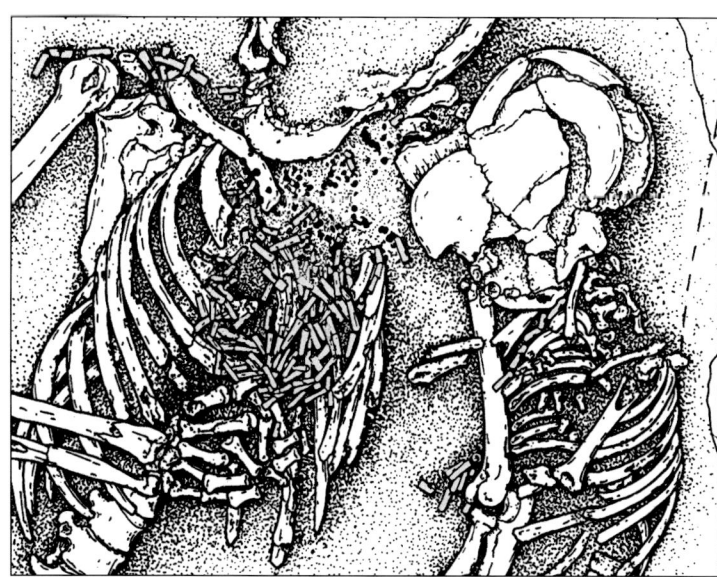

Figure 7. Double burial at La Chapelle Saint-Mesmin (Loiret), early Neolithic. Excavation by G. Richard, Ch. Verjux, and H. Duday, plan by H. Duday.

woman has a more complex furnishing made of many shells and small discoid lignite beads. Such elements in Neolithic burials are generally interpreted as large pectoral ornaments laid across the garments. But in this case all the dentalia have fallen into the axial region in the cavity created by decomposition, when the sternum and the cartilages connecting the ribs to the sternum have fallen into the thoracic cavity. Had it been a pectoral ornament, these elements would have also fallen sideways, which did not happen. These observations therefore lead us to envisage a central ornament composed of a necklace in several loops or several necklaces. In order to reconstruct the arrangement of ornaments or dress, it is necessary to take into consideration the changes in the volume of the corpse during its decomposition.

3.2. The archaeology of funerary behaviour or the archaeology of rites?

With reference to the previous discussion, it may be argued that if an action is intentional then it can be considered ritual. At this point it is important to understand the symbolic meaning behind the intentional action. The aspiration and objective of funerary archaeology are to understand better the religious thought of past populations. However this is not possible on the basis of archaeological observations alone, unless other sources of information are used, for example written texts. Pier Francesco Fabbri has given an outstanding example of this in the analysis of necropolis A at Entella, an ancient and medieval city in Sicily. He found many burials laid parallel to one another, each a narrow grave containing an individual laid on its right side with its head turned towards the southeast (Figure 8). Since this type of burial was found for

Figure 8. Rocca di Entella (Sicily), necropolis A, tomb 19. Photograph by F. Fabbri.

several dozen individuals, it can be inferred that the action is intentional and therefore ritual. These are characteristically Islamic burials, since the dead look towards Mecca (and not the southeast). Texts and architecture reveal the Islamic occupation of Sicily. Their cemetery occupies the site of an earlier Hellenistic graveyard and most stones used for these structures were taken from Greek tombs. By using knowledge derived from the historical context and texts, it is therefore possible to find correspondences between excavation observations and systems of religious and symbolic thought. Here a remarkable leap can be made from field observations to their interpretation.

The archaeology of rites studies actions and tries to understand the religious background to them. When working on more ancient periods, we might want to substitute texts with ethnographic comparisons, but this is generally destined to fail. The observations that anthropologists have derived from the living populations of other continents during the 19th or 20th centuries cannot be blindly applied to European prehistoric populations. The same actions can obviously be manifestations of different systems of thought. If we ask two different modern populations about the significance of using the colour red in burials, we will obtain different answers. For one this colour might represent extra energy for the journey to the afterlife, for the other the vital energy of the individual that is passing into the earth and dissolving in the soil. When we lack sources of information to complement our field observations, it is possible to carry out only an archaeology of actions and not of rites, since the latter derive from the interaction of action and thought.

3.3. Identifying a primary burial through the analysis of anatomical connections

A primary burial is one in which the corpse is laid in its final place of burial where decomposition takes place. It is now necessary to demonstrate the elements on the basis of which a burial can be argued to be a primary deposit. It is well known to archaeologists that primary burials can be recognised from the presence of anatomical connections, and that the presence of these connections allows us to reconstruct the original position of a corpse, even when some decomposition-related changes have occurred.

Returning to our example of Entella in Sicily (Figures 8 and 9), a body was laid on its right side with the upper left limb, the left hand and the hip joint still in anatomical connection. The part of the rib cage laid on the bottom of the pit has kept its natural shape, which is rare, while those which were above the void created by decomposition of the lungs and bowels have fallen and seem more oblique. There are also elements that are not in anatomical connection. The spinal column is partly disassociated, the sacrum lies inside the cavity within the pelvis and the left forearm is inside the coxal bone. In order to establish whether this is a primary burial, we cannot rely only on the anatomical connections since not all are preserved but must also consider other factors.

Some joints disappear before others. Let's imagine for example, that an interphalangeal joint breaks down on average in three weeks (this is a theoretical estimate, which only has value for the sake of an example and is not an objective fact). If this connection is

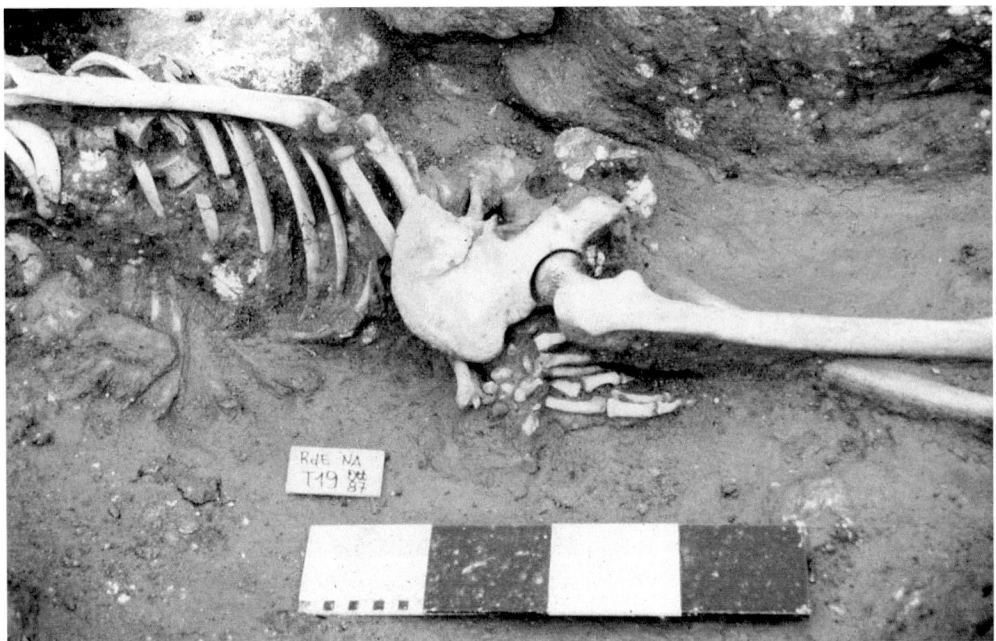

Figure 9. Rocca di Entella (Sicily), necropolis A, tomb 19 (detail). Photograph by F. Fabbri.

present, then it can be assumed that less than twenty days have passed between the death of the individual and burial. If, instead, only the anatomical connection of the knee is still present, which is much slower to break down (let's say, for example, that eleven months are needed to destroy these ligaments), this means that less than eleven months have passed between death and burial, but this might mean one day or ten months.

The joints which break down most rapidly during decomposition ('unstable' or 'labile' joints) are the most useful for establishing whether a burial is primary because, if they appear to be still connected, then a short time has elapsed between death and the deposition of the corpse. The joints that break down more slowly can be called 'persistent'. I prefer this term, since it refers explicitly to the duration of time, to 'resistant' which might also signify mechanical resistance. In the wrist, for example, which is very resistant from a mechanical point of view, there are many thin ligaments going in all directions which break down simultaneously and rapidly. The carpal is therefore resistant from the mechanical point of view but its joints break down rapidly from the taphonomic point of view. In conclusion, a primary burial can be reliably claimed where anatomical connections are still present between the joints that break down more rapidly.

The time taken for joints to disappear may vary and depends on the funerary treatment of the body and on the place of burial. In cremation, for example, all joints break down rapidly. If a corpse is buried inside a glacier, all will be persistent because of the cold temperature that inhibits the decay of organic materials. This could also happen in a very dry environment or in a bog, in fact in every environment which promotes natural mummification.

Where a body is buried in temperate and relatively humid environments the joints that break down more rapidly are those of the hand (carpals, metacarpals and phalanges), the distal part of the foot (metatarsal-phalangeal and interphalangeal joints), and the cervical vertebrae. The muscle masses between the scapula and rib cage also break down quickly. The more persistent joints are generally those which bear the heavier weights, such as the lumbar, lumbo-sacral (between the fifth lumbar vertebra (L5) and the sacrum) and sacro-iliac vertebrae, the knee, ankle, tarsal and metatarsal. However although they bear the weight of the body, hip joints break down more rapidly because the head of the femur is inserted so perfectly into the acetabulum that powerful structures to retain it are not needed: the ligaments are formed of fibrous strands that surround the joint capsule.

The Entella burial discussed above is therefore in effect a primary burial, since the interphalangeal joints, which are among those which break down most easily in the body, are preserved. However the sacro-iliac, which is generally one of the most persistent, is not. This apparently paradoxical situation can be simply explained. When the body was laid in the pit, all the joints were obviously connected, since this is, as we have seen, a primary burial. The corpse started to decay quite quickly and the ligaments of the left hand disappeared but since this rested on the bottom of the pit, the bones of the carpal, metacarpal and phalanges have remained in their original arrangement. The ligaments of the more persistent joints broke down much later. Since the body was laid on its side, the sacrum, which was vertical, has fallen into the void created by the disappearance of the intra-pelvic organs and the left coxal bone has slipped, taking with it the femur, since the head of the femur was closed within the acetabulum (the hip joint cavity). In reality the image which is seen at excavation derives in part from the position in which the body was laid at burial and in part from the gradual action of gravity on the bones as the ligaments disappeared. The force of gravity is universal and in this case there is no re-working of the burial. This term must be reserved for disturbance produced by an exogenous element. No-one would refer to re-working in relation to the flattening of the rib cage.

It is therefore normal that in a primary burial all the joints should be in close connection (we will see later that this can be verified, but only in very particular conditions). To demonstrate the primary character of a burial, it is enough to demonstrate that connections are maintained in some joints, as long as these belong to the group of joints that break down more rapidly. If the bones are not well preserved, and if, more precisely, the spongy parts are destroyed, it is not possible to check for the presence of anatomical connections proper. The latter are defined as the preservation of articular relationships and the articular zones are almost all found in those zones whose internal structure comprises spongy bone (short bones and flat bones, the extremities of long bones). It is possible to demonstrate the primary character of the deposit through the preservation of the general topography of the burial: it is not rare that remains of the cranium and the mandible, as well as fragments of diaphysis corresponding to the medial part of the limb long bones, mark the outline of the skeleton, with each element in a logical position.

The primary character of the burial is therefore recognised from the presence of connections relating to the joints that break down more rapidly and, secondarily, from adherence to the overall order of skeletal remains. But contrary to what is often seen in the archaeological literature, the absence of connections does not constitute sufficient proof of the secondary character of the deposit. This absence of connections can be caused by disturbances linked, for example, to the circulation of animals or water, or to collapses of the tomb: it is generally enough for these re-workings, whatever their cause (including human intervention), to happen a long time after deposition when all the ligaments have disappeared. Furthermore, a primary burial can change naturally over time, even in the absence of re-working, towards a state in which no anatomical connection survives. This happens, for example, when the deceased is placed on a wooden support (a funerary bier) or a hammock. It is sufficient in this case that the perishable support should collapse some time later, when all the ligaments have disappeared. The bones of the now decomposed corpse fall to the ground in disorder, losing their anatomical connections. Here even if the burial is primary, there are no connections. It is always necessary to maintain a critical approach to the interpretation of the data.

The above description of decomposition related to various types of joints, based on whether they break down more rapidly or their more persistent character, is based on observations made during many excavations. European societies do not allow the use of corpses for experiments or to observe the behaviour of the joints during decomposition. Corpses given to science are made available to medicine, not to archaeology. In the United States however, experiments on corpses can be carried out, including for example the research carried out by W.M. Bass at his 'body farm', the fame of which is largely due to Patricia Cornwell (Bass 1984; 1997).

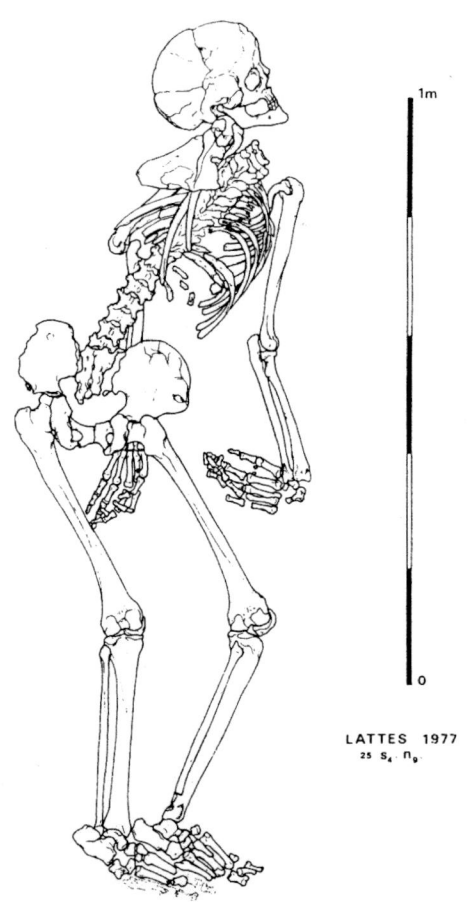

Figure 10. Lattes (Hérault, France), 6th century BC. Excavation by H. Prades and H. Duday, plan by H. Duday.

The following example illustrates how the observations made in excavation can

3 Individual primary burials: additional aspects

help expand the reference collection for the relative chronology of the disassociation of joints. A skeleton of the sixth century BC, buried in a flood layer beneath the water table, at Lattes, a harbour city in southern France, belongs to an older woman who had probably drowned. It is a primary deposit, as demonstrated by the perfect preservation of certain joints that break down more rapidly (the bones of her hands are in perfect connection). However, some displacements are visible in the arrangement of her bones (Figure 10). The left ribs are disturbed and the left scapula has an anomalous orientation: its spine is vertical and almost parallel to the vertebral column. This position is anatomically possible if the arm is raised with the elbow above the head, but this is not the case here since the left hand was found lying on the pubis. The vertebral column is interrupted at C4 and a disjunction can be noticed between the atlas (that appears in lateral aspect like the cranio-facial region and the mandible) and the axis, which, like C3, presents its superior aspect. The olecranon process of the left ulna has passed in front of the distal extremity of the humerus, which is still connected to the radius. Finally there is a gap of seven centimetres between the distal extremity of the left forearm and the hand (Figure 11).

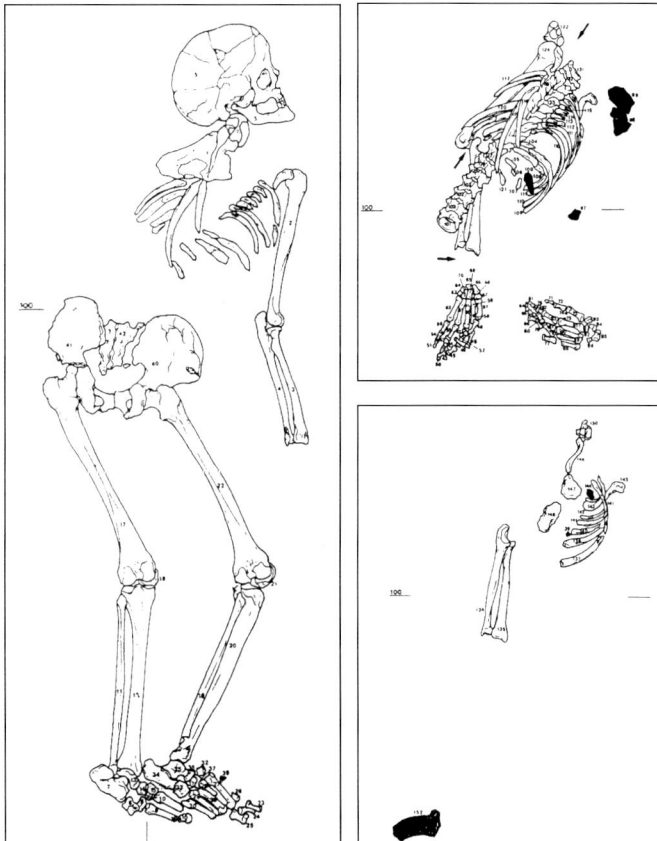

Figure 11. Lattes (Hérault, France), 6th century BC, plans of successive layers. Excavation by H. Prades and H. Duday, plans by H. Duday.

These anomalies depend on the semi-liquid nature of the sediment, in which were areas of greater or lesser pressure. The head has in fact slid towards the left when a depression was created behind the back of the cranium. Ligaments between the mandible and the cranium and between the atlas and occipital were still joined. The axis has followed the atlas, but during displacement or soon after it rotated, remaining linked to the third cervical vertebra (C3). The complete interruption between C3 and C4 shows the absence of (surviving) ligaments here.

At the same time, the upper limb has been pulled up. The scapula, humerus and the clavicle are connected, showing that the shoulder ligaments were in place when the displacements happened. The elbow ligaments were loosening (connection between humerus and radius, disassociation between humerus and ulna). At wrist level, the joints had already decomposed, since the hand has remained in its original position while the forearm has followed the arm as it moved up.

These observations do not have a specifically archaeological interest because the drowning of an old woman is a chance event, insignificant for the cultural history of ancient populations. Yet they give us useful information on the relative chronology of the disappearance of ligaments. In conjunction with the observations made in excavations of other burials, they permit us to construct a reference system for future analyses.

On archaeological sites the discovery of human remains is not always to be related to burials. The skeleton at Lattes belongs to a woman who had probably died accidentally by drowning and cannot be explained as an intentional funerary deposit. A more meaningful example is the reliquary of Saint Fidèle (Figure 12), which is exhibited in a small chapel in the south of France. Inside a tiny gilded wooden case of 18th century date, a cranium with its mandible is arranged on a shelf supported by a tibia, in turn held up two 'columns' made of the distal half of a femur and the proximal part of a tibia. Above, two proximal halves of femora form an arch, of which the keystone is the iliac wing. In the lower part of the reliquary are visible a crown of human vertebrae and flowers made of fabric and gilt metal. At the bottom some ribs and vertebrae are scattered. Although this belongs in a particular religious and cultural context, it would be certainly wrong to consider it as representative of the funerary rite used in France either at the beginning of the 21st century or during the 18th century AD or during the period of Saint Fidèle. We shall return later to the notion of burial.

3 *Individual primary burials: additional aspects* 31

Figure 12. Shrine at Saint Fidèle (Alpes Maritimes, France), 18th century. Photograph by A. Colomer.

Lecture 4

Relationships between the internal and external environments of the corpse (I): the analysis of environmental conditions within the burial

This chapter shows how observations on the taphonomy of a corpse can provide us with useful information on the micro-environment in which a decay process takes place, and, indirectly, on burial architecture: the corpse may be buried either in a filled space or in a void.

4.1. Decomposition in a void

Let us begin with an example of a Middle Neolithic burial excavated at Villeneuve-Tolosane on the outskirts of Toulouse. The complex, 17 hectares in size, belongs to the middle Chasséen. During this period in the south of France, all the burials took place in earth graves. A burial is in an 'earth grave' when the corpse is placed either in an existing hole or in a pit cut into the ground for this purpose. The hole or pit is filled in afterwards immediately and the fill directly touches the body, its clothes or the shroud in which the corpse is tightly bound.

In this case the individual is lying in a pit on his left side in a crouched position (Figure 13). Since the connections that break down more rapidly are still preserved, this is a primary individual deposit. Wild boar canines and a vessel are present as offerings. The right ribs have fallen into the thoracic-abdominal cavity left free by the decomposition of the internal organs, while the left ribs have remained in their original position at the bottom of the pit. The vertebral column is slightly displaced: when excavated, it is generally found to be divided in segments (most commonly from two to five) of three or four vertebrae in strict connection. Between those segments, it is possible to observe a shift, rotation or change of angle at one of the inter-vertebral spaces. Save where the body is laid perfectly symmetrically on soft sediment, the vertebral column is subject to forces which exercise a double torsion. As long as ligaments hold, these forces do not generate any movement, but when the linkages break, one of the three types of displacements described above occurs in the space where the ligaments first yield. This movement absorbs the action of the forces on the vertebral column, unless another should happen a little further away at the intervertebral space which gives up second, and so on. David Persinotto, who is working on his Ph.D. dissertation at Bordeaux on corpse taphonomy, has showed the systematic occurrence of a displacement at the first or second lumbar vertebrae. At this point in front of the vertebral column is the transverse colon, containing faecal matter and bacteria which have been proliferating

4 Relationships between the internal and external environments of the corpse (I) 33

Figure 13. Villeneuve-Tolosane (Haute Garonne, France), burial P4–3, middle Neolithic (Chasséen culture). Excavation by J. Vaquer, J-P. Giraud and H. Duday.

since the moment of death. These attack tissues and rapidly cause a zone of precocious destruction.

The photograph further shows that the sacrum has fallen, dragging with it the L4 and L5 vertebrae, causing a very clear rupture at the space between L3 and L4. When the ligaments of the sacro-iliac joint came apart, the ligaments of L4–L5 and L5–S1 still held, whereas those of L3–L4 had already decayed. Here we see how excavation data may give us important information on the chronology of joint breakdown.

A few cervical and upper thoracic vertebrae have moved away from the space originally occupied by the corpse. There must have been a void since a vertebra obviously cannot move in the earth by itself. Many animal holes have been observed in the sides of the pit and although none have been found by the neck, a burrowing animal might have caused a disturbance. However even if a hole constitutes a void, this is of no archaeological interest because it does not provide us with any relevant information about the original structure of the tomb.

The upper part of the right limb is still in connection, while on the left, of the hand only the thumb and little finger remain in place, partly covered by the face. The central part of the carpal and the second, third and fourth metacarpals are connected, but away from the space originally occupied by the body, near the elbow. Since these joints break down more rapidly, the displacement should have taken place soon after deposition. During the initial phase of decomposition, there would have been a void around the corpse.

In conclusion, the displacement of skeletal elements proves the existence of an original void. Since this void provides information on the structure of the tomb and on the environment within the grave, it is necessary to demonstrate its existence at the initial phase of decomposition. This excludes the possibility of later re-working not related to burial practices.

In this case the causes of displacement are quite simple to explain. The upper part of the body leans slightly upwards on the side of the pit and, during decay, the cranial skeleton has slipped downwards towards the rib cage. It seems that the skeleton 'has no neck' (it is clear that at the same time the cervical and thoracic vertebrae shifted backwards). Moreover part of the left hand has slipped along the forearm bones during decomposition. Putrefaction in fact produces a rather viscous mass that may slide under the force of gravity. I have observed this mechanism in several cases, for example when corpses are buried on their back with their knees raised. Usually the patella does not fall vertically but after the quadriceps muscle is destroyed remains connected to the tibial tuberosity, through the patellar tendon. Then it slips towards the lower third of the leg, pulled by the fluid produced by decomposition.

'Archaeothanatology' therefore allows clues to be identified related to the presence of a void at the moment of burial. Archaeological observations, for example of traces of wood, nails or differences in fill would probably clarify what type of structure might have caused this void, coffin, burial chamber, wooden framework *etc* . However, a void can also be detected in the absence of architectonic elements. There are cases of individuals buried under covers of leather, a thick and rigid material that creates a void around the corpse, seen in the displacement of bones away from the space originally occupied by the body, since the cover decayed long after the corpse did.

Another example is a Middle Neolithic burial found at Berriac, near Carcassonne, in the south of France. Here grain storage pits were sometimes later used as graves. In our example the body was found laid on its back, with knees folded under its femora and an ox rib laid on its thorax (Figure 14). The head, that originally rested on the side of the pit, had fallen dragging with it the mandible, atlas and axis (in this case, the break is between C2 and C3) still attached to the base of the cranium; the first two cervical vertebrae had later fallen to the bottom of the pit, beneath the *foramen magnum*. This means that decomposition took place within a void and that a wooden cover which had closed the pit subsequently disappeared.

Displacements are linked to the effects of the force of gravity and depend on the position of the corpse at burial. When the body is laid on its back (as usually happens in Christian cemeteries as well as among other human groups) in a fairly wide space, the disappearance of ligaments is followed by the collapse and disarticulation of the pelvic structure. After the displacement of the coxal bones, a lateral rotation of the femora occurs, with the heads still engaged in the hip joint, along with the falling of the patellae away from the knees (Figure 15). It is therefore very important to record the exact position of the patella during excavation.

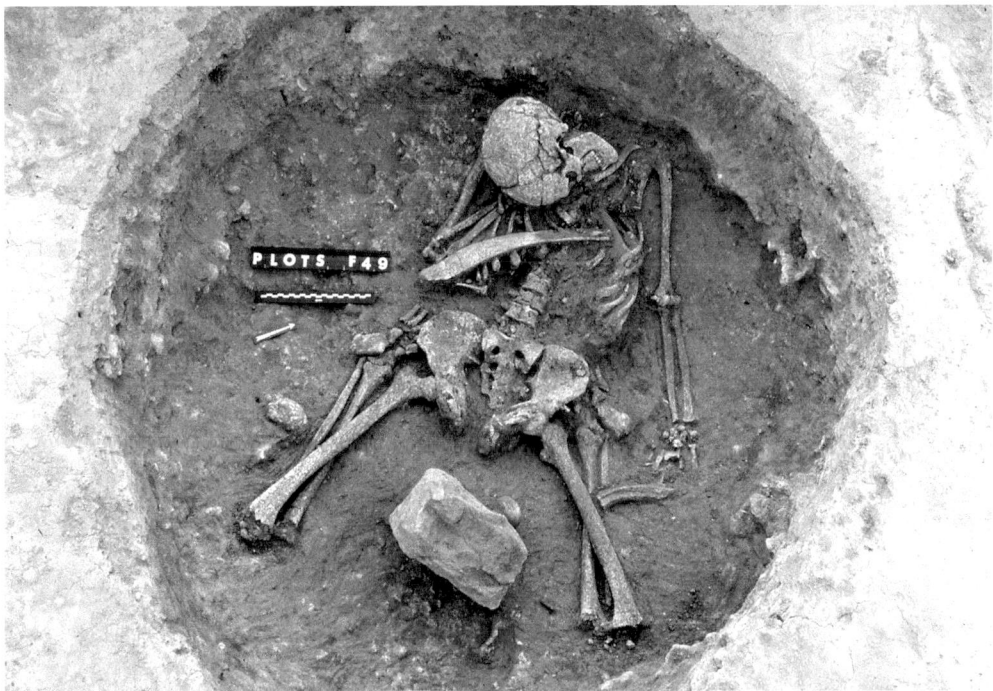

Figure 14. Les Plots at Berriac (Aude, France), middle Neolithic (early Chasséen phase). Excavation by J. Vaquer and H. Duday.

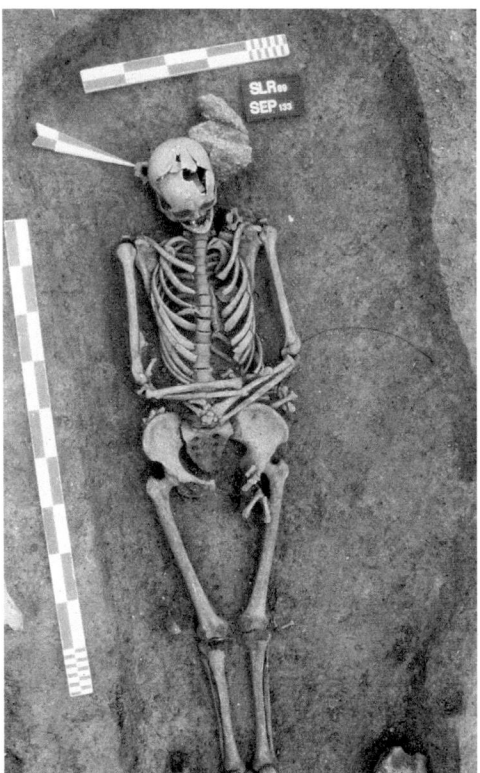 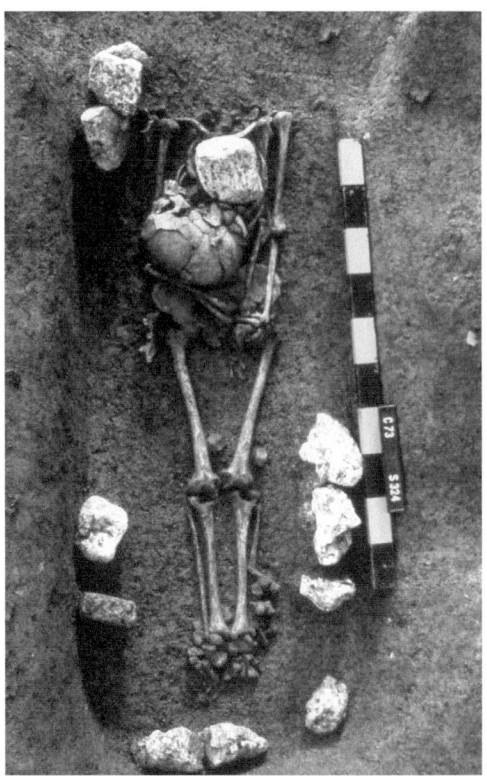

Figure 15. Serris, Les Ruelles (Seine-et-Marne, France), burial 133, early medieval. Excavation by B. Foucray, F. Blaizot, F. Gentili and H. Guy.

Figure 16. Cemetery of Saint Cheron at Chartres (Eure-et-Loir, France), burial 324, 4th–5th century AD. Excavation by D. Joly and P. Courtaud.

There are multiple potential causes of alteration to the original deposit. To the action of gravity we could add, for example, a partial collapse of the coffin, as in the case of a fifth century AD burial found at Chartres (Figure 16). The skeleton is in a wooden coffin (which is different to the bier: the latter transports the corpse from home to the place of burial). A displacement of the foot bones can be observed; the right patella has fallen outside the knee because of gravity, while the left has fallen inside because of the medial rotation of the femur. The cranio-facial region has been pushed forward onto the torso by the collapse of the wooden wall behind the head.

A medieval burial at Serris-les-Ruelles provides another example (Figure 17). There are important disassociations in the area of the head, with an upwards displacement of the cranio-facial region, mandible, upper and middle cervical vertebrae (the series has turned but remained connected), scapulae, clavicles, left humerus and some upper ribs. The upper part of the body has generally preserved its original position, but with some disjunctions in the vertebral column (there is a widening of the intervertebral space

4 Relationships between the internal and external environments of the corpse (I)   37

between L2 and L3) and especially of the bones of the right forearm. The radius has rotated (with the distal end by the elbow and proximal end seemingly in articulation with bones of the right wrist). The leg bones (tibiae and fibulae) and those of the feet have kept their anatomical connections, but there is an important overlap at the knees: the patellae have retained their relationship with the tibiae but not the femora. The overall impression is that the skeleton has been divided into four separate blocks: (1) the head, the neck and the upper part of the thorax, (2), the remainder of the thorax and the first two lumbar vertebrae, the left forearm and the left hand (the latter situated a little above and within the right elbow), (3) the last three lumbar vertebrae, pelvis and thighs, with the right forearm and the right hand which lies on the left hip and (4) the legs and feet. These indications suggest that the base of the coffin split along three fracture lines that were more or less perpendicular to its longitudinal axis, perhaps because wooden beams had been positioned under the coffin. The other parts then slipped one over the other like tectonic plates (for a detailed analysis of the collapse of a wooden container, see Duday et al. 1990).

On the same site, another burial (Figure 18) shows a large zone of disconnection in

 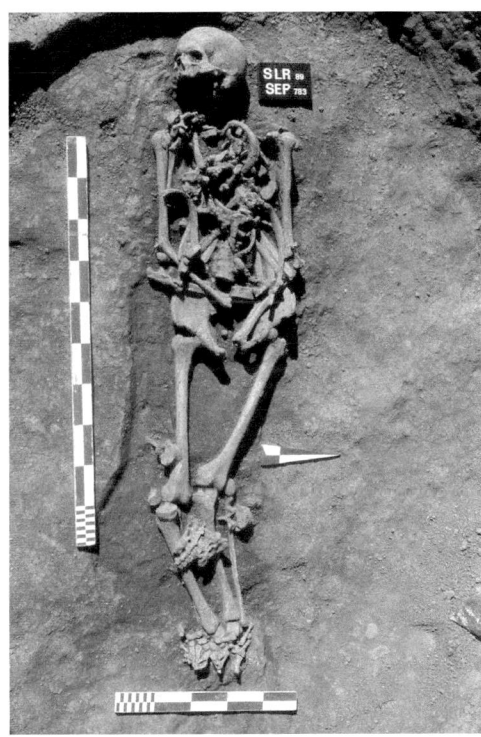

Figure 17. Serris, Les Ruelles (Seine-et-Marne, France), burial 342, early medieval. Excavation by B. Foucray, F. Blaizot, F. Gentili and H. Guy.

Figure 18. Serris, Les Ruelles (Seine-et-Marne, France), burial 783, early medieval. Excavation by B. Foucray, F. Blaizot, F. Gentili and H. Guy.

Figure 19. Cemetery of Saint-Cheron at Chartres (Eure-et-Loir, France), 4th–5th century AD. Excavation by D. Joly and P. Courtaud.

the area of the thorax; the last two lumbar vertebrae and the sacrum have moved about 50 cm. towards the knees. These anomalies are probably due to fluctuation of the water table and micro-currents within the burial which have floated and moved the smallest bones. Obviously this can only happen in a void.

Some displacements may be due to human intervention long after the inhumation. An example is given by a fifth century AD burial from Chartres in the cemetery of Saint Cheron (Figure 19). The bones of the upper part of the left limb had been moved towards those of the right one. They are certainly still within the volume originally occupied by the corpse, but the left humerus and the left ulna have rotated, making them pass temporarily into the space outside this original volume. This disturbance was caused by the excavation of a later pit which cut the side of the coffin. Rather than throwing them away the bones were replaced in the position described.

Whatever their cause, all these displacements suggest that a void existed at the moment of burial.

4.2. Decomposition in a filled space

This section discusses a middle Neolithic burial found at Berriac, near Carcassonne (Figure 20). It is a primary burial, with the individual laid prone, the head turned to the left and the right hand holding the right knee (Figure 21). The bones of the hand are connected and the distal phalanges of the fingers are pushed straight into the ground, against the upper part of the right tibia. Generally, if a bone is in potential disequilibrium in relation to the space occupied by the body, it will fall into this space when decay of the soft tissue frees it. If this does not happen, something has prevented its fall.

4 Relationships between the internal and external environments of the corpse (I)   39

Figure 20. Les Plots at Berriac (Aude, France), burial F36, middle Neolithic (early Chasséen phase). Excavation by J. Vaquer and H. Duday.

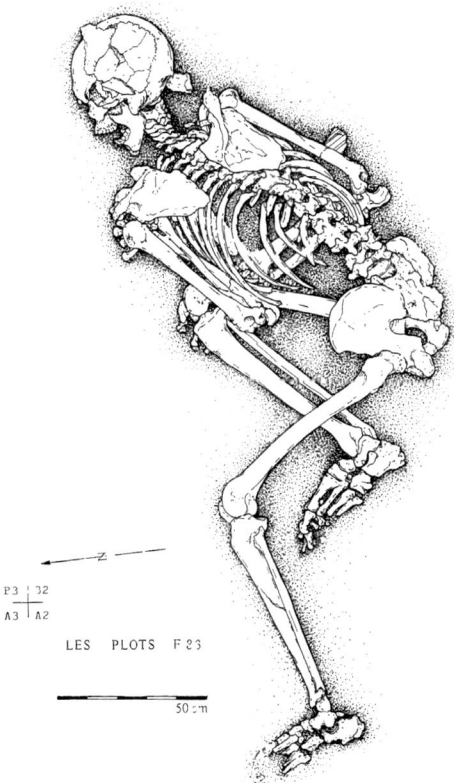

Figure 21. Les Plots at Berriac (Aude, France), burial F36, middle Neolithic (early Chasséen phase). Excavation by J. Vaquer and H. Duday, plan by H. Duday.

This would demonstrate the existence of an obstacle that provides some support. The archaeological observations may allow us to identify that element, which could be:
- the edge of the pit (not the case here);
- a border in perishable material in contact with the corpse at some distance from the edge of the pit (but in this burial the effect caused by the obstacle can be observed at a distance from the line that joins the outermost points of the skeleton, the face, the left shoulder and the left foot);
- the pit fill (the bones are prevented from falling beyond the space occupied by the corpse because this space is already filled).

In this case, it is likely that the earth was in contact with the corpse and served as an obstacle to prevent the bones from falling. This would then be a burial in a filled space.

These obstacles have effects of two different sorts:
- a 'supporting' effect, which we have just described (a burial is defined as in a 'filled space when the grave fill provides the obstacle, supporting the bone),
- a 'linear delimitation' effect, seen when all the bones on one side of the corpse are aligned against a physical limit, for example the side panel of a coffin, the edge of a pit, the base of a wall *etc*.

The demonstration of the existence of an obstacle is not therefore sufficient in itself to prove that a burial is in a filled space. An early medieval burial at Serris-les-Ruelles gives an example (Figure 22). The corpse is supine and the pubic symphysis has not separated, the femora are in an anterior position and the patellae are at the distal extremities of the two femora. The body has been buried in a particularly narrow pit. The characteristics of the grave cut here prevent the displacement of the bones. A narrow container may both delimit and hold the burial, so that the bones line up against the side and remain in equilibrium.

A 'supporting' effect can be observed even when decomposition has undoubtedly taken place in a void. In a 17th century AD samurai cemetery in Japan, some tombs have the shape of small circular chests (Figure 23), buried with a void within and a wooden cover above. The wood is very well preserved due to the permanent humidity. The corpse was buried in a sitting position inside the container: at the bottom were the pelvis, which has opened, and the lumbar vertebrae, as well as the head, which has fallen, and the scapula showing its posterior aspect. The lower limb bones however have remained in their vertical position, leaning against the wall.

4.3. The Grotte de Foissac: some observations on taphonomy in an underground environment

In 1965 cavers exploring a network of unknown galleries in the Grotte de Foissac in the south of France came across the bed of a subterranean stream which they decided to follow. They reached the original entrance of the cave, the surface of which was covered with intact Neolithic vessels, arrow heads, foot and hand prints *etc*. In order to reach the site, now visited by many tourists, a shaft had to be dug.

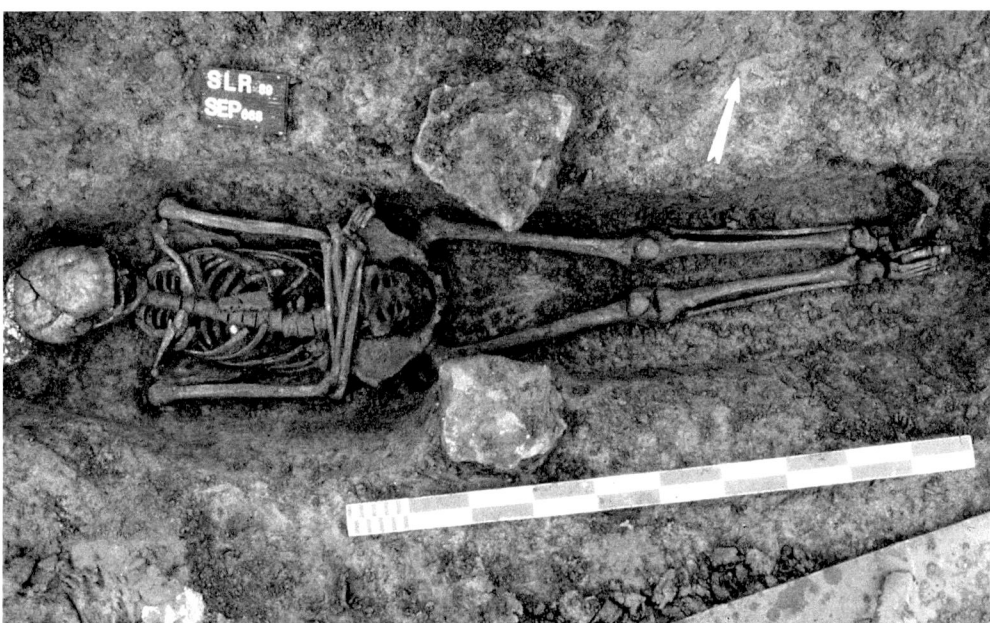

Figure 22. Serris, Les Ruelles (Seine-et-Marne, France), burial 688, early medieval. Excavation by B. Foucray, F. Blaizot, F. Gentili and H. Guy.

Figure 23. Sendaï (Japan), Samurai cemetery, 17th century. Photograph by T. Nara.

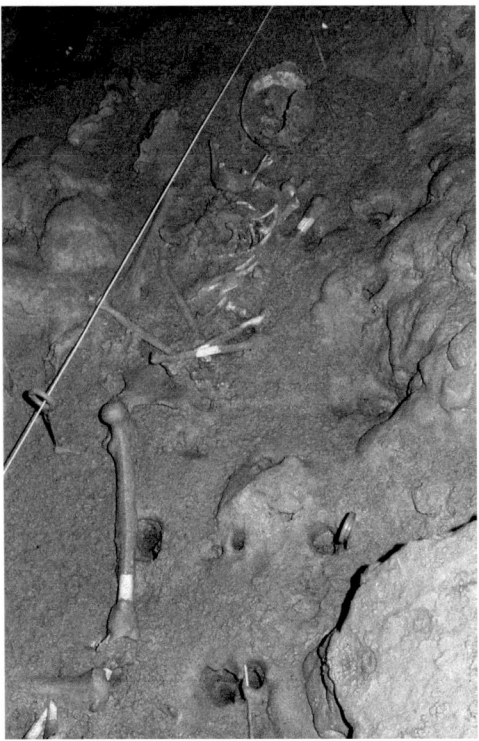 

Figure 24. Grotte de Foissac (Aveyron, France), burial 1, Eneolithic. Excavation by H. Duday, photograph by F. Rouzard.

Figure 25. Grotte de Foissac (Aveyron, France), burial 1, Eneolithic. Excavation by H. Duday, photograph by F. Rouzard.

About 4500 years ago, the cave was a clay pit, with platforms to facilitate extraction of the clay. On these platforms skeletons have also been found. The clay has preserved everything, impressions of basketry, of a stick with a rope knotted around it, tool marks and, against the wall, a child's footprint. The burials were found on the platforms cut into the clay along the shore of the stream, placed on the surface and not in pits. During floods, water mixed with soil covered the bones. Drops of water, falling from stalactites, then washed the bones of the clay which had encased them.

In one sector of this site, the skeleton of an old woman was found (Figure 24), mostly with anatomical connections preserved but with some disturbance. Animal bones present included a pig's rib cage placed under the left leg of the skeleton which was laid on its back. During decomposition the head moved upwards and backwards, the upper limbs were partially dissociated and the foot bones disappeared.

At the proximal extremity of the right tibia and fibula, an osteolytic lesion, whose surface is slightly porous, could be an osteitis. The other fibula shows an eroded zone, black in colour, in a position corresponding to the zone of erosion on the woman's right leg (Figure 25). This spatial indication shows that the alteration of the bones depends on

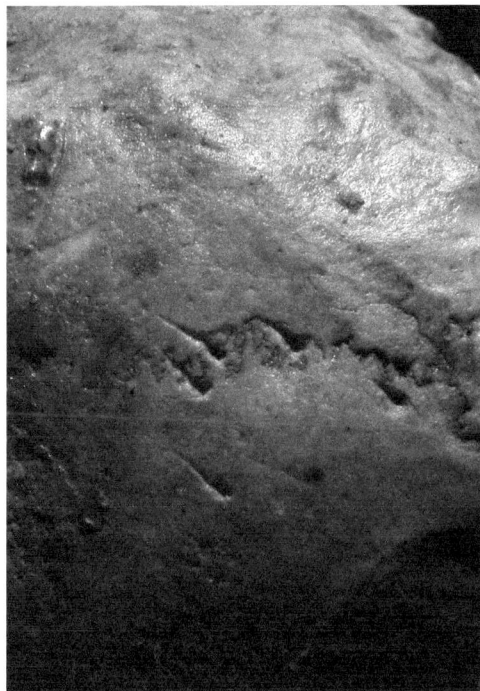 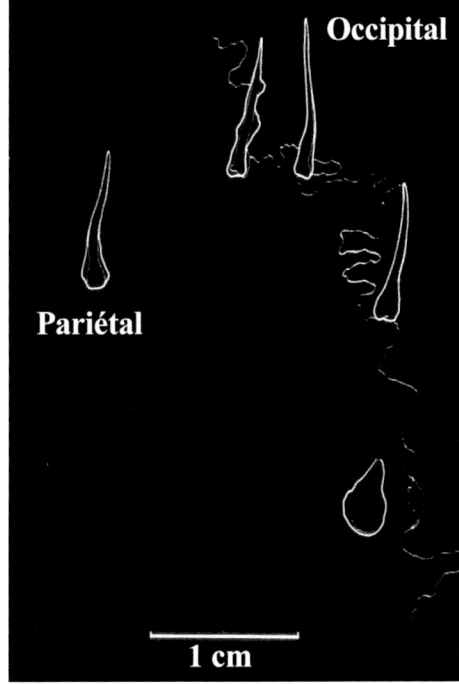

Figure 26a. Grotte de Foissac (Aveyron, France), burial 1, Eneolithic. Claw marks on the parietal-temporal region. Excavation and study by H. Duday, photograph by F. Rouzard.

Figure 26b. Grotte de Foissac (Aveyron, France), burial 1, Eneolithic. Drawing of claw marks by H. Duday.

the position in which the corpse was laid and is not a pathological lesion. This alteration has been caused by the water falling from the stalactites above and the black colour is due to deposition of manganese.

There are also disturbances to the torso and the head. Some vertebrae have shifted, paradoxically moving in a direction opposite to that of gravity. On the cranium there are five deep comma-shaped marks, corresponding to the left front paw of a small animal, a mustelid, perhaps a skunk (Figure 26). The displacements are therefore taphonomic and due to the passage of the skunk. The cranio-mandibular dissociation is not to be interpreted here as evidence for a headrest.

In another, higher area, above the flood level, was the burial of a seven-eight year old child. The head was detached from the bones and fresh fractures were visible on the skeleton. Beside the skeleton were some small clay blocks and many bones were displaced. The child was crouched on its back, with the knees folded up to the thorax, so that the tarsal bones were found by the pelvis (Figure 27). The mandible is complete, but the left mandibular condyle has broken and is by the right shoulder. The right ribs are in position, while three left ribs, apparently in relation with each other, have

Figure 27. Grotte de Foissac (Aveyron, France), burial 1, Eneolithic. General view after excavation.

shifted towards the side of the platform, but not down the slope, as might be expected. A metatarsal was found behind the lumbar vertebrae and as excavation continued, four foot phalanges were found. The child was probably deposited in a sitting position, with his back resting against the wall. After an early stage of decomposition, some bones, including those of the distal area, became detached from the skeleton.

Lecture 5

Relationships between the internal and external environments of the corpse (II)

5.1. 'Verticalization' of the clavicles

This topic can be introduced with the example of another medieval burial found at Serris-les-Ruelles (Figure 28). It is a primary deposit in a void of a body with its connections that break down more rapidly still preserved. The left patella has fallen outside the knee, and the foot bones and some cervical vertebrae have been displaced. The 'verticalization' of the clavicles can be observed, with their lateral extremity pushed upwards and the medial downwards. This position is a consequence of transversal compression at the shoulders and can only occur when the body has been placed in a very narrow coffin or has been wrapped in a shroud (a double effect of 'linear delimitation' can be seen at a certain distance from the edges of the pit, on the right side of the skeleton).

The clavicles also become vertical or shift to a very oblique position in 'anthropomorphic' tombs dug into rock or clay. The corpse lies in a pit cut to its shape and the grave narrows

Figure 28. Serris, Les Ruelles (Seine-et-Marne, France), burial 125, early medieval. Excavation by B. Foucray, F. Blaizot, F. Gentili and H. Guy.

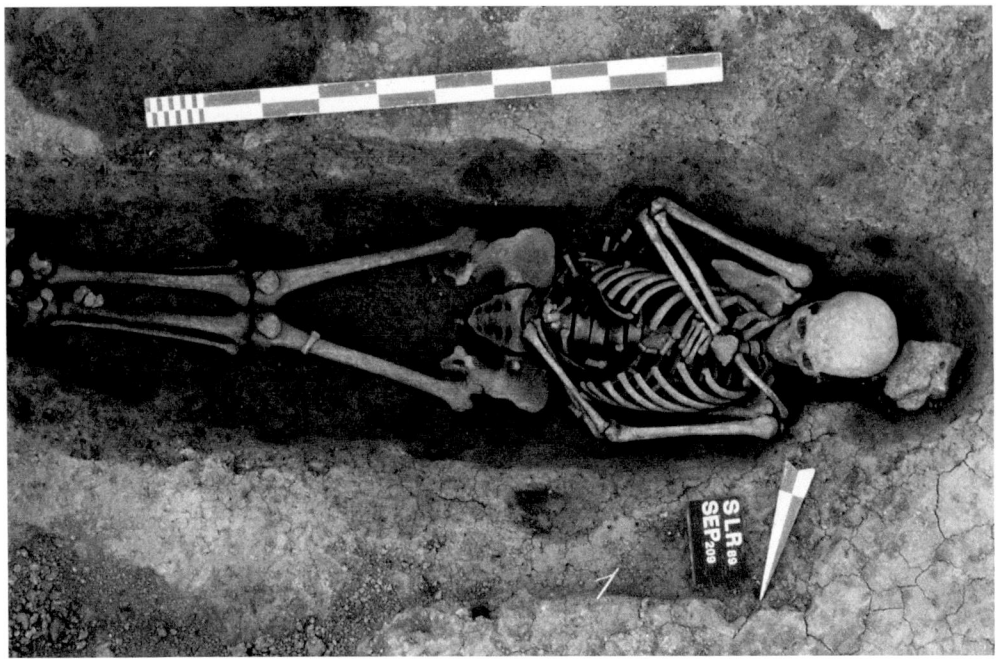

Figure 29. Serris, Les Ruelles (Seine-et-Marne, France), burial 209, early medieval. Excavation by B. Foucray, F. Blaizot, F. Gentili and H. Guy.

at the neck to a niche for the head. The shoulders are pushed forward since they lie where the pit narrows for cutting the niche for the head, which is often slightly higher than the bottom of the pit (Figure 29).

The 'verticalization' of the clavicles simply indicates that the shoulders were pushed upward, forward, and towards the interior of the space occupied by the body. The observations made during excavation give information on the mechanism for this and on the taphonomic dynamics. To interpret them correctly, the archaeological information concerning the characteristics of the pit should be carefully considered.

5.2. Voids that form around the corpse

Let us now examine burial 175 of the fourth century BC necropolis at Aleria in Corsica, a site already discussed in relation to the arrangement of grave goods. This tomb does not seem to have been robbed in antiquity; the door of unfired brick was still closed when the tomb was found. This closed off access to the burial chamber, which was formed by a ledge on each side where the corpses were placed and a central pit where grave goods were laid (Figure 30). Sand has infiltrated to cover the skeletons and protect them when the tomb ceiling collapsed. One individual has a bronze brooch on its chest, beads, a scarab made of glass paste near the right elbow and a bronze ring on a phalanx

5 *Relationships between the internal and external environments of the corpse (II)*   47

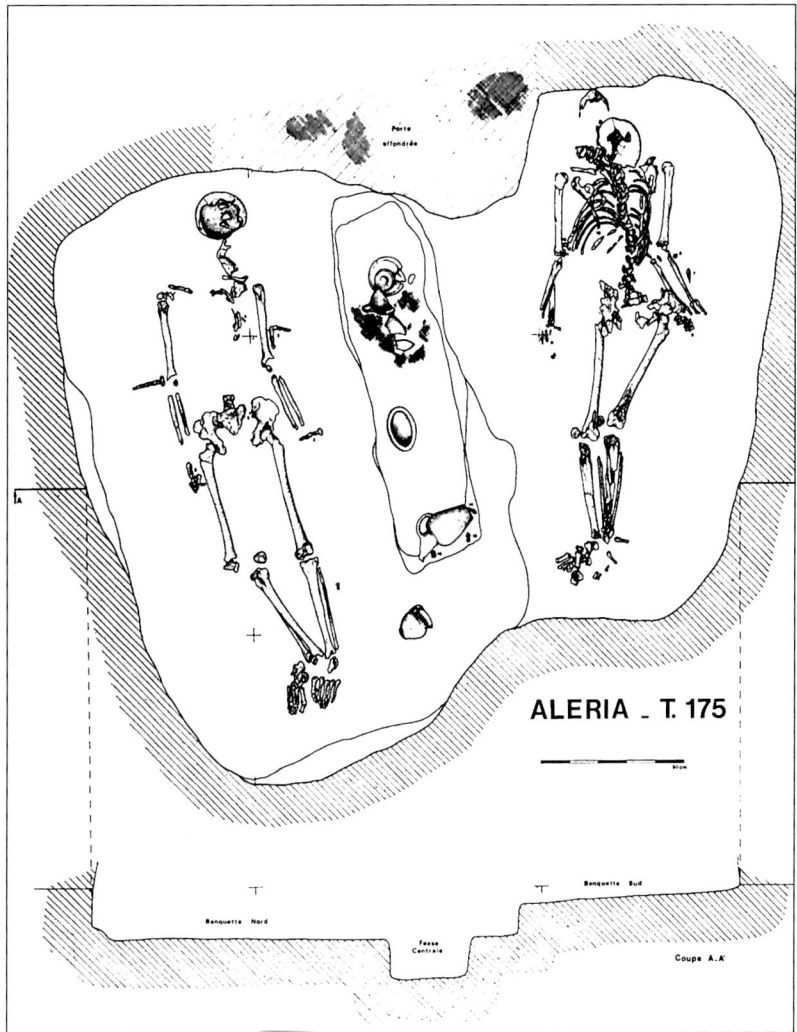

Figure 30. The pre-Roman necropolis of Aleria (Corsica), burial 175, 4th century BC. Excavation by J. Jehasse and H. Duday, plan by H. Duday.

on the left hand. This burial is of interest not only for its rich grave goods, but also for what has happened to the head. The mandible is in a vertical position against the side of the chamber. The cranio-facial region with the atlas connected to the occipital has fallen to the left of the neck, while the vertebral column, still in connection up to the axis, has leaned towards the right (Figure 31). This is the typical position taken up by the bones when a perishable element that supports the head decomposes (for example a cushion or small wooden structure, like a headrest). A supporting element can leave traces among the bones only if made of material that decays after the ligaments of

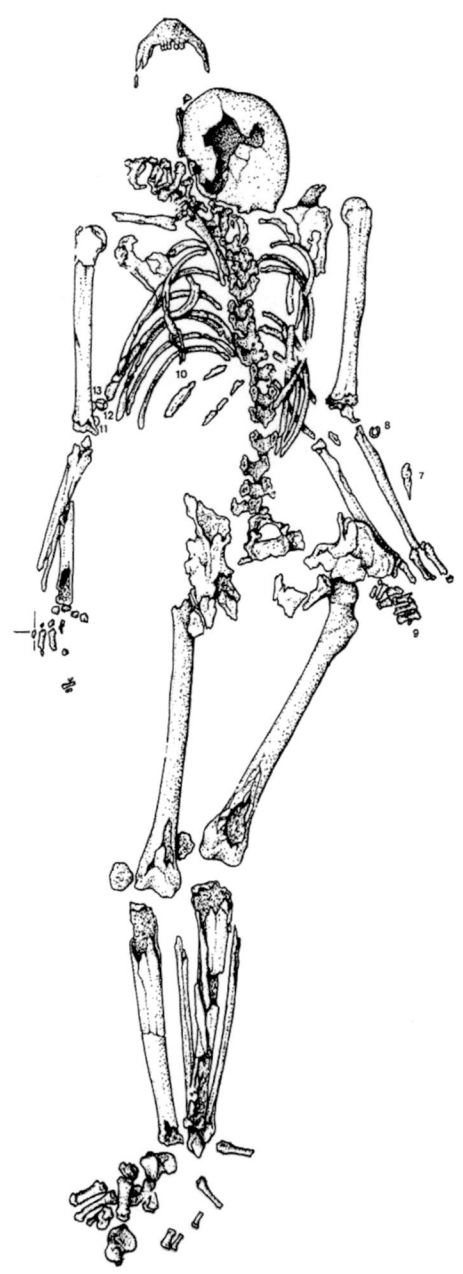

Figure 31. *The pre-Roman necropolis of Aleria (Corsica), burial 175, 4th century BC detail. Excavation by J. Jehasse and H. Duday, plan by H. Duday.*

the temporo-mandibular and cranio-vertebral joints have decomposed.

A similar situation can be seen in a fifth century AD burial in the St Cheron cemetery at Chartres (Figures 32 and 33). The corpse was put in a coffin (whose nails have been found *in situ*) inside a very narrow pit. The corpse was laid on its back with limestone blocks placed beneath, one below the upper part of the thorax and head and the other beneath the feet. The head has rolled against the side of the pit, detaching itself from the vertebral column, and the cervical vertebrae have been scattered, while the mandible is on the same side as the cranio-facial region, from which it is nevertheless separated. The organic matter produced by the decomposition of the corpse soaked the wooden coffin and caused its destruction. The collapse of the base of the coffin, held up by the limestone blocks, has caused the displacement of the bones. The elements from the central part of the body have fallen to the bottom of the pit, while the extremities have remained in an elevated position where they came to rest on the blocks. From above the tomb looks the same as in the previous case, even if the changes undergone by the skeleton are different, as shown by the different levels of the individual bones. In the tomb at Aleria, all the bones are on the same level (the ledge), while here the bones of the head, neck and feet are elevated in relation to the rest of the skeleton.

In a medieval burial in the cemetery of Saints-Côme-et-Damien at Montpellier, in the south of France, a hyperextension of the head can be seen with an exaggerated opening between the occipital and the atlas and between the atlas and axis (Figure 34). The cause is a hole made by an animal that passes just behind

5 Relationships between the internal and external environments of the corpse (II) 49

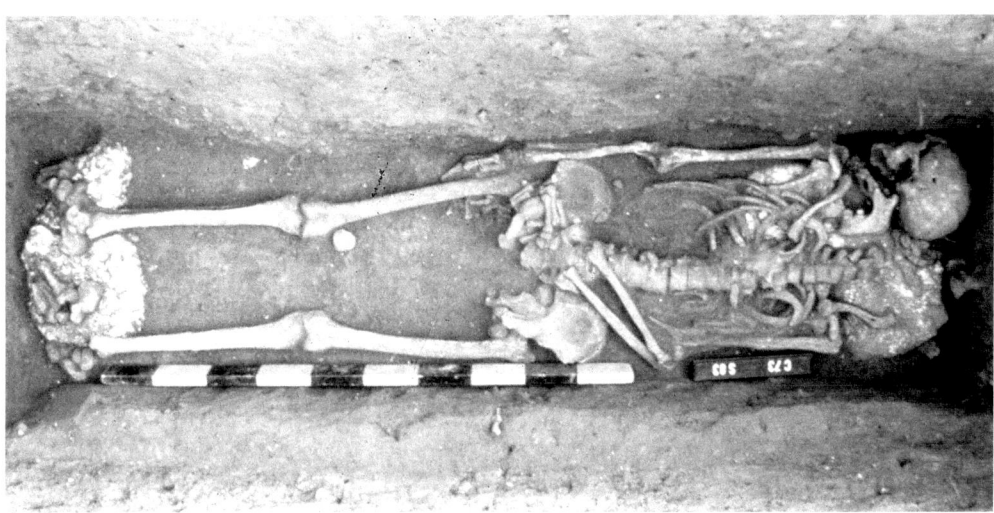

Figure 32. Cemetery of Saint-Cheron at Chartres (Eure-et-Loir, France), burial C73, 4th–5th century AD, general view. Excavation by D. Joly and P. Courtaud.

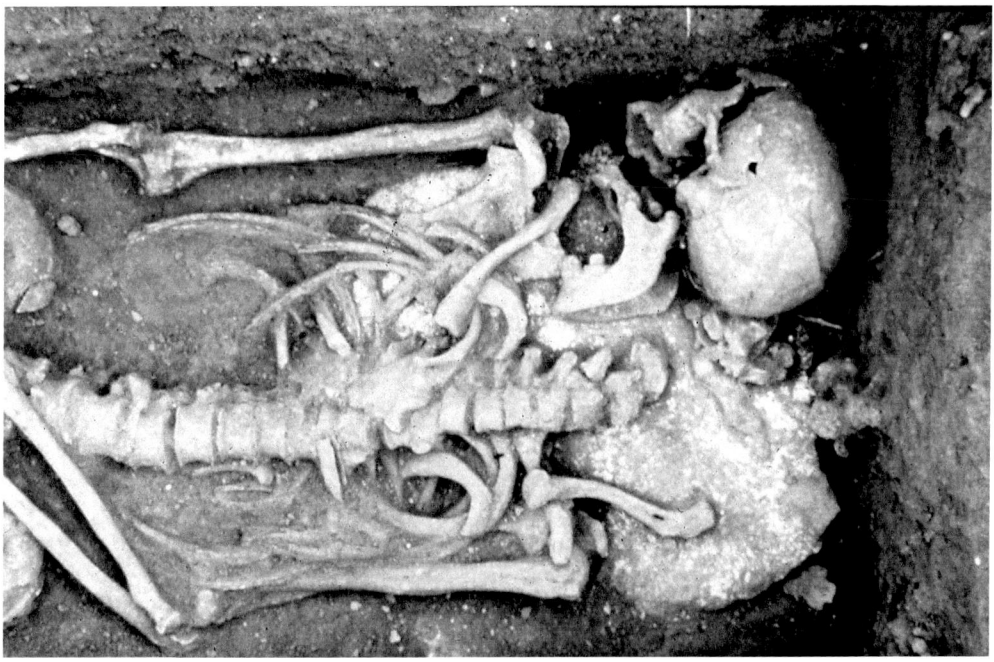

Figure 33. Cemetery of Saint-Cheron at Chartres (Eure-et-Loir, France), burial C73, 4th–5th century AD, details of thoracic region and upper limbs. Excavation by D. Joly and P. Courtaud.

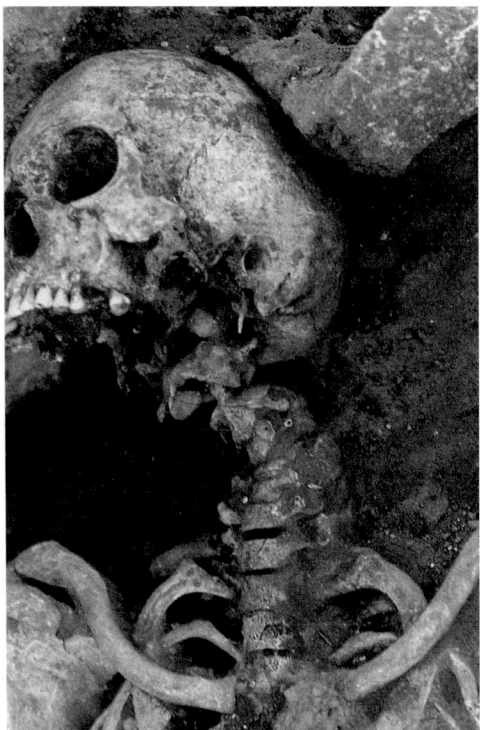 

Figure 34. Cemetery of Saints-Côme-et-Damien at Montpellier (Hérault, France), Middle Ages. Detail before the removal of the cranio-facial region. Photograph by E. Crubézy.

Figure 35. Cemetery of Saints-Côme-et-Damien at Montpellier (Hérault, France), Middle Ages. Detail after the removal of the cranio-facial region. Photograph by E. Crubézy.

the head (Figure 35). The hole has collapsed and pulled the head into it. Even if the disassociation between vertebrae and cranium can be seen from above, measurement of their relative depth reveals that the occipital is lower than the rest of the skeleton.

These considerations concern the displacement of the bones towards voids which are created during the 'history' of the burial. The discussion may sometimes be more complex but also richer in information in those cases that imply later human interference. In a burial in the cemetery of Saint Cheron, Chartres, the individual is supine and while the original anatomical logic is preserved, the skeleton is extremely compressed transversally on the median line through the burial (Figure 36). The femora are behind the coxal bones on the median line; the right femur appears in anterior view, while the left is in posterior view and their heads touch. The vertebrae are in front of the ribs which are oriented downwards and towards the interior of the burial and converge on the median line. The upper limbs can be found under the skeletal elements of the torso, at a greater depth (Figure 37).

5 Relationships between the internal and external environments of the corpse (II)

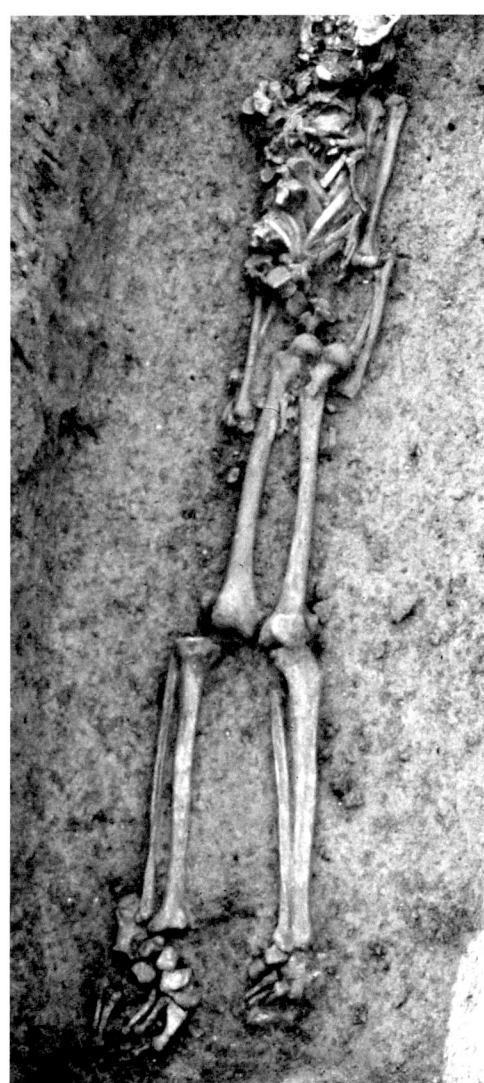

Figure 36. Cemetery of Saint-Cheron at Chartres (Eure-et-Loir, France), burial 98, 4th–5th century AD, first excavation layer. Excavation by D. Joly and P. Courtaud.

Figure 37. Cemetery of Saint-Cheron at Chartres (Eure-et-Loir, France), burial 98, 4th–5th century AD, second excavation layer. Excavation by D. Joly and P. Courtaud.

This would seem to be a case of an anomalous disturbance but is actually the natural evolution of a primary burial of a body laid on its back in a V-section coffin. As decomposition frees the bones, they move toward the median line of the burial, moving down the slope. The scapulae are freed faster than the ribs, so that the upper limbs slip behind the thorax. The heads of the femora, having joints that break down more rapidly, move out of the hip joints and pass below the coxal bones toward the median line; during this movement the left femur has rotated. We know that rib joints disassociate quite fast because of the decomposition of the rib cartilage. They are followed by the destruction of the joint between the rib head and the vertebral bodies, so that only the joint between the costal tubercle and the transverse processes of the vertebra remains connected. At this point the rib cage flattens, a phenomenon we have already discussed. Usually, when a corpse lies on a flat surface, the ribs rest on it and spread symmetrically in relation to the vertebral axis, while the sternal extremities are displaced. When the container has a V-section, the sloping support causes the anterior part of the rib to be pulled backwards and to the middle and finish behind the vertebral column (an inversion of the normal relationship between ribs and vertebrae).

These mechanisms are known thanks to the observations made by François Lambach in his study of protohistoric burials at Nordhouse (Alsace), where many individuals were buried in tree trunks dug out in U- or, rarely, V- shaped sections. Since the wooden containers were well preserved, in the second case he could observe the pulling backwards and towards the median axis of the coffin of the bones freed by decomposition of the ligaments. In a V-section coffin, a particular space develops during the decomposition of the corpse. This space becomes accessible only when the bones are freed from the ligaments.

Lambach's observations have made it possible to understand this type of burial and interpret others. The observations made during excavation provide substitutes for experiments and help us to understand corpse taphonomy. The displacements reveal an interaction between the corpse during its decomposition and the structure that contains it. This might initially be a V-shape, but sometimes it could be a flat support which has later split in two parts along its longitudinal axis. These two sections then slope towards the median line. If this break occurs quite early, then the bones freed by putrefaction are under the same mechanical conditions as those observed when the container was originally V-shaped in section.

5.3. The filling of the internal volume of the corpse

A corpse ready to be buried still has internal organs and muscles. The 'soft parts' which characterize the primary deposit disappear and are replaced by the fill which is found when the burial is excavated. It is important to examine this 'transubstantiation', the apparent transformation of flesh into fill, which clearly constitutes the main difference between the time of burial and of excavation. Paradoxically the archaeological literature seems to overlook this process completely. When does the filling of the internal volume of the corpse occur and what are its causes?

5.3.1. The chronology of filling the volume freed by the decay of soft tissue
5.3.1.1. Delayed filling
Generally the filling is staggered over time, as the various examples discussed earlier testify, in particular the flattening of the rib cage or the separation at the inter-vertebral

5 Relationships between the internal and external environments of the corpse (II)   53

spaces (see for example Figure 13). The decay of the thoracic (lungs, heart) and abdominal organs (liver, spleen, stomach, and bowels) frees a space which lasts for a certain time. The bones are subject to various forces (for example gravity, torsion of the vertebral column *etc*) and when freed by the breakdown of ligaments, move under the action of these forces. The sediments later invade the interstitial spaces and block the bones in their new position. They will only be freed by further disturbance, for example excavation.

A little known consequence of the delayed filling of the volume freed by the decay of soft tissue is the closing of the intersegmental angles of the body, *i.e.* the angles which are created by the different segments of the limbs, like the arm and forearm (elbow) or thigh and leg (knee). For example, in the Chalcolithic burial chamber of Devois de l'Etang in the lower valley of the Rhône, a corpse was found crouched in a particularly contracted position (Figure 38). Many archaeologists interpret skeletons in this position

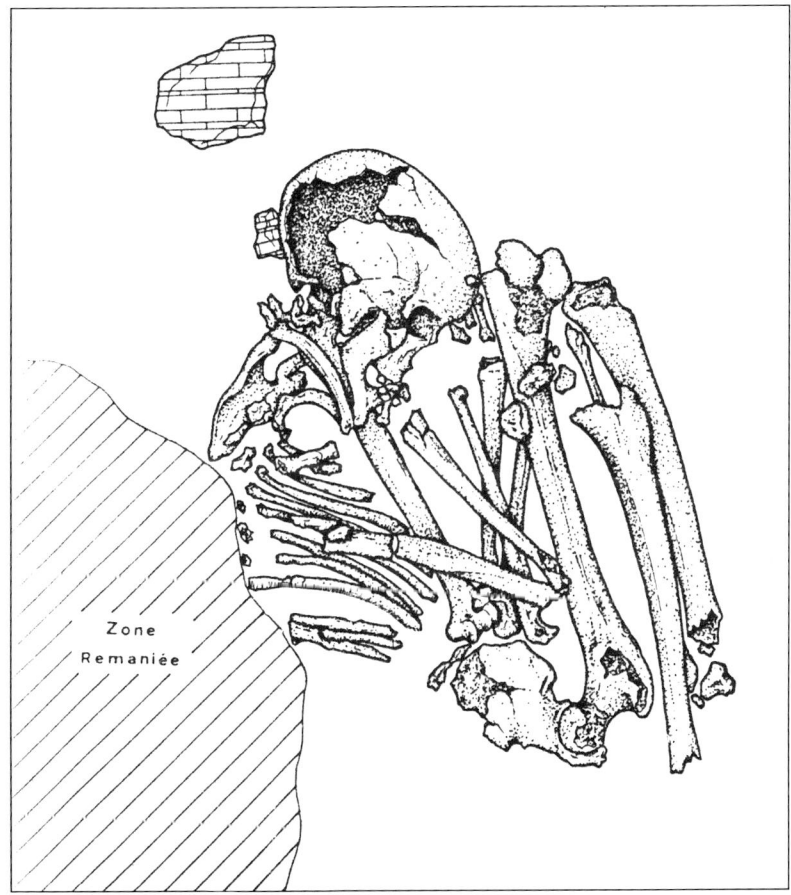

Figure 38. Burial chamber at Devois de l'Etang at Laudun (Gard, France), Chalcolithic. Excavation by A. Colomber, J. Coularou, X. Gutherz, A. Raux and H. Duday, plan by H. Duday.

as evidence for corpses having been buried in bags or tightly bound. This is possible but difficult to prove. When a corpse is buried in the earth, the sediment around it exerts pressure and gradually, as muscles and ligaments progressively decay, closes the intersegmental angles between the bones. Obviously this phenomenon does not occur when the joints are extended or lightly flexed.

5.3.1.2. Progressive filling

Let us take the example of a fifth century BC skeleton of an eight to ten year old boy, a primary burial found at Coteau de Montigné, in the west of France (Figure 39). Two small fragments of the base of the cranium have been displaced from the space originally occupied by the corpse, but they cannot be considered proof that decomposition has taken place in a void, since a burrowing animal has made a hole beneath the head. The rib cage has partly retained its original volume. A difference of four to seven cm. in depth was measured between the anterior-lateral and posterior extremity of the ribs. Flattening of the pelvis was also not noted. At this age, the coxal bone comprises three independent bones, ilium, ischium and pubis, linked by cartilage that naturally decays during decomposition of the corpse, when each of these bones would go its own way. In child burials these bones usually fall within the pelvic basin, but in our example they have been found in their original position (the pubic symphysis is still tightly connected). The hands, too, are in their original position. The right hand lies at a level which corresponds to the forward part of the abdomen, where it had been laid when the body was buried. The left hand lies in a place corresponding to the super-lateral part of the left hip, with the first two fingers passing forward and inside the anterior-super iliac crest. Although these bones were potentially in disequilibrium with respect to the internal space of the corpse, they maintained their original position exactly. This occurred because the volume left by decay of the soft tissue had been progressively filled with sediment.

The filling of spaces with sediment can therefore be either deferred, *i.e.* staggered, or progressive, *i.e.* when it replaces the organic elements little by little as these decompose. The former case is more common.

5.3.2. The mechanisms of filling the volume freed by the decay of soft tissue

Three mechanisms have been identified in the process of filling. The first is the force of gravity: the sediment that has built up above the corpse falls into the spaces left empty by the disappearance of the soft tissue. The second is the increase in volume of clay sediment when wet, as Michel Pichon, engineer at the Institut National de Recherche en Archéologie Préventive, suggested to me: decomposition fluids from the corpse soak the sediment and, if clay, this expands to fill the empty spaces. The third is disturbance caused by the actions of small animals, particularly earthworms. While digging tunnels they swallow the soil and later expel it. Such animals particularly seek out humid areas where the sediment is rich in organic matter, like those near burials.

Worm action may radically change the sediment near the tomb. When excavating a burial, one of the first tasks is the identification of the edges of the burial pit. If the tomb has been excavated in rock and filled with earth then this is easy, but if the burial has been made in an alluvial deposit and has been filled with the soil excavated when it was dug then it is more problematic. Often archaeologists interpret as pit fill a zone where the sediment is darker, softer, and lumpier than usual (they sometimes call this 'organic' sediment). In such cases I have often noticed that the pits seem very large compared to the skeletons. Archaeologists often think they have completed excavation when they have recovered the skeleton and the grave goods. However if they continue to excavate they may notice the presence of this sediment for some centimetres beneath the level of the skeleton. This is because the sediment interpreted as pit fill is soaked with decomposition fluids which worms have then worked in all directions. As a result the size of the pit and in particular its depth may be overestimated. This may be misleading for the identification of intersections between tombs or circulation spaces around them.

We turn now to cases where it has been possible to identify a progressive filling of the volume left by the decomposition of soft tissue. The first example is a Neolithic burial from Djibouti in eastern Africa (Figure 40). Since the sediments of this area comprise very fine powdery sands, tiny vacuum pumps were used in excavation. This was the burial of a young woman, laid on her left side in a contracted position. With the head turned towards the left, her face rested on the bottom of the pit. Inside the mandible is the hyoid bone. This is a U-shaped bone, lacking in real joints and suspended among the muscles, attached to the body through the greater horns. In adults of advanced age it is a single bone, whereas in children and in young adults it is formed of three portions linked by cartilage. After the disappearance

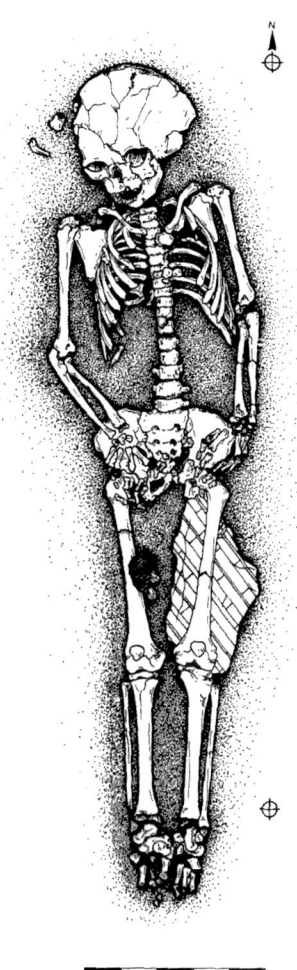

Figure 39a. Funerary circle at Coteau de Montigné, Coulon (Deux-Sèvres, France), burial P9, 5th century BC. Excavation by J-P. Pautreau and H. Duday, plan by H. Duday.

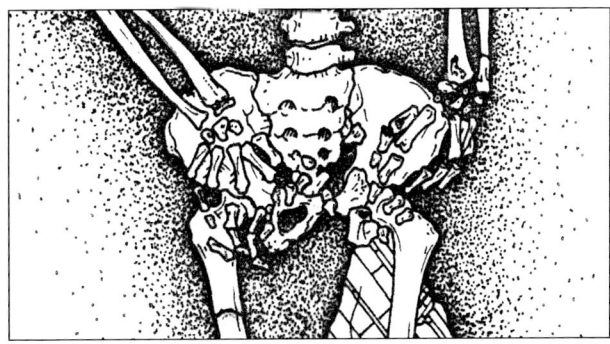

Figure 39b. Details of abdominal region and hands.

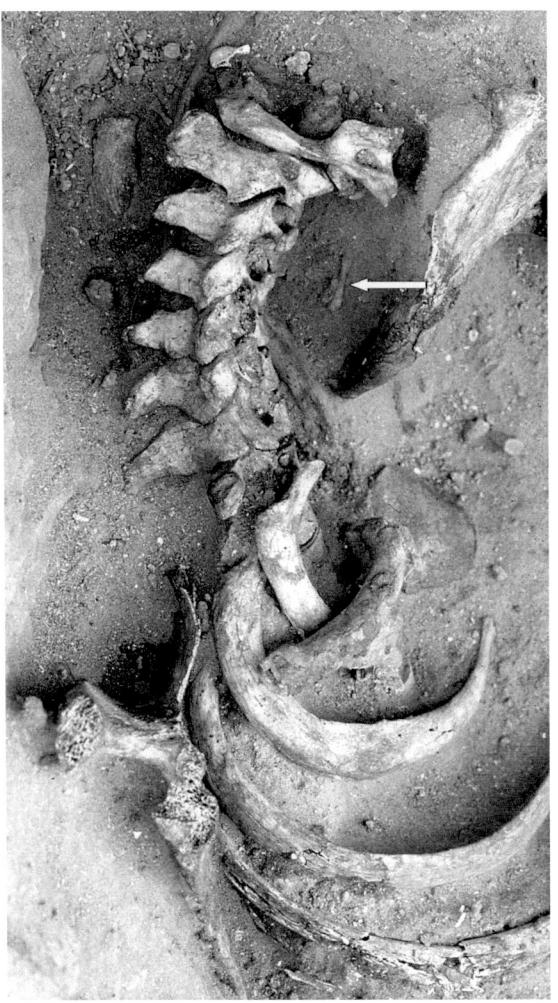

Figure 40. Asa Koma (Republic of Djibouti, eastern Africa), early Neolithic. Excavation by X. Gutherz, R. Joussaume, J.-P. Cros and H. Duday.

during decomposition of the muscles that surround it, the hyoid bone generally falls and separates. However, in this case it has been found in its original position: the white arrow shows the large right horn of the hyoid bone. This proves that this very fine sediment has progressively filled the empty space left by the muscles' decay. This has been called the 'hour-glass' effect (Duday 2005).

In the Neanderthal burial at Kebara in Israel the hyoid bone was also found in its original position in a primary deposit (Figure 41). The body of the hyoid bone and the large horns are linked and were found *in situ*. Since the sediment is also fine and powdery, we again conclude that the filling of the space was progressive.

An early Neolithic burial (of 'Cardial' type and with impressed Ligurian pottery) found in Abri Pendimoun at Castellar, near Nice provides another example (Binder *et al.* 1993). The corpse was buried in a pit on its left side and in a contracted position, with one hand under the mandible (Figure 42). Again the sediment here is very fine. Some traces of later disturbances caused by a burrowing animal have been found, including the displacement of the fifth lumbar vertebra. The left hand is still in anatomical connection and is in potential disequilibrium, because of which it should have fallen under the action of gravity. This has not happened because the sediment has filled the volume left with the disappearance of the soft tissue. The hyoid bone appears transversally inside the mandible. The left foot seems smaller than the right, but this is only an optical effect, since it was in a vertical position against the side of the pit. A distance of 15.5 cm. can be found between the distal extremity of the hallux and the posterior aspect of the calcaneus. Under the head of the first metatarsal the sesamoid bones were found (their name derives from their sesame seed-like shape). The sesamoid bones of the first metatarsal are about 6.5 mm. long and have remained in their original position. Usually during decomposition the feet fall into the space left by the decay of the muscles under the plantar surface. This is evidence that decomposition occurred in a filled space in which the volume occupied by the corpse was progressively filled with sediment after the decay of soft tissue.

In all burials of this type, the sediment turns out to be extremely fluid (sandy, ashy or very fine). This phenomenon is only possible when burials are in a filled space and cannot be true if there is originally a void around the corpse.

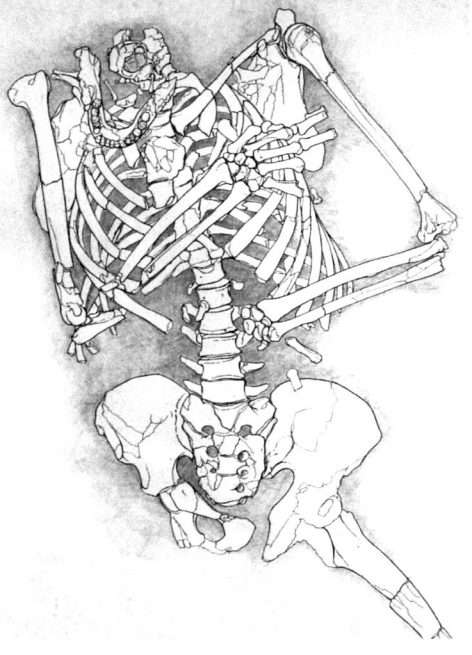

Figure 41. Cave at Kebara (Israel), middle Palaeolithic, plan by D. Ladiray.

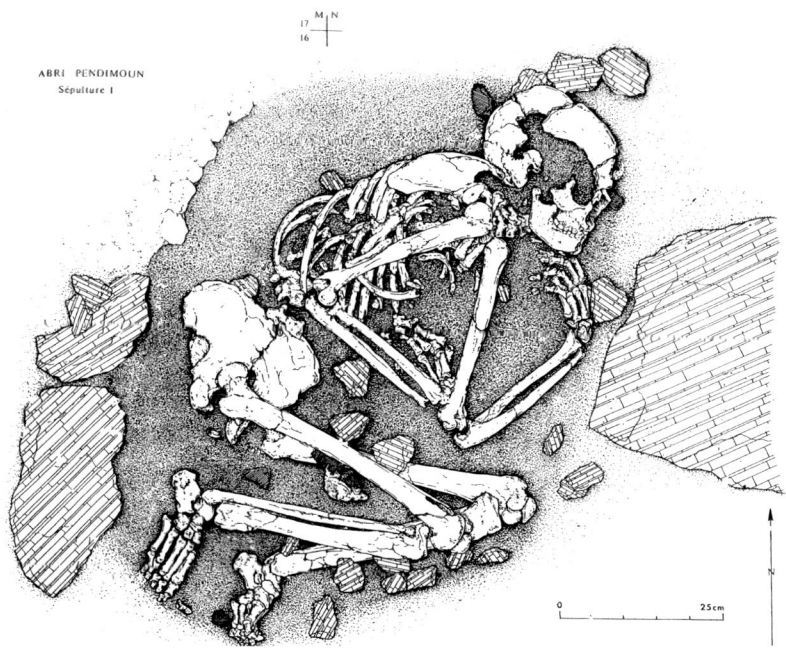

Figure 42. Abri Pendimoun at Le Castellar (Alpes Maritimes, France), early Neolithic. Excavation by D. Binder and H. Duday, plan by H. Duday.

Lecture 6

Burials of babies who die within the first six months of life

In all societies, one category of the dead is subject to particular funerary practice, stillborn children or babies who die within a few days of birth. Nearly all populations have had different ways of dealing with them. Until the 20th century in the Basque region in south-west France, for example, stillborn children were buried under kitchen floors. In 1870 the priest of a village in Languedoc wrote to the civil administrator of the community to congratulate him for having reserved an unconsecrated area in the new cemetery for the burials of stillborn children. This would stop, he said, the burial of stillborn babies in farmyards.

Today women give birth in hospital and the family of a stillborn child does not usually ask for its body and lets the hospital take care of it. We can therefore hypothesise that when future archaeologists dig our cemeteries they will not find a full population sample. Christians believe that an unbaptised child cannot be considered a son or daughter of the church and if it dies without the sacrament then it dies in a state of original sin and can only be buried in unconsecrated ground within the cemetery. If excavation takes place in an area of the cemetery from which unbaptised children have been excluded, then a misleading picture of mortality rates will be obtained. The factors that select individuals to be buried are fundamental for understanding how the society of the living is reflected in the cemetery.

The bodies of stillborn babies are usually not more than 55 cm. long and they are often buried in shallow pits. If the place of burial is later farmed, with time ploughing will remove these small bones and selectively destroy important information. These are important considerations for the study of palaeodemography and above all for evaluating how representative a sample is.

Our first example concerns the Chalcolithic village of Cambous in the south of France. Its stone-built houses are sometimes more than 20 m. long. During this period caves and dolmens were used as burial places. Archaeologists have explained the systematic absence of small children in these as a taphonomic phenomenon related to differential preservation. Children were actually however deposited in vessels beneath house floors (Figure 43). This is an example of a funerary practice particular to children.

Another well-documented example concerns the *oppidum* of Plan de la Tour at Gailhan in the south of France, dated to the fifth century BC (Dedet *et al.* 1991). Excavating the skeleton of a very small child requires very careful attention (we might call this a 'bonsai' excavation). Here the skeleton of a child which died in the perinatal period was found. It had been buried with its head raised and resting on a stone (Figure 44). The ribs were found spread in a fan shape. This is frequently seen in the tombs

6 *Burials of babies who die within the first six months of life* 59

Figure 43. Village at Cambous (Hérault, France), Chalcolithic. Excavation by H. Canet and J-L. Roudil.

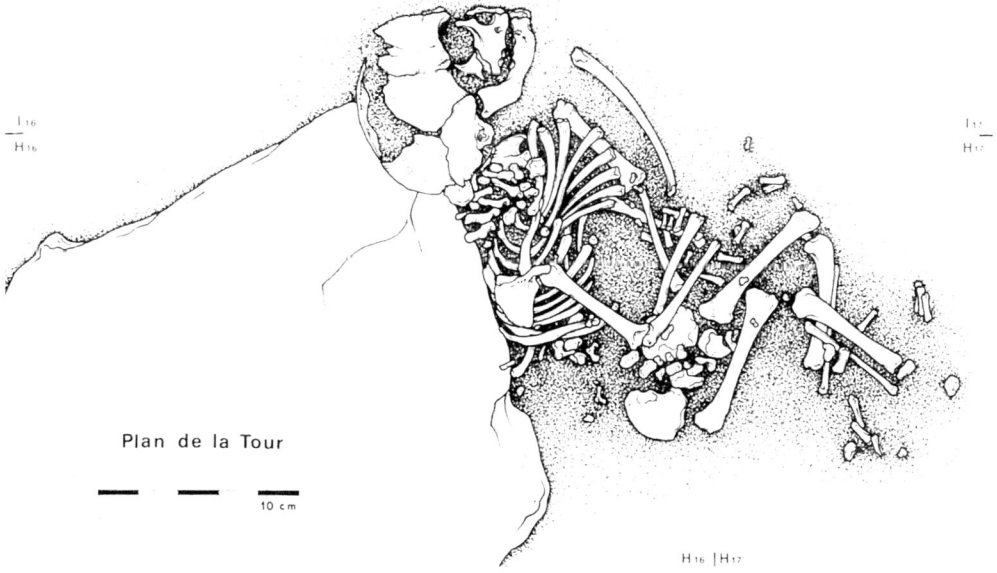

Figure 44. Oppidum of Plan de la Tour at Gailhan (Gard, France), burial in sector I-H/16–17, 5th century BC. Excavation by B. Dedet and H. Duday, plan by H. Duday.

of very young children since at this age the ribs are not yet arranged obliquely, which explains the nearly cylindrical aspect of a child's thorax.

Studies of anatomy have identified small ossification centres at the knee, called the Béclard nucleus. These are the centres for the formation of the lower extremity of the femur and are very useful in determining age at death. This is usually calculated from long bone dimensions. Height increases with age and by measuring the bones one can derive the stature of the individual, but it is important to consider the margin of error related to variations in the proportions of different parts of the body, even if stature is the same. We know that children of the same age can have different dimensions and that children of the same height can have different ages. Today in Western Europe, for example, the height of a child born after nine months of pregnancy varies between 45 and 55 cm. With this 10 cm. variation, age can be estimated with an approximation of ± 20–25 days.

The determination of age will be more precise if we consider the degree of maturation of the skeleton. For example the distal extremity of the femur starts to ossify at the end of pregnancy: this can be noted in excavation since it appears to be a small atypical bony nodule (Figure 45). In order to be certain of its identification it should be recognized *in situ* and not during sieving. The study of the calcification of the tooth buds may also help (Figure 46). At birth the enamel is very porous and absorbs the soil pigments, becoming browner or greyer. Their colour, size (a few millimetres wide) and fragility make it difficult to identify them during excavation. However during the cleaning of the dental arcades in the laboratory they can be recovered in the earth remaining in the sockets.

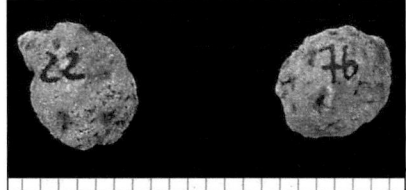

Figure 45. Distal epiphyses of both femora belonging to the individual whose burial is shown in Figure 44.

Figure 46. Buds of the lower right teeth belonging to the individual whose burial is shown in Figure 44.

The use of a trowel in excavation risks destroying neonate burials, so it is important to act as soon as the first bones appear. The excavation team for a large funerary complex should include a specialized funerary archaeologist who can identify the bones and organize the excavation of burials. However problems derive from the fact that the burials of very small children are found on sites which are not previously recognised as funerary. It is not seldom that these small skeletons are not recognized as human and often only the larger bones are collected, as is the case for animals. Generally we see only what we have learnt to recognize. There is, above all, a training problem here and it is necessary for archaeologists excavating settlements to have first had the opportunity to see neonate skeletons. In 1982 a burial was excavated at the *oppidum* of Gailhan and presented to local archaeologists at a seminar at Montpellier. In the following year twenty-four burials of children who died in the perinatal period were found in that region, as many as had been excavated since the beginning of the 19th century. The exception to this is the extraordinary site at Mailhac in southern France, where more than 50 years ago Odette and Jean Taffanel were able to recognize the burials of about 40 very small children.

Another child skeleton has been excavated at the *oppidum* of Gailhan (Figure 47). Its arms have moved away from the thorax, while the ribs are open like a fan. The thorax volume is perfectly preserved, with a difference of 5.5 cm. in level between the anterior and posterior extremities. This situation arises from the particular shape of the tomb, formed by a narrow central pit, where the body lies and two slightly raised ledges on both sides where the arms have been laid (this is the so-called 'gutter effect', described above). Here the same taphonomic dynamics apply as with adults. If the excavation is performed with sufficient care, the methods of 'l'anthropologie de terrain' can also be applied to the tombs of very small children.

The fifth century BC skeleton of a child who died in the perinatal period and which was excavated at Coteau de Montigné allows us to take the methodological discussion further. It was found in a large circular funerary pit, 17 m. in diameter. A site on such a scale needs to be excavated by appropriate means, which explains why the first stroke of the trowel has scattered most of the foot bones and some lumbar vertebrae.

In children, the cranial vault is formed by several elements that are separated by fibrous membranes. These elements can buckle at birth, to allow the child's head to emerge. As soon as the membranes and the brain decay, the bones fall within the cranial cavity, preventing us from determining the original orientation of the head (Figure 48). In this case, two tiny bones of the internal ear, the left malleus and incus, were found next to one another. These are the only bones that have the same morphology and size in adulthood and at birth, so that they seem relatively large with respect to the rest of the skeleton. They are situated inside the eardrum, a fibrous membrane that disappears during decomposition. If the head appears in front view, they remain deep in the middle ear. If the corpse is laid on one side, the auditory ossicles that are turned towards the higher part of the tomb fall into the deep part of the middle ear, while those of the opposite ear will fall to the bottom of the pit, by the external auditory meatus. Their identification allows us to figure out the original position of the ear and, consequently, to deduce the original position of the head. Only the use of small tools will allow such elements to be found.

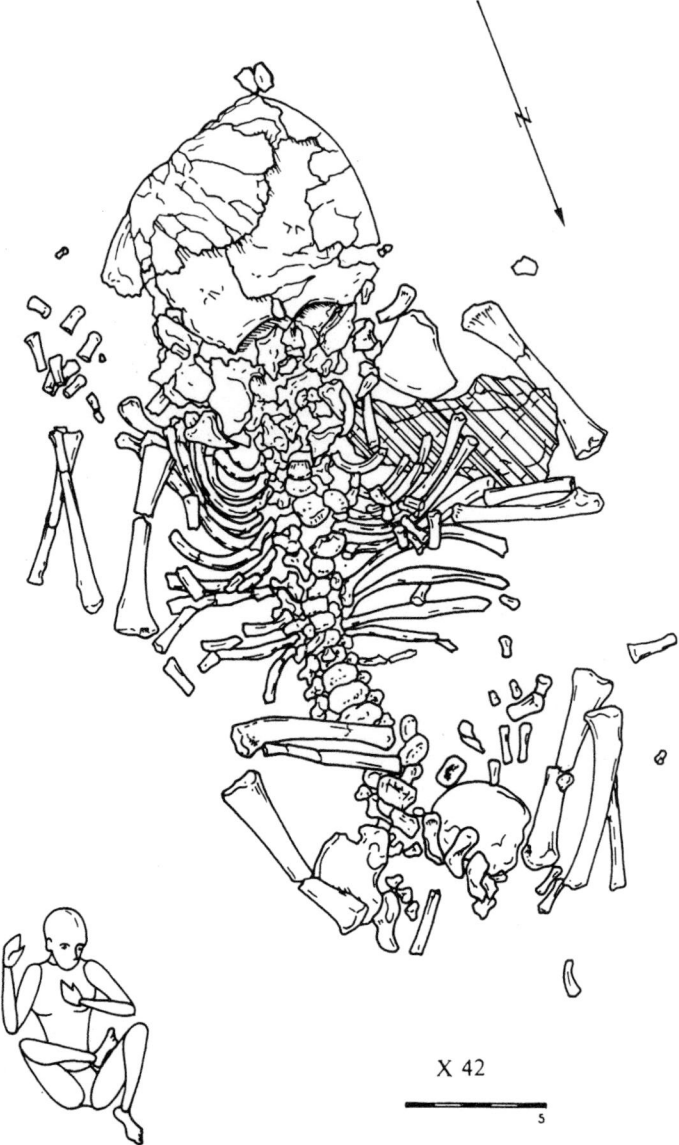

Figure 47. Oppidum of the Plan de la Tour at Gailhan (Gard, France), burial in sector X42, fifth century BC. Excavation by B. Dedet and H. Duday, plan by H. Duday.

The activity described above is important for studying not only children's burials, but also those of larger subjects, in particular to understand the original position of the head if it has later been moved. If the head is absent, the discovery of ossicles shows that the skull was originally present in the tomb (so that we may distinguish the removal of

COULON – 1983

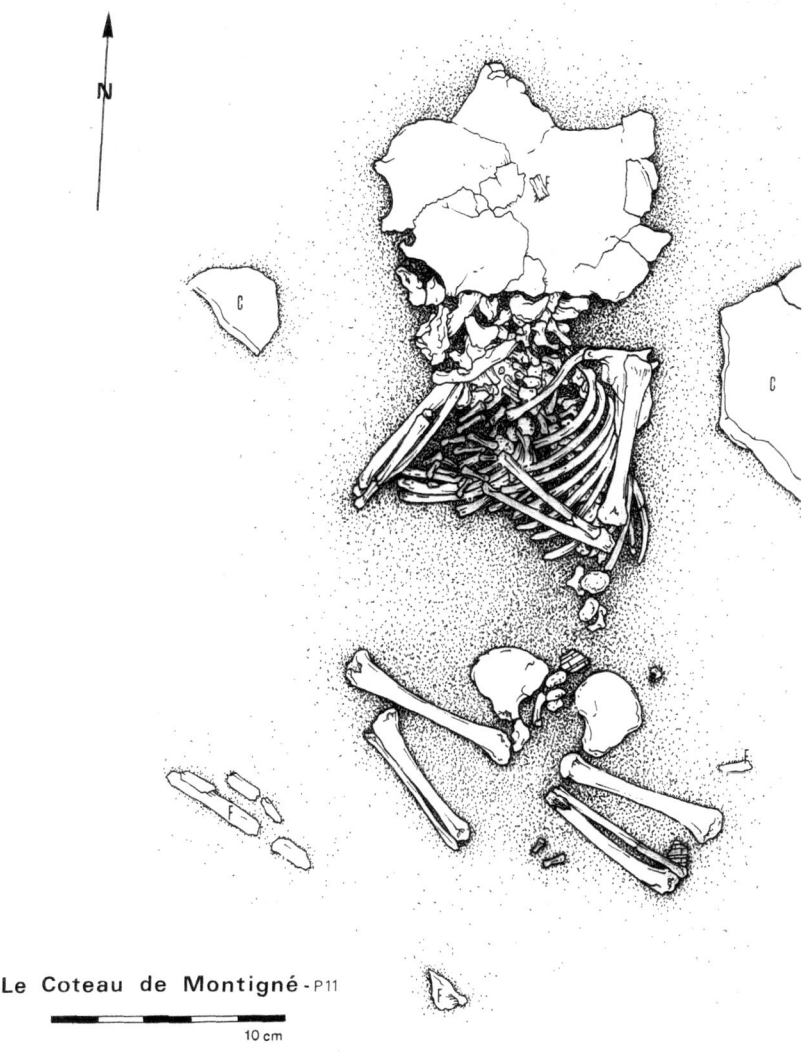

Figure 48. Funerary circle at Coteau de Montigné, Coulon (Deux-Sèvres, France), burial P11, fifth century BC. Excavation by J-P. Pautreau and H. Duday, plan by H. Duday.

the cranium and mandible after decay from the deposition of a decapitated individual) and gives us information on its position in the tomb.

We now examine a Gallo-Roman potter's workshop of the first century AD at Sallèles-d'Aude near Narbonne (Duday *et al.* 1995, 146). After the conquest of this region, Rome

Figure 49. Gallo-Roman potter's workshop at Sallèles-d'Aude (Aude, France), first century AD. Excavation by F. Laubenheimer, A. M. Tillier and H. Duday.

gave land to colonists who developed viticulture. Many workshops related to this were created, especially for making containers for transporting wine, as was the case for the workshop under study, in which a room measuring seven metres long and four metres wide was used for drying vessels and amphorae. Under each of the roof tiles found along its walls a child burial was documented (Figure 49).

To carry out the excavation, the diggers worked from platforms supported by metal scaffolding. To remove the soil small vacuum pumps, like those of dentists, were used. Plans were made at a scale of 1:2 or 1:1. Each bone was numbered and its anatomical orientation and depth were recorded (Figures 50 and 51). All these processes can be completed in 12 to 14 hours by a person with specialized training.

This excavation was made more difficult to carry out by the clay soil of the site with its small stone inclusions. The first burial discussed shows a small zone of disturbance caused by an animal's passage. The individual is prone (Figure 50) and the arrangement of the ribs allows us to read the position of the thorax directly. If the person is laid on his back, the first rib lies on the second, the second on the third, and so on. If the person instead is laid on his stomach, the lower ribs rest on the upper. Within the pit an alignment can be seen, with the right foot folded under the right leg.

Another burial from the same site was that of a three-month old baby. The cranium has been compressed (Figure 52): the bones of the cranial vault have fallen inside the

6 Burials of babies who die within the first six months of life

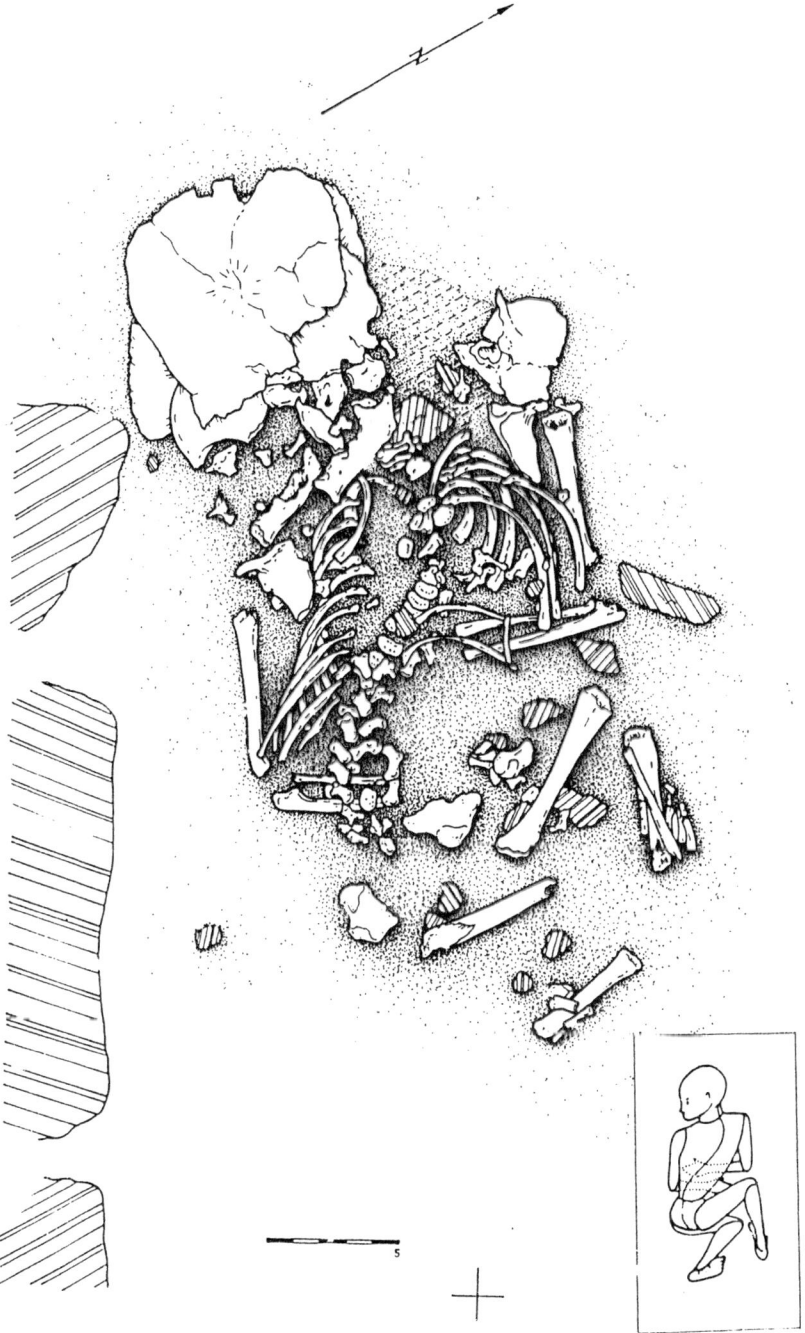

Figure 50. Gallo-Roman potter's workshop at Sallèles-d'Aude (Aude, France), first century AD. Composite plan of the burial of a still-born baby by H. Duday.

Figure 51. Gallo-Roman potter's workshop at Sallèles-d'Aude (Aude, France), first century AD. Plans of three successive excavation layers of the burial shown in Figure 50. The composite image in Figure 50 has been created from these partial views.

6 Burials of babies who die within the first six months of life

Figure 52. Gallo-Roman potter's workshop at Sullèles-d'Aude (Aude, France), first century AD. General view of the burial of a few weeks old baby.

space left by the disappearance of the brain and the parietal bones have folded on themselves. Some bones of the vault have clearly moved beyond the original space occupied by the cranium. The burial has a bronze brooch with some plant fibres attached which probably belonged to clothing. The zygomatic bone and some bones of the hands and feet have been displaced from the space originally occupied by the corpse. This then was a primary burial in a void (Figure 53), covered by a roof tile.

13 burials were found in this workshop, with ages at death from birth to six months. During the Roman period cremation was the most common funerary rite in France but texts by Pliny and Juvenal record that the burning of children who did not yet have

Figure 53. Gallo-Roman potter's workshop at Sallèles-d'Aude (Aude, France), first century AD. Composite plan and longitudinal section of the burial shown in Figure 52, plan by H. Duday.

their teeth was forbidden. This would explain the choice of a workshop as a burial place and the treatment of the bodies related to their age at the death. It was in fact possible to show a variation in burial practice for these children according to age at death. If the baby was stillborn or died soon after birth it was laid in a small pit, in a contracted position and with no grave goods. Decomposition took place in a filled space and a

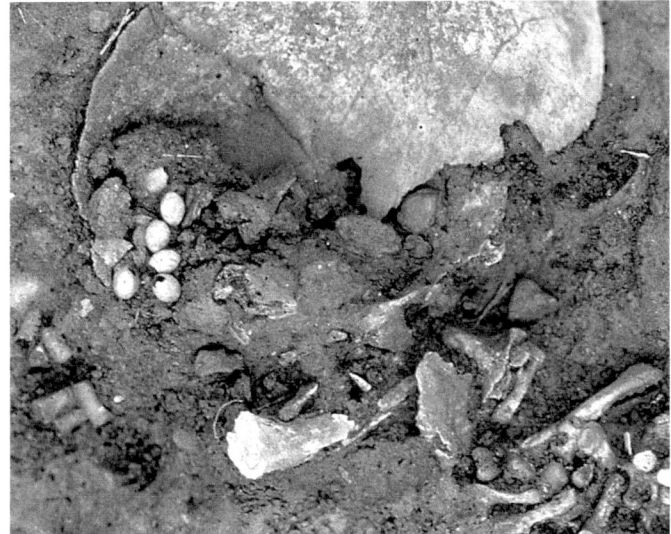

Figure 55. Testacella sp. egg (scale in millimetres).

Figure 54. Gallo-Roman potter's workshop at Sallèles-d'Aude (Aude, France), first century AD, A detail of the cranium of a still born burial as it is dismantled during excavation.

roof tile fragment above marked the burial. If the baby instead lived for a few months, it was laid in a larger pit and in a slightly more extended position, in one case with a brooch. Since the roof tile placed above it served as a cover, decomposition occurred in a void. Finally, in the single case of a baby which died at the age of *c.* six months, the body was placed in a small coffin formed by roof tiles and accompanied by grave goods (oil-lamps, ceramic and glass vessels, a bead and a bronze needle).

In one case two children were buried one on top of the other in the same pit which was clearly dug to accommodate both. It is much deeper than the other pits which contain only one corpse: the two deposits are therefore simultaneous. The lower individual died in the perinatal period and its decomposition occurred in a filled space while the upper individual, who lived for *c.* three months, decomposed in a void. This leads us to conjecture about the relationship between these individuals, given that they could not have been brothers. Calcified eggs with a maximum diameter of *c.* seven mm. long (Figures 54 and 55) were found in the cranial cavity of the lower child. They had been laid by a snail that carried a small shell on its tail, from which its name (*Testacella* sp.) derives. This carnivorous snail specifically predates on earthworms. Their presence therefore implies that of worms which are, in turn, abundant near burials where the sediment is enriched with decomposing organic matter. The finding of *testacella* shells and eggs suggests the primary character of the burial. A secondary deposit of defleshed bones would have produced neither these organic fluids nor a concentration of earthworms.

It is sometimes possible to find deposits of even younger individuals, for example in

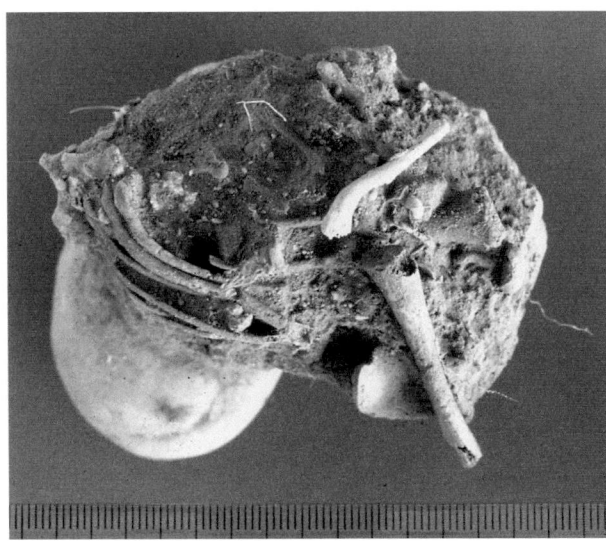

Figure 56. Lattes (Hérault, France), first century BC. Photograph by V. Fabre.

a first century BC burial under the floor of a house at Lattes, near Montpellier. In the bottom of an urn was a white pebble, a carved goat's astragalus, a small lead plaque and the bones of a five and a half month old foetus (Figure 56). The baby had been born prematurely and died. Ancient texts give us no information on the treatment reserved for children born prematurely, indicating the importance of this discovery. This exceptional discovery is due to my student Véronique Fabre, *ingénieur* at the Institut de Recherche en Archéologie Préventive.

We conclude with a discovery made in the Grotte de Montespan at the foot of the Pyrenees, famous for its upper Palaeolithic art, in particular a statue of a bear modelled in clay. A skeleton was found in a depression in a rock and was interpreted as that of a Magdalenian (*c.* 16,000–9,500 BC) neonate. The cranium is missing, probably because it has been taken away by a caver, and the mandible has rotated. The excavation and plan have allowed us to determine the position of the body, extended on its back; the left hemithorax has preserved part of its volume, since it rested on a clay projection on which the left forelimb was found still in perfect anatomical connection. Here it is possible to see, on one side only, the 'gutter' effect with a ledge at the side, as at the tomb at Gailhan (Figure 47). However the morphology of the humeri was not human, since the skeleton was that of a neonate bear (Figure 57)! It is curious that the body of this small bear has been buried within the footprint of an adult bear. This find is important, since it gives detailed information on the morphology of the small immature bones (vertebrae, limb extremities) of a breed of bear that died out 10,000 years ago.

6 Burials of babies who die within the first six months of life   71

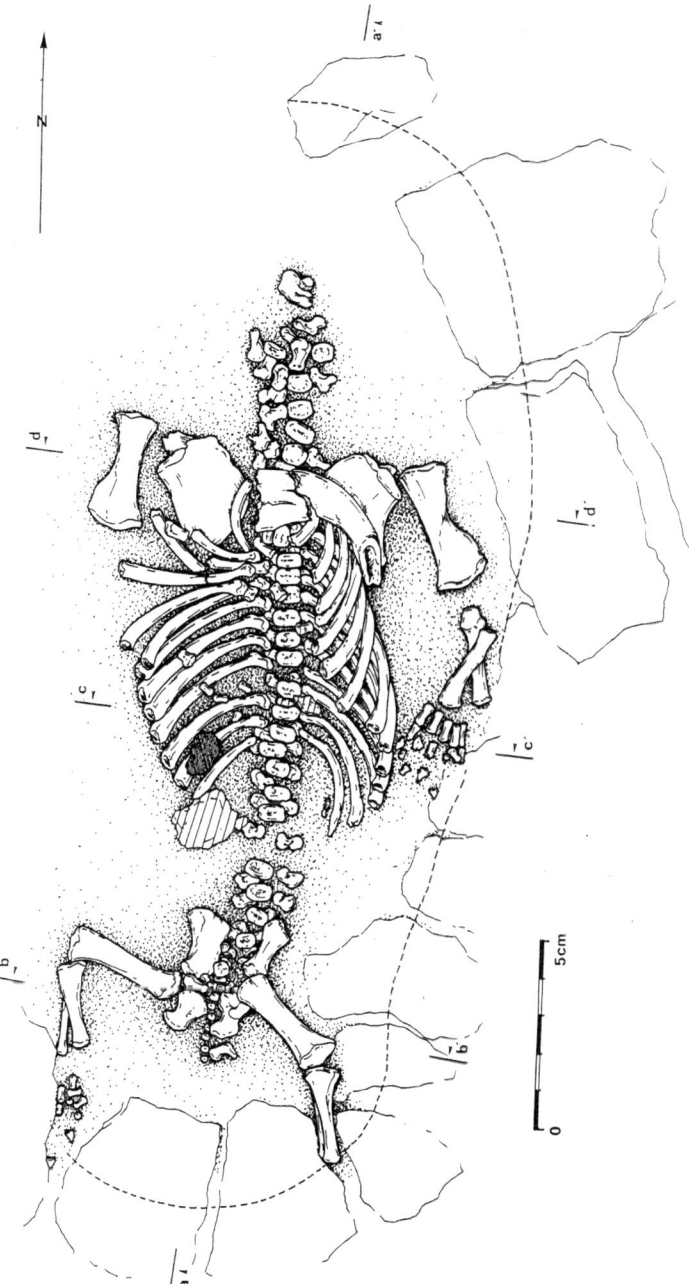

Figure 57. Grotte de Montespan (Haute Garonne, France), Upper Palaeolithic. Excavation by M. Garcia and H. Duday, plan by H. Duday.

Lecture 7

Double burials and 'reductions'. Remarks on the notion of burial. Palaeopathology and archaeology

7.1. Burials containing the remains of two individuals

When a burial contains the remains of two individuals, it is necessary first to understand whether they have been deposited simultaneously or separately over a long period.

7.1.1. Asynchronous deposits: 'reductions' and related acts

Sometimes a 'reduction' (see below) of the skeleton of the first corpse can be identified. In tomb 582 at Serris-les-Ruelles (Figure 58), a corpse has decomposed in a void. Traces of wood from the bottom of the coffin can be seen, as well as the displacement of some bones and a 'linear delimitation' effect especially visible along the right side of the skeleton. Between the coffin and the side of the tomb can be seen the heaped up remains of another individual who was buried much earlier, since the bones were no longer linked by ligaments.

Another burial from the same site (Figure 59) shows clear evidence of 'linear delimitation' between the right side of the first individual, whose skeleton is transversally compressed with the 'verticalisation' of its clavicles, and a second individual, whose remains are piled up in some disorder between the side of the coffin and the side of the pit.

There is a tendency to think that these bones have been 'reduced', but we should reflect on the meaning of this term. Normally, 'reduction', by definition, takes place within the same container, for example when a sarcophagus containing one individual is re-opened much later to accommodate the remains of another. The bones of the first individual are then moved to one end of the sarcophagus, but remain within it. A distinction should be drawn between 'reduction' inside the same container and 'reduction' outside, along the sides of a pit or above a cover. In the latter case, the second individual is buried inside the structure, while the bones that previously occupied that space are heaped on the lid. If this collapses, the bones that have been laid on it will fall inside the container overlying the more recently buried remains, causing a statigraphic inversion.

The problem here is to understand whether the two individuals have really been deposited in the same structure or in the same container. If the bones of the first were collected inside the tomb at one end or outside, against the side of the tomb or on the cover, this should probably be considered as 'reduction' proper: the aim of the gesture is to clear the necessary space for depositing the second individual. However where grave diggers have come across an older tomb, the collection of the larger bones may

 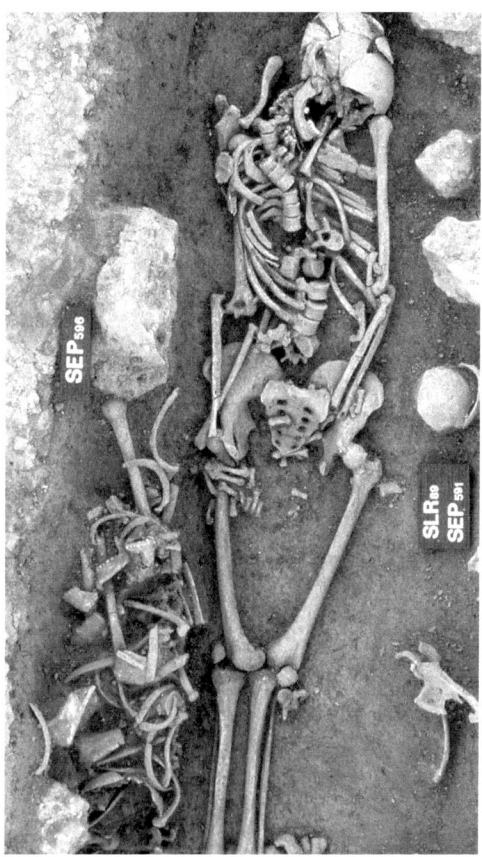

Figure 58. Serris, Les Ruelles (Seine-et-Marne, France), burial 582, early medieval. Excavation by B. Foucray, F. Blaizot, F. Gentili and H. Guy.

Figure 59. Serris, Les Ruelles (Seine-et-Marne, France), burial 591, early medieval. Excavation by B. Foucray, F. Blaizot, F. Gentili and H. Guy.

reflect a wish to clear the space – thus a case of 'reduction' – but can also mark a gesture of respect towards bones unearthed by chance and recognised as human.

7.1.2. Double burials

In the Grotte Gazel at Sallèles-Cabardès, an early Neolithic burial in a niche in the rock contained the remains of two individuals, a woman and a four-five year old child (Figure 60). Looking at their position, we can infer that it is a simultaneous deposit, a double burial. The child's body covers the woman's right upper limb, but it is covered with her left lower limb, and the woman's left wrist is under the child's armpit. The same impression might however have obtained in the case of two consecutive deposits, made within a very short time interval. The child might have died a few days after the woman and have been buried with her, perhaps because of kinship or because of a non-genetic relationship. Somebody would have arranged the placing of the child's body between the woman's arms, manipulating a corpse that was already in an advanced state of decomposition. To our way of thinking these gestures would be considered disgusting. Even today however many people deal with such bodies as professionals, for example forensic pathologists and the police. There are populations in Polynesia that collect decomposition fluids to include them with food, rice for example. This is a highly ritualized gesture to respect the dead. We must refrain from projecting our sensibilities on the people of the early Neolithic.

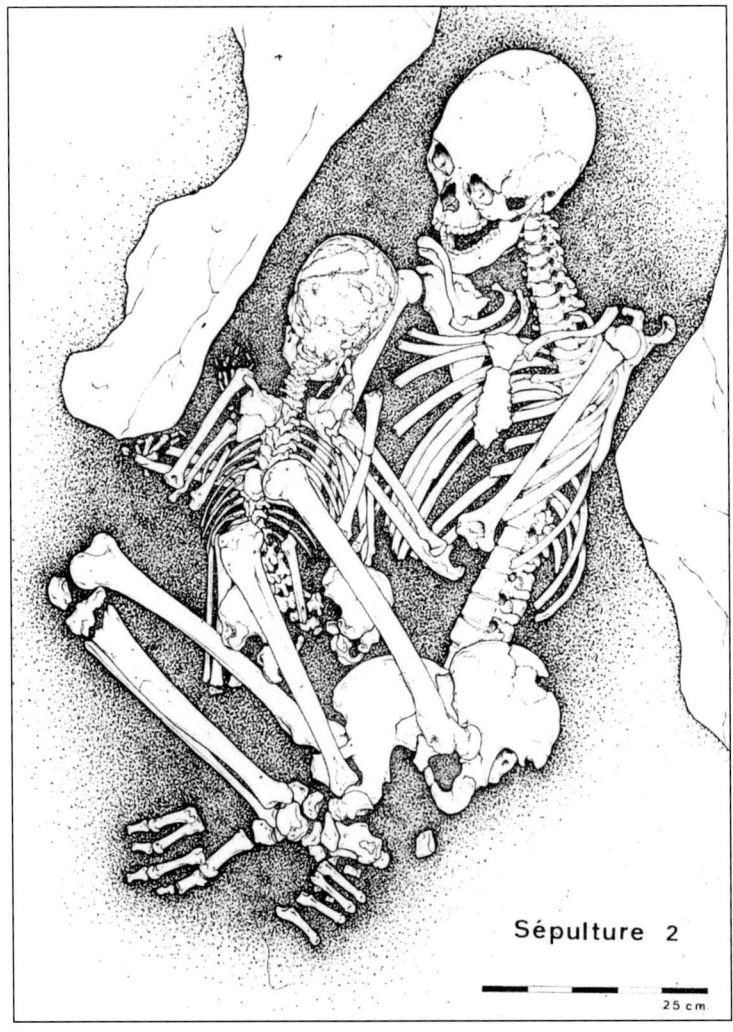

Figure 60. Grotte Gazel, Sallèles-Cabardès (Aude, France), early Neolithic. Excavation by J. Guilaine, plan by H. Duday.

As long as the ligaments hold, the corpse can be handled and the skeletal elements remain connected. In the example at the Grotte Gazel, the burial could be a simultaneous deposit or two deposits made with an interval of a week or two. It is not possible to be more precise and to distinguish between a double burial proper and two depositions separated by a short interval, since the ligaments of the joints that break down most easily would not yet have disappeared.

In the late Neolithic (*c.* 2500 BC) fortified site of Chatelliers-du-Vieil-Auzay (Large *et al.* 2004, 686), there are three structures, each containing two individuals, an adult and a sub-adult, each of which has a vessel above or near the head (a vessel is missing in one instance, but its absence is probably due to the cutting of a pit in the Bronze Age which had disturbed this area).

In structure 2 there are two individuals (Figure 61) in a primary deposit where decomposition has taken place in a filled space, with the obstacle to the bones caused

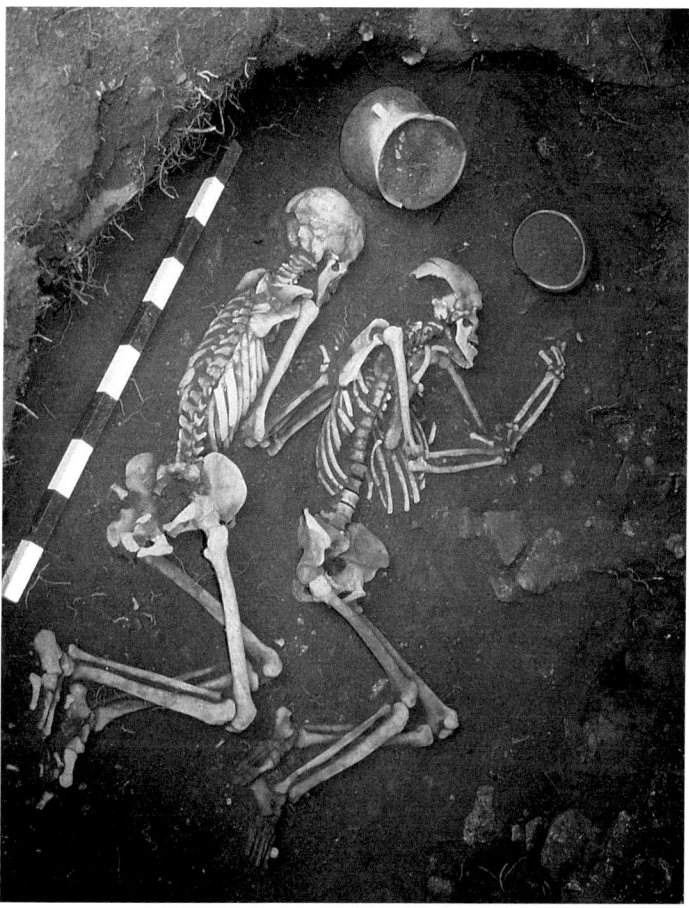

Figure 61. Les Chatelliers du Vieil-Auzay (Vendée, France), structure 2, later Neolithic. Excavation by P. Birocheau, J-M. Large and J-P. Cros.

by the fill. Although the original structure created a void, fine sediments very quickly penetrated to cover the corpses soon after their deposition: evidence of decomposition in a filled space is clearly visible. As for the relative chronology of the two deposits, the individuals touch through elements that break down particularly easily. If the individual on the right was the first to be deposited, then his scapulo-thoracic junction was still intact when the second individual was buried, since the hands of the latter have not disturbed it. On the other hand, if the corpse on the left was the first to be buried, then his hand joints were still intact when the corpse on the right was deposited. Both corpses retained their anatomical integrity when they came in contact with each other. It may have been a simultaneous deposit or two successive deposits made over a short time period.

7.2. Reflections on the notion of burial

The three structures at Châtelliers-du-Vieil-Auzay enable us to address another important issue, the identification of whether or not the deposit is a 'burial'. At first sight, everything seems to indicate that these are burials. There is a structure deliberately made to house the remains of the dead, who were provided with vessels and in one case with stone tools. The deliberate character of this deposit cannot be doubted (Figure 62). Nevertheless we must always bear in mind that the very concept of funerary practice implies a positive connotation in relation to the dead. If a murderer hides the corpse of his victim by burying it in a pit, this is obviously not a burial because the purpose is to escape justice. Yet in this case too there is a structure, a corpse, a deliberate deposit and 'grave goods', if the

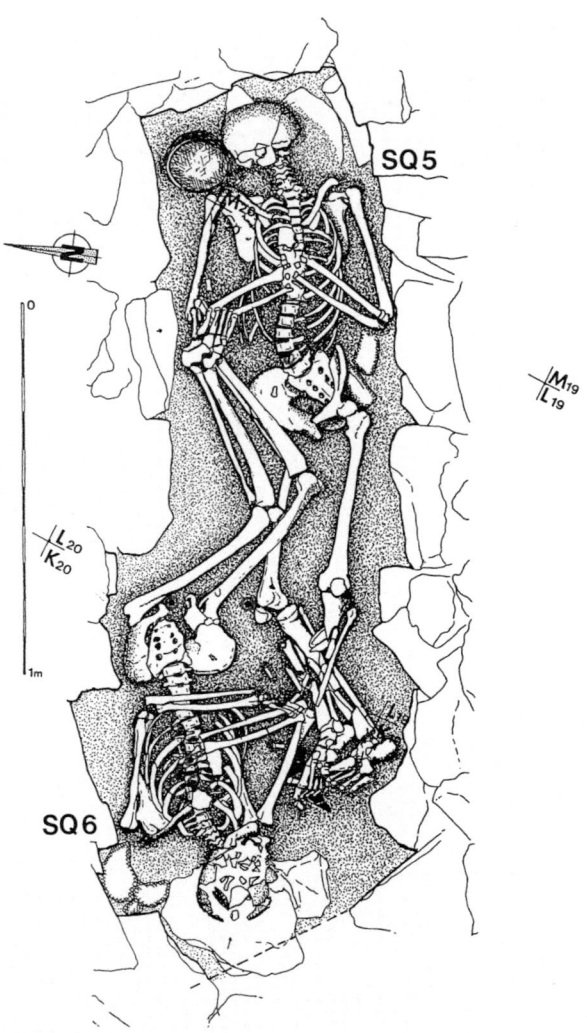

Figure 62. Les Chatelliers du Vieil-Auzay (Vendée, France), structure 3, later Neolithic. Excavation by P. Birocheau, J-M. Large, and J-P. Cros, plan by P. Birocheau and J-M. Large.

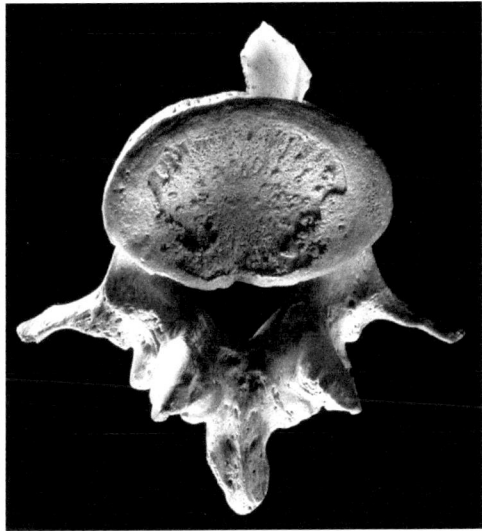

Figure 63. Les Chatelliers du Vieil-Auzay (Vendée, France), structure 3, skeleton 5. Photograph by F. Houët.

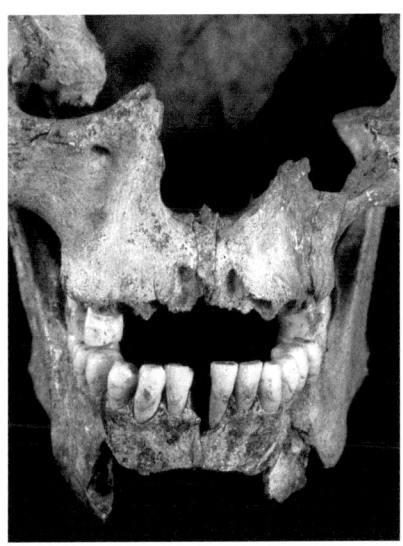

Figure 64. Les Chatelliers du Vieil-Auzay (Vendée, France), structure 3, skeleton 5. Photograph by J-P. Cros and H. Duday.

corpse has not been stripped of its dress, jewels, *etc*. If the murderer out of remorse makes the sign of the cross and prays for the dead, it becomes a burial. The difference cannot be seen at all through the material traces that excavation can give us.

In this case our uncertainties about its status as a burial relate to the cause of death. Examining the vertebral column of one individual, we note a flint arrow head embedded in the left antero-lateral aspect of the fourth lumbar vertebra (L4) (Figure 63). This is where the abdominal aorta bifurcates. If struck this will haemorrhage, causing death within a few minutes. We cannot be sure that this was the real cause of death in this case. The same individual also received a blow by a blunt instrument full in the face which has caused the loss of his chin and teeth through the violent impact (Figure 64). This would be a fatal wound, as would be the injury from the axe blow to the posterior aspect of the occipital (the same injury is on each of the six crania found). The other individual deposited in the same structure has an arrowhead in the rib cage, broken from contact with the vertebrae, and shows traces of an axe blow to the back of his head.

On several skeletons, some cranial fragments are white in colour. These have fallen into the cranial vault and have been soaked with matter from the decomposition of the brain. Two individuals have a circular wound on their crania (Figure 65) with clean edges and fissures, caused by a blunt instrument (Figure 66). The small bone roundel detached by the blow has been found inside the cranium: it has a very characteristic impact trace (Figure 67). Another has seven blows to his cranial vault and an axe blow to the back of the skull.

By observing these numerous traumatic lesions, we may conclude that these

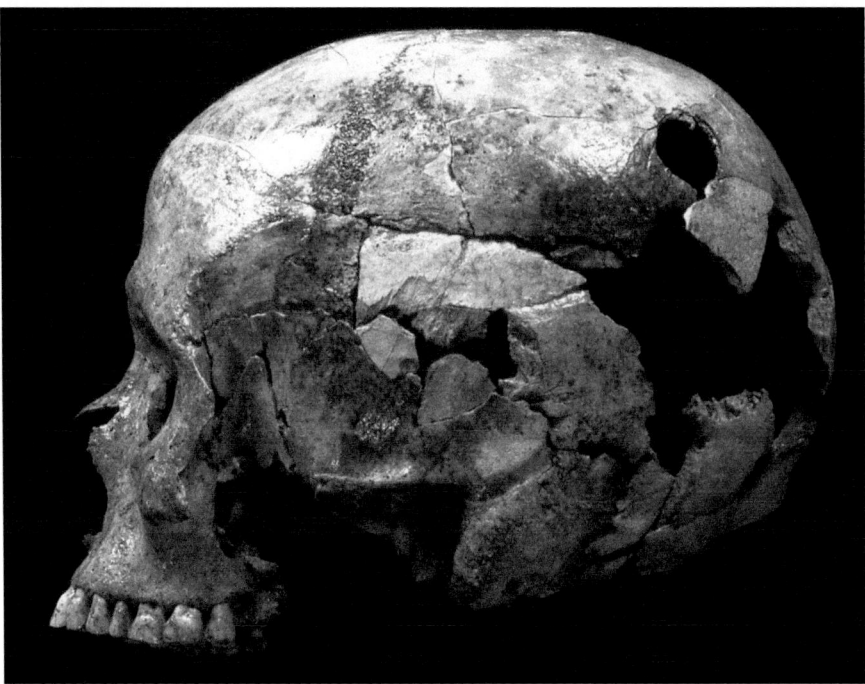

Figure 65. Les Chatelliers du Vieil-Auzay (Vendée, France), structure 2, skeleton 4. Photograph by J-P. Cros and H. Duday.

individuals have been spectacularly killed by many blows to their crania. Some of these blows have been repeated identically on two or three of the six individuals examined and traces of the axe blow that shattered the external occipital protuberance have been found on all six. We get the feeling of a *mise en scène* in this killing and deposition. It is certainly possible that these corpses have been buried, but we cannot exclude human sacrifice. We may hypothesise that they have been deposited as offerings, like the vessels, to some unknown deity. So a deliberate deposit (of a body) need not be a burial. An individual may be killed either as punishment or as a sacrifice and deprived of his human *status* by reducing him to an object through the reification of the corpse.

7.3. Palaeopathology and archaeology

Palaeopathology is a discipline that deals with the diagnosis of lesions, the history of disease and the therapies practised by past populations. It is almost always practised in the laboratories of faculties of medicine, where the archaeologist or anthropologist brings the bones they consider anomalous. It is of great importance that there is a constructive dialogue between these three disciplines of archaeology, anthropology and palaeopathology, in order to establish an active collaboration which puts a disease in its historical context (we shall examine later burials due to mortality crises caused by

7 Double burials and 'reductions'

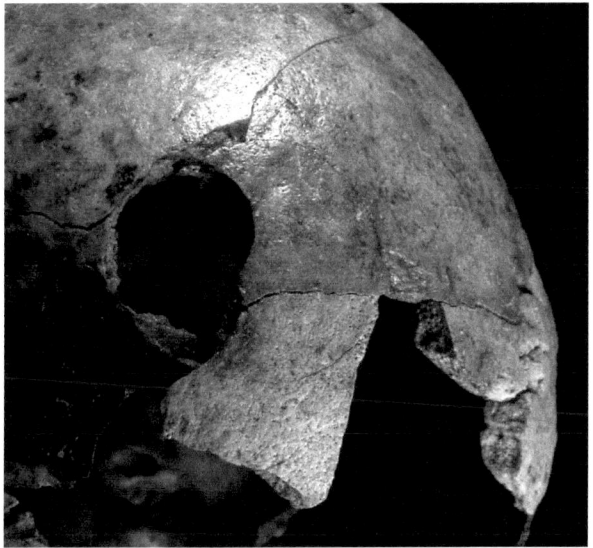 

Figure 66. Les Chatelliers du Vieil-Auzay (Vendée, France), structure 2, skeleton 4. Photograph by J-P. Cros and H. Duday.

Figure 67. Les Chatelliers du Vieil-Auzay (Vendée, France), structure 2, skeleton 4. Photograph by J-P. Cros and H. Duday.

epidemics). In reality palaeopathological analysis should take into account observations made during excavation.

7.3.1 Documenting a physical handicap

Let us return to the example of the Mesolithic burial at Bonifacio in Corsica (Figure 2). The very fine sediment has blocked the woman's left hand in the original position in which she was buried. This hand is extended from the forearm, with the last two fingers bent back on themselves, the other two half flexed while the thumb is not bent. This is the position that the hand spontaneously adopts in case of paralysis of the ulnar nerve (Figure 68) ('claw hand'), but this observation is not enough in itself to diagnose a paralysis. On the left ulna in lateral view a swelling of the distal part is visible, a callus formed after an ancient fracture (Figure 69) that is well healed and consolidated. One of the most

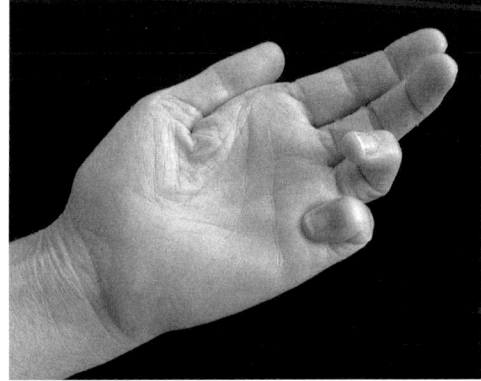

Figure 68. Characteristic position of the fingers in a hand of an individual affected by paralysis of the ulnar nerve.

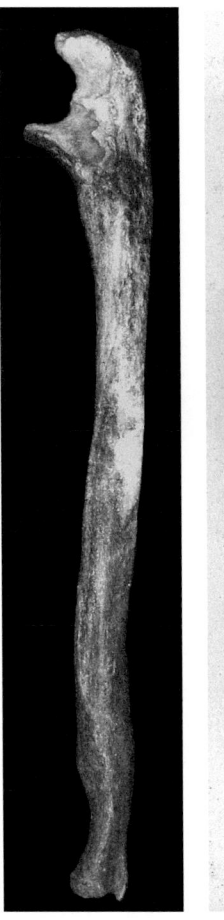 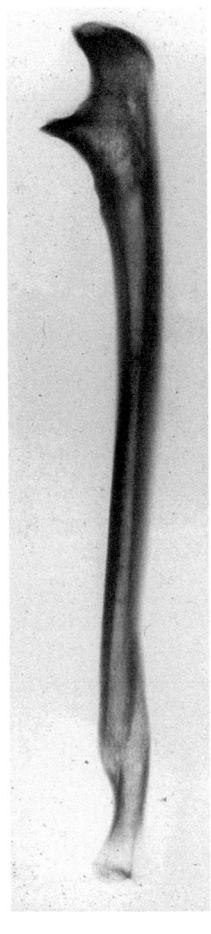

Figure 69. Rock shelter at Araguina Sennola at Bonifacio (Corsica), Mesolithic. Lateral view and radiograph of profile of the left ulna.

frequent causes of paralysis of the ulnar nerve is known to be a blow to the distal extremity of the ulna itself, where the nerve runs in direct contact with the bone. From the radiographs a slight convexity can be seen on the third left metacarpal, where a fracture has been well healed. The fifth left metacarpal shows much more obvious anomalies (Figure 70). It has an irregular surface, is shorter than it should be and the whole bone is incorporated in a callus. On this bone the lateral ligaments of the phalangeal-metacarpal joint are partially ossified and the radiograph shows a sesamoid immobilised by a callus. The little finger was therefore ankylosed and bent. In an ulnar paralysis the bending of the last two fingers can be passively reduced for a while, but later these contract again, giving rise to an irreducible contraction which is obviously much more of a handicap.

It is well known that when a part of a limb is immobilized its bone will demineralise. This process may be identified here by weighing the bones, since a demineralised bone is obviously lighter. All the bones of this left hand are notably lighter then those of the right, except for the fifth metacarpal, which has artificially reintegrated minerals following the formation of the callus. The direct measuring of the degree of bone mineralisation objectively confirms this phenomenon, along with an increasing density in the central part of the diaphysis of the third left metacarpal where another callus is visible.

We can conclude that the distal part of the woman's left limb had undergone one or more traumas many years before she died. One of her lesions is a typical cause of ulnar paralysis. There is evidence of 'claw' ankylosis of the phalangeal-metacarpal joint of the fifth finger as well as the demineralisation of the whole hand. These observations from laboratory study clarify the meaning of the position in which the woman's hand was found at excavation, but the position of the hand is itself an essential element for diagnosis. It is almost certain that she suffered post-traumatic ulnar paralysis during the last years of her life. She also presented other chronic lesions, including inflammation of the gums due to calculus, an apical cyst, vertebral arthrosis, evidence of trauma at the right ankle (an ossified haematoma), chronic inflammation of the serous bursa which allowed the slipping of the Achilles tendon on the posterior aspect of the left calcaneus and, finally, interphalangeal arthritis

7 Double burials and 'reductions'

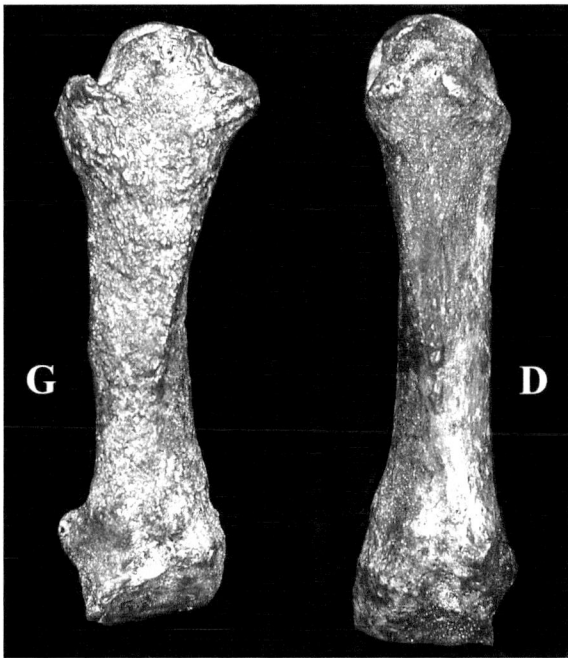

Figure 70. Rock shelter at Araguina Sennola at Bonifacio (Corsica), Mesolithic. Dorsal view of the fifth left metacarpal (G) and the corresponding right one (D). Photograph by M. Thouvenot.

of the right hallux. Some of these pathologies are quite debilitating and this woman would have found it difficult to obtain food and other means of existence on her own. We may assume that the group to which she belonged took care of her, perhaps because she possessed knowledge important for the community or perhaps simply out of love. This is, of course, only one piece of data, but concerns an aspect of culture for which we generally lack any other information, especially for periods without documentary records, *i.e.* the position of handicapped individuals in ancient societies.

In the study of an early Neolithic burial in Northern Africa, Jean Dastugue has also described the case of a woman whose pelvis had a healed fracture and with destruction to some of the sacral nerve roots, which would have prevented her from getting up and would have made her incontinent. Somebody therefore had to take care of her in order for her to survive.

At Shanidar too, in Iraq, Neanderthal skeletons have been found, among which was a poly-traumatized individual whose survival surely depended on the care of relatives. Erik Trinkaus, who has studied his skeleton, has concluded that he had been probably assisted during his life. Taking care of a handicapped individual among a group of Neanderthals casts new light on our image of these fossil people which contrasts with the brutality, not to say bestiality, which many attribute to them. In my view, information

82   *The Archaeology of the Dead*

of this sort has as much historical value as our knowledge of the way Neanderthals worked flint.

There are also examples from much more recent periods of severely handicapped individuals whose survival was due to the care of the group to which they belonged. Some very developed degenerative lesions show us sufferers who continued to exercise their locomotive function, even though the cartilage in their joints was completely destroyed (see for example the articular damage and visible remodelling of the femoro-patellar joint in an individual of the 18th century, Figure 71).

7.3.2. *Determining the cause of death*

It is rare and difficult to discover the cause of death of an individual by examination of the skeleton alone. Sometimes there may be various traumas, all potentially fatal (see the case of Châtelliers-du-Vieil-Auzay considered above).

The first example we will consider concerns an early Neolithic burial of the Danubian culture found in the Paris region in the Aisne valley. The anatomical connections are generally preserved. The left femur has a double fracture and is about 10 cm. shorter than the right (Figure 72). Is this an *ante mortem*, *circa mortem* (the expression *circa mortem* is preferable in my view to the term *peri-mortem* which is a Greek-Latin hybrid), or *post mortem* lesion? There is no scarring and not even a sign of hypervascularization to suggest the formation of calluses: the fracture might have been immediately *ante mortem* or *post mortem*. The joint of the left hip is still connected. The shortening is therefore

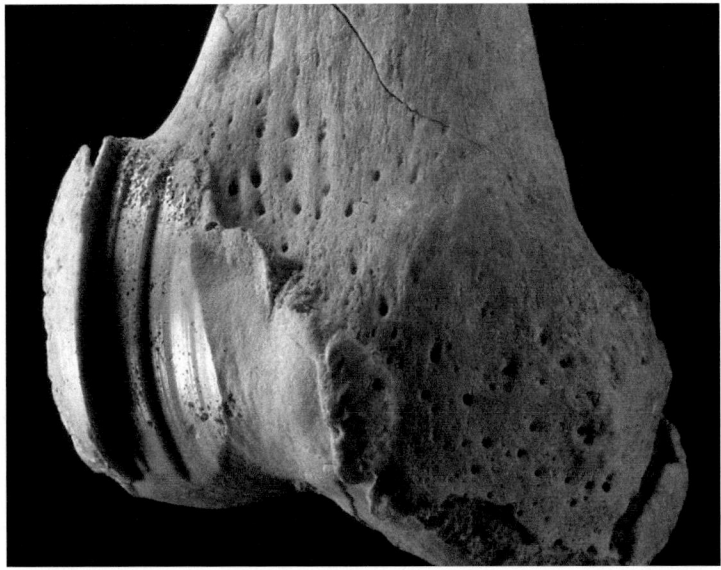

Figure 71. Cemetery at Pézenas (Hérault, France), 18th century. Illustration by J.-P. Vion, photograph by H. Duday.

linked to the rising of the lower femoral fragment which lies under the double fracture. In its displacement this has pulled with it the entire lower left limb. The knee, ankle, tarsal, metatarsal and toe joints are all tightly connected. The interphalangeal joints of the foot are among the tissues of the body that break down most easily: when the lower part of the femur rose, all the ligaments must therefore still have worked. We conclude therefore that this happened immediately *ante mortem* or very soon after deposition.

This must be the result of a very violent trauma given that the femur at its diaphyses is the most resistant bone in the body. However, the femoral artery passes at this point and if this breaks a massive haematoma is created (the quantity of blood may very soon reach 2.5 litres) and the individual cannot survive for long. The shortening presupposes a considerable force, since, in its rising, the lower part of the femur has pulled the thigh muscles. It is a real possibility that the displacement is due to the contraction of the quadriceps muscle caused by the haematoma. This is not then a taphonomic event, but a direct consequences of the trauma that would have caused the death of the individual. In this case it is obvious how useful excavation data can be for aetiological discussion.

In the excavation of multiple depositions that correlate with epidemics, DNA analysis may contribute to isolating the bacterium or the virus responsible for the disease. In other cases we can only identify a plausible cause but without any certainty. Let us return to 'la Dame de Bonifacio', whose pathologies have already been described. We now enquire into the cause of her death. First, her cranium, rotated towards the right, is well preserved but in the view from above shows a vast zone of fracture in the right

Figure 72. Neolithic burial of Danubian type in the Aisne valley (France). Photograph by Y. Guichard.

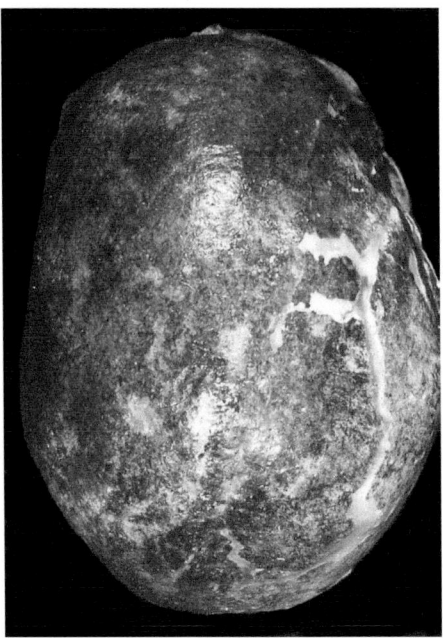

Figure 73. Rock shelter at Araguina Sennola at Boniface (Corsica). Mesolithic. Upper view of the cranium. Photograph by M. Thouvenot.

temporo-parietal region (Figure 73), where part of the lamina has fallen inside the cranial cavity. The problem is to determine whether a violent trauma has caused her death (there are no signs of scarring on the bone) or if the fracture has occurred after burial. At the time of discovery the endocranial surface was covered with a *c.* 0.2 mm. thick crystalline deposit that was shiny, pale yellow and very fine and spread across the entire surface, following endocranial relief perfectly. The X-ray diffraction spectrum showed this layer to be composed of calcite, a calcium carbonate with a crystalline structure that almost never forms in the organism, forming in exceptional cases in the pancreas and in the biliary calculi (gall stones). Therefore it is almost certainly a post-mortem deposit: the water had become rich in calcium carbonate by percolating through the strata above, had infiltrated the cranial cavity and then evaporated inside the void left by decomposition. The minerals in suspension had then been freed in crystal form. In conclusion the cranial fragmentation was a taphonomic event, perhaps linked to the collapse of part of cave roof some millennia later, during the early Neolithic. It is not related to the woman's death.

The mandible lacks its lower right first molar, where a zone of destruction to the bone tissue is visible, with signs of hypervascularization. This is an osteitis, *i.e.* an inflammation of the bone, where an enormous abscess has destroyed part of the mandible (Figure 74). The missing tooth was found slightly displaced and broken in three. The fine deposit of calculus on the fracture lines shows that the fragmentation has taken place *ante mortem*. If we replace the tooth in its socket, lining up its occlusal surface on the occlusal plane, we note that the roots no longer have contact with the bone. Therefore when the woman died, the tooth was floating in infected tissue, in pus. The body generally eliminates quite quickly a hard element if it is embedded in necrotised tissue (in pathology this phenomenon is called a *sequestrum*). At the moment of death this woman had an infective lesion in progress on her face. Before the age of antibiotics, serious infections of this kind frequently caused death because there are many blood vessels between the face and the endocranium: a septic embolism (with bacteria entering the blood circulation) may produce meningitis or encephalitis which can be fatal without appropriate care. These observations suggest that the mandibular osteitis may be a cause of death, but it is not possible to exclude that the real cause could have been violence (poison, strangulation, *etc.*).

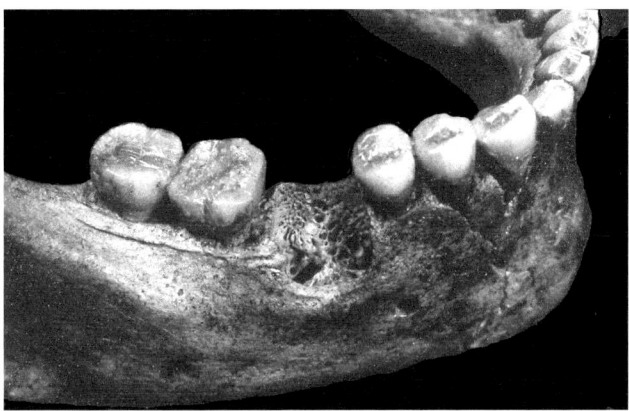

Figure 74. Rock shelter at Araguina Sennola at Boniface (Corsica). Mesolithic. Antero-lateral right view of the mandible. Photograph by M. Thouvenot.

7.3.3. Biological calcifications and ossifications

So far we have referred to only osteo-articular and dental pathologies. Occasionally excavation also provides other solid pathological elements. In the dolmen at Prayssac, for example, the archaeological material found included a small ovoid stone 42 mm. long (Figure 75). It was first interpreted as a 'cave pearl', a particular type of calcite concretion that forms in puddles inside caves. On its damaged face was evidence of growth in concentric layers, suggesting that it was an exogenous stone deposited as an offering near a skeleton. The X-ray diffraction spectrum however shows that it is formed by a hydrated phosphate of calcium and iron and it turns out to be a urinary calculus of the bladder. The presence of quartz derives from the clay that had impregnated its external surface. Again the archaeologist's observation is crucial. François Rouzaud was wrong in interpreting the stone as a cave pearl, but the essential thing is that he immediately understood that it was an exogenous element. This suggests that we should sieve all

Figure 75. Dolmen of Bertrandoune at Prayssac (Lot, France). Eneolithic. Illustration and photograph by F. Rouzaud, study by H. Duday.

the soil coming from burial excavations before attempting palaeoepidemiological analysis of the frequency of lithiasis among past populations, but this is impossible.

Other excavations have revealed calcified faecal matter in the digestive tract, pleural plates, calcified uterine fibroids, and in one case the peripheral calcification

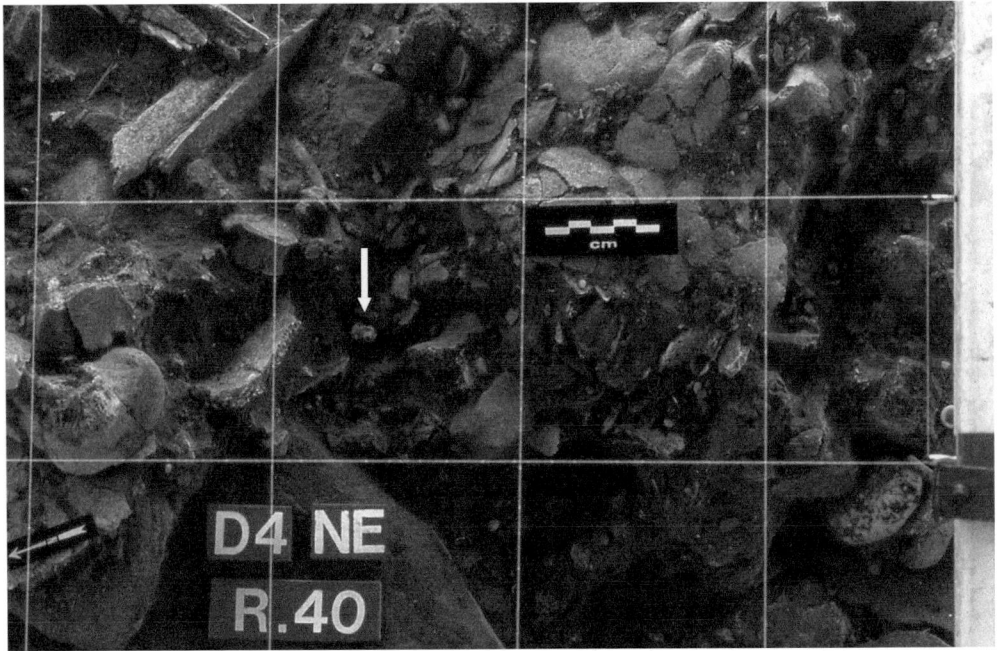

Figure 76. Dolmen of Peirières at Villedubert (Aude, France), Eneolithic. The arrow shows the calcified ganglion. Photograph by H. Duday, analysis by C-A. Baud.

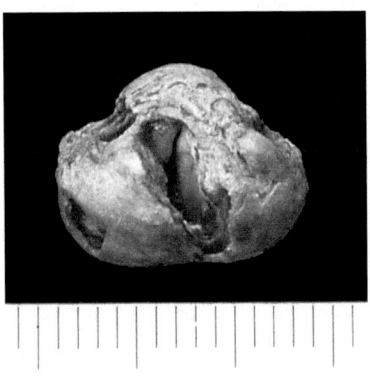

Figure 77. Dolmen of Peirières at Villedubert (Aude, France). Eneolithic. View of the tuberculous calcified ganglion. Photograph by H. Duday, analysis by Ch-A. Baud.

of a cyst, which corresponds to a parasitic disease due to the *taenia echinococcus* (human tapeworm) that generally attacks the liver. In the Neolithic dolmen at Les Peirières, near Carcassonne, was found a small object, 13 mm. long (Figure 76) with a particular structure. Its centre was made of two yellow nuclei and its outer part of thin concentric mineral layers (Figure 77). It was recorded during excavation as a biological calcification but laboratory analyses carried out at Geneva's Medical School by Charles Albert Baud have shown it to be a calcified tuberculous ganglion of the pulmonary hilus. In his view it was the oldest evidence of pulmonary tuberculosis ever known. If we consider the consequence of this disease for human groups, we realize the historical importance of such a discovery. Here too, if we consider archaeological research as a genuinely anthropological investigation, we must recognise

Figure 78. Barrow cemetery at Nordhouse (Haut-Rhin, France). Final Bronze Age – Early Iron Age. The white pins show the positions of the calcified ganglions. Excavation by S. Plouin and F. Lambach, photograph by F. Lambach.

that this evidence is of a historical importance at least equivalent to the ways in which Chalcolithic people decorated their pottery or worked flint.

In a burial in one of the barrows at Nordhouse, in Alsace, (dating to the transition between the late Bronze Age and early Iron Age), a skeleton of a woman with rich grave goods was found. François Lambach has identified *in situ* calcifications, probably due to tuberculosis, related to the subclavicular lymph glands (Figure 78). Again in Alsace, during excavation of a Neolithic burial at Enzheim, he immediately noted the peculiarity of the cranium, which had one orbit smaller than the other. He excavated the orbits and inside the smaller one found a bony capsule formed by concentric layers (23 mm. long) with a small orifice (Figure 79). This is a choroidal osteoma. The choroid is one of the eye membranes. Being an organic element, it disappears during decomposition but a rare

Figure 79. Choroidal osteoma found inside an orbit of a Neolithic cranium from Enzheim (Alsace, France). Illustration by F. Lambach, photograph by H. Duday.

disease may cause its ossification and consequent preservation. The ossification is quite slow and it may take ten years to form. It develops only in a blind eye, so this individual lost his sight in his childhood and the eye muscles later atrophied. The small orifice, completely atrophied, was where the optic nerve once passed.

Palaeopathology does not give us information on funerary rituals but on the conditions of life and death for past populations. The examples examined above have highlighted the importance of observations made during excavations for palaeopathological diagnosis. They also led us to reflect on the socio-cultural dimension of illness and on the status of diseased individuals in ancient societies. This research can no longer be considered as simple curiosity or as a secondary branch of medical science but should be fully integrated into historical dialectic.

Lecture 8

Secondary burials

Secondary deposition concerns dry bones that have become separated from their organs and ligaments. It is important to emphasise the notion of 'pre-planning' to distinguish a secondary burial from a mere secondary deposit (see the abovementioned double burials). In the literature of funerary archaeology, reference is often made to secondary burials, but it is important to understand the criteria which allow their identification.

A frequently used criterion is that of 'disorder' in the arrangement of the bones, an expression currently used to indicate that they are not anatomically connected. The argument runs as follows: if the corpse is first deposited to decompose in a place suitable for that purpose and the bones are later collected and deposited elsewhere then they will no longer be in anatomical connection. However in certain cases some particularly resistant connections may survive, for example that between the atlas and the occipital which sometimes disappears only after several years. At the same time there are primary burials where the anatomical connections are missing. This may happen when the corpse has been laid on a hammock or on a funerary bier, for example. If the supporting element collapses, the bones will fall to the ground in disorder. Dispersal may also be due to the passage of water or animals. Disorder is not then by itself conclusive in demonstrating the secondary character of the burial.

Another frequently cited criterion is the absence of bones, especially those of small dimensions. Their absence may be explained by their being forgotten, by the selection of bones in the *pourrissoir* (structures in which a corpse is placed to decompose – see Chapter 1), by their fall during transport, for example if they were brought to the final tomb inside coarse-woven baskets (a hypothesis formulated by some writers which would imply a somewhat surprising negligence towards the remains of the dead, what we might call a 'Hansel and Gretel theory'). That some bones remain in the temporary place of deposition is attested in practice, which makes this argument valid enough, and the range of bones represented in the *pourrissoir* shows what might be the missing elements from the secondary deposits. But because the observation is potentially significant, it is necessary to eliminate more banal causes. The first and most frequent is the poor quality of some excavations, where the sediment has not been sieved. In a chamber in the lower part of the Enlène cave a collective burial site of the middle Bronze Age was excavated about a century ago. In recent excavation by Robert Begouën and Jean Clottes all the soil from the earlier excavation was sieved. The bones recovered are absolutely analogous to those found in a *pourrissoir*, bones of the carpal, small bones of the tarsal, phalanges, fragments of long bone, unfused epiphyses of immature individuals, as well as many isolated teeth. This situation is perfectly understandable for such an old excavation but is not acceptable today.

Moreover, if moisture variations are significant, cracks up to three centimetres wide will form as clay dries. If a corpse has been laid on the ground its smaller bones may fall into these cracks which can be up to ten centimetres deep. If the moisture level rises, the cracks may close, trapping what has fallen inside them. The same can happen to small bones that may be 'sucked' down by the collapsing of animal burrows dug into the clay beneath. These mechanisms, often seen in caves, can be considered as a 'natural sieving' that subtracts some of the smallest elements from the deposit. Because the lack of bones is a significant criterion when defining a burial, we need to research the causes of their absence systematically, in particular by excavating the soil for at least ten centimetres beneath the burial.

Another frequently mentioned criterion relates to traces of defleshing on the bones, in particular cut marks. It should be noted that these correspond to a particular funerary practice which comprises the removal of soft tissues with a cutting tool. There is no reason to find them on bones gathered after natural putrefaction, unless those carrying out the rite have carefully scraped the bones and removed the last traces of ligaments when they have collected them in the *pourrissoir*. Cut marks can also be due to other causes such as surgery (trepanning, *etc.*), autopsy, injuries (a knife can cut a bone during a fight, not only during the funerary process), as well, obviously, as cannibalism. Much depends on the historical period to which a burial belongs.

Indicators of cremation, *i.e.* applying fire to the corpse, are often mentioned as evidence for secondary burial. A burial is considered to be secondary when a corpse is burnt on a pyre. Its flesh disappears while the bones are collected and preserved in a vessel that can be buried at some distance from the pyre. In this case the place in which the organic substance of the corpse disappears should be distinguished from the final tomb where only its mineral fraction (*i.e.* what remains of the skeleton) is deposited. The particular characteristic of this treatment is that the disappearance of the soft tissue has been accelerated by fire. Sometimes there can be primary cremation deposits, for example, when the corpse is placed on a pyre which collapses into a pit beneath, which is then filled (in the Roman period this is usually called a *bustum*). The place where the body is burnt is the final tomb and the treatment of the body happens in a single phase only. Not all cremation burials are therefore secondary.

Among some groups cremation does not relate to funerary practice but to cannibalism. Many such cases have been described for the prehistoric period. Moreover, when a fire has been lit in a space previously used for burial, it is not rare to find human bones with traces of burning. In the Neolithic the deposition of the corpse on the surface was common. In these cases it is important not to confuse a funerary practice with an occasional chance phenomenon.

All the criteria suggested here to define a secondary burial are therefore logical, but not sufficient in themselves. The first depend on negative considerations, *i.e.* the absence of small bones or anatomical connections. By contrast the identification of primary burials relies on positive characteristics, such as the preservation of anatomical connections at the joints that break down more rapidly. The identification of secondary burials is therefore rarely made with absolute certainty. It is often difficult to distinguish between a robbed primary burial and a true secondary deposit. The only cases which do not present these problems are those of secondary cremation burials in which the bones have been collected in an urn (since it is certain that the corpse has not been burnt within the vessel!).

8 Secondary burials

In conclusion, the extremely heterogeneous character of behaviour related to secondary burials and the difficulties in interpreting them should be underlined. The excavations led by E. Vigneron (1985) in Polynesia in a *marae* (a cult building) in Tahiti serve as an example where deposits containing human bones have been identified. In one pit were found a vertebral column with ribs still anatomically connected, the scapulae, elements of the pelvis, one forearm (radius and ulna) and bones of one hand and the feet (Figure 80). An anatomical logic has been respected here. The individual has been laid on his back with the lower limbs bent in front of the torso (this explains why the patella lies by the rib cage and the feet are near the pelvis). Most of the long bones were missing and were found in a nearby pit. The corpse had therefore been deposited and, after decomposition of the soft tissue, the long bones had been collected and placed in another pit. This is therefore a primary burial, but part of the skeleton has been removed to create a partial secondary deposit, indeed perhaps two deposits, since the skull and the mandible have been removed to a place that has not yet been identified. How should we label all the elements of this complex? Has the corpse been at the same time the subject of a primary burial that has later become incomplete and also of a partial secondary burial? After the removal of the long bones and the cranial skeleton, the pit containing the elements that preserve their anatomical connections may have been 'ignored' (becoming a particular type of *pourrissoir*) or may have preserved its status as the tomb proper, continuing to require commemorative rites.

This situation was repeated in another pit a few metres away, but in this case the long bones, gathered in a bundle, have been replaced in the same pit, above the skeleton of which the torso remained in anatomical connection. The dry bones have been manipulated (a humerus and a femur are both in an unlikely position with their proximal extremities pointing downwards). The secondary deposit has taken place within the space in which the body has decomposed (Figure 81). Is this to be considered a 'reduction' (Chapter 7)? Certainly not! In a third pit nearby, there are long bones belonging to an adult whose remaining skeleton has not been found.

Even if this complex contains structures that have several similar characteristics,

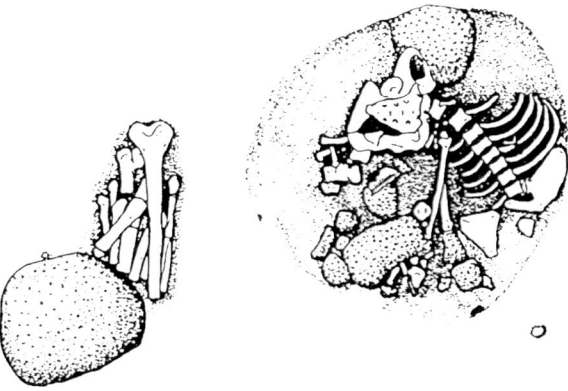

Figure 80. Marae Maraetahata (Tahiti, Polynesia). Detail of a funerary structure. Excavation and plan by E. Vigneron.

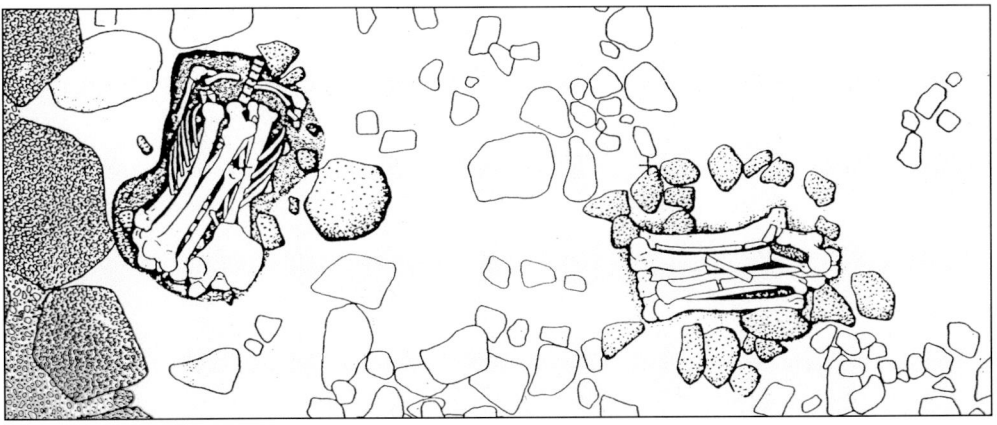

Figure 81. Marae Maraetahata (Tahiti, Polynesia). Details of two other funerary structures. Excavation and plan by E. Vigneron.

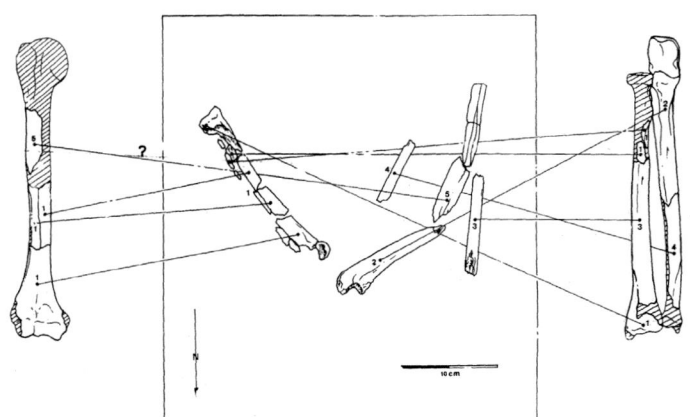

Figure 82. Saint-Michel-du-Touch (Haute-Garonne, France), tomb A185, middle Neolithic. Partial plan based on photograph of the "restored" bones. Excavation by L. Méroc and G. Simonnet, study by H. Duday.

a typology that is too strictly defined might lead us to classify them in very different categories, especially if the classification is based on the distinction between the place of decomposition and the place of deposit. It is, however, important to identify and reconstruct funerary behaviour rather than struggling with nomenclature.

The second example concerns the excavation of a middle Neolithic structure at Saint-Michel-du-Touch (near Toulouse), a wide chamber containing rich grave goods and the remains of two individuals. One was found in a contracted position on his side. The two humeri were placed in a line as if to represent the upper limb. In this way, the appearance of the individual had been reconstructed using bones that were already defleshed. This is a very particular secondary deposition. In another part of the same structure there were various large fragments of diaphysis, a bone apparently *in situ* and a flint blade (Duday 1979). The bone, which is apparently complete, is in fact formed from fragments of the humerus and radius to give the appearance of a long bone (Figure 82). This is also a secondary deposit, but it is difficult to define it as a burial.

Lecture 9

Funerary complexes (I)

'Funerary complexes' are those sites that contain the remains of a greater or lesser number of individuals.

9.1. Cemeteries and necropolises

The first category includes cemeteries and necropolises. These may be enclosed by a wall or ditch, which are archaeologically visible, or a hedge, for which archaeological evidence is less easy to identify. The scale of the work being undertaken and the means at the disposal of archaeologists often make it impossible to conduct extensive investigation of all the area concerned. These complexes are generally formed by the juxtaposition of individual elements, in the simplest cases individual tombs. A cemetery of this type is studied by considering not only the funerary ritual for each individual burial but also the organization of the complex as a whole, its evolution over time and the relative chronology of deposits. For example in the cemetery of Saint-Cheron at Chartres, excavated by Dominique Joly and Patrice Courtaud, it was noted that the tomb of a child was deeper but later than the two tombs of adults which it cut (Figure 83). This observation makes us think about the limits beyond which the marking of a tomb ceases to be visible, what we might call the duration of memory. In this instance we note that the long bones of the two tombs that were cut have been collected in the later grave. The respectful handling of remains recognised as human is not part of the typology of burials, but reveals something of the attitudes of past populations.

Each burial is studied by examining parameters related to chronology (relative or absolute date, stratigraphic relationships), topography (location, orientation), architectural form (type of container, materials used, size of tomb or pit, superstructure) and grave goods (nature and quantity, position in the tomb and in relation to the corpse *etc.*). The original position of the corpse is also taken into consideration, both as a whole (on its back, side or stomach, extended or flexed) and in its parts (possible rotation of the head, position of the hands *etc*), the space in which it has decomposed (a void or filled space) is assessed, and, more generally, all the criteria applied to the study of individual burials are considered as a whole (Figure 84). The burials are classified according to the differences found in the parameters considered. The normal analytical procedure consists in comparing these different classifications in order to find significant associations.

The various archaeological characteristics are then compared with the anthropological and biological parameters. Characteristics related to the sex and the age of the deceased are considered first, two key elements for placing individuals in the funerary complex

Figure 83. Saint-Cheron cemetery at Chartres (Eure-et-Loir, France). Excavation by D. Joly and P. Courtaud.

and in the society from which they derive. The age of the deceased is established from indicators of dental and skeletal maturity for immature individuals (such as the appearance and synostosis of the secondary ossification centres) and from indicators of ageing for adults, although these are much less precise.

The pelvis is the most significant skeletal element for establishing sex, particularly the coxal bones, whose morphology is shaped by adaptation to pregnancy and childbirth. Other indicators based on differences in height and robusticity are less reliable as there are obviously tall sturdy women as well as small thin men. Thanks to the introduction of molecular palaeo-biochemistry (for example the analysis of ancient DNA), it has been possible to determine the sex of children. Some elements of ornament and dress, such

Figure 84. La Favorite cemetery at Lyon (Rhône, France). Late antiquity. Excavation by L. Tranoy and V. Bel.

as brooches or earrings, may be specifically feminine, while weapons are commonly reserved for men. These associations may change over time, for example the torc in Gaul. In the Corded Ware culture from the end of the Neolithic in central Europe, the position of the dead and of grave furniture varied according to sex.

It is very important to indicate by which method sex has been determined and to assess its reliability. If a researcher attempts a synthesis of the sex specificity of an element of grave furniture, for example a brooch, s/he must base the analysis on tombs where sex diagnosis has been made from the skeleton and exclude tombs labelled as female because they contained a brooch.

The biological study of skeletons allows us to obtain very detailed information which helps us to evaluate correctly the funerary complex as a whole. The term necropolis is significant because it refers to a 'city of the dead' and suggests that within it there is an element of urban planning proper, as applies to the city of the living. In a necropolis there are roads, spaces to move and zones in which individuals are grouped according to criteria such as geographical origin, kinship, economic position, profession or religion, *i.e.* generally according to social criteria. Therefore the structure of the cemetery reflects, more or less faithfully, the organisation of a community and is a dynamic phenomenon that evolves over time. From the 1960s so many Muslim families have emigrated from Algeria to France that Islam is now the second religion. Consequently zones have been created in cemeteries for their dead, generally along the edges of cemeteries already in existence. Exclusively Muslim cemeteries have rarely been built. The funerary complex here reproduces the transformation of society with the birth of different zones characterised by names and rituals different from the original complex.

The cemetery generally gives a precise, if not always objective, reflection of the history of a society. The random distribution of the dead within it is very rare. The very image that the community of the living offers to itself through the ordering of its burial space reflects an extremely significant aspect of the culture of the society to which it refers, the importance of which exceeds by some degree the contribution provided by 'l'anthropologie de terrain'. The direct use of biological data in the study of funerary complexes is doubtlessly one of the most significant recent developments in funerary archaeology. It is important to understand the criteria on the basis of which individuals are distributed in the funerary space. In the course of life, the skeleton registers permanently information that is more or less directly related to living conditions, for example growth and development, nutrition, health status, muscular activities, anomalous postures and trauma.

If a child at a certain stage of growth suffers a serious attack on its organism, for example famine bringing malnutrition, psychological stress-inducing anorexia or serious infantile illness, then some functions cease that require significant amounts of energy but do not immediately affect survival. Such circumstances may halt the formation of tooth enamel. If the child overcomes the period of difficulty, this interruption is signalled by a transversal defect, a linear hypoplasia due to deficient development in the tooth enamel (Figure 85). Each line is therefore a non-specific stress indicator, since it suggests a trauma experienced by the body but does not specify its nature. The

Figure 85. Linear hypoplasia of the tooth enamel on a left central upper incisor from the Kitsos cave (Laurion, Greece), Neolithic. Photograph by N. Lambert and H. Duday.

most recent episode of stress is indicated by the line nearer to the neck of the tooth (the junction between the crown and the root) since the enamel begins to form from the occlusal surface and the formation of the crown develops towards the root. To some extent it is therefore possible to estimate the age at which the stress took place. If an individual lives in a condition of chronic malnutrition, then s/he is much more sensitive to attack and more exposed to disease. The quantification of linear hypoplasia therefore helps us to identify the individual's social position.

Radiographs of long bones may reveal some small transversal lines of denser ossification. These are Harris lines (Figure 86) and relate to the accumulation, or rather deposition, of mineral in a bone whose longitudinal growth has been slowed or interrupted. The oldest line is therefore the furthest from the epiphysis. These lines can, however, be reabsorbed during the individual's lifetime (especially in women after menopause) and cannot then be identified on the skeleton. If the long bones are broken, the earth that has penetrated the diaphysis must be extracted with great care since too rough a cleaning would remove these thin lines of denser spongy fabric. From this point of view enamel hypoplasia lines are among the most reliable of the non-specific stress indicators. However, the formation of teeth enamel ends relatively early, around the age of ten, but bone growth lasts much longer, providing us with information for the whole period of adolescence.

Various traumas can be recorded that are work or activity related. The identification of enthesopathies, *i.e.* ossifications in the form of small spurs that develop in the muscular or ligament structures when they are overworked, allows us to obtain information on the type of work that is being undertaken. The skeleton may also record the habitual posture of an individual. If a person works while squatting, for example, and exerts a very strong pressure on the knees and ankles then additional articular facets develop, essentially extensions of the joint surface. Trace elements present in bone such as zinc, strontium and calcium give us information on nutrition, whether it is based on meat, fish or vegetables. The skeleton reveals therefore a certain number of events that have marked the life of the individual and which often correlate to the conditions of his or her everyday life.

Physical anthropology seeks to establish kinship relations between individuals within

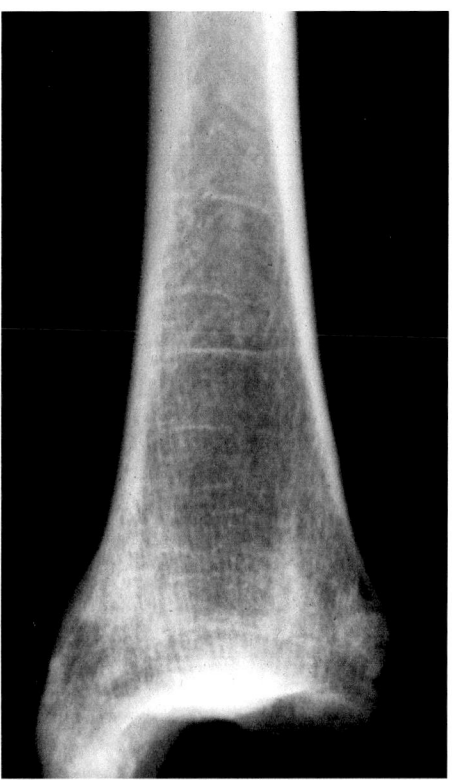

Figure 86. Harris lines visible on the radiograph of a medieval tibia. Illustration by E. Crubézy.

a cemetery. For several decades these studies have been based on the assessment of discontinuous anatomical variables, 'non-metric traits', which are either present or absent. The study of DNA now opens new research perspectives, allowing genetic relationships between individuals to be established with greater precision. It is important though to bear in mind that the study of DNA helps us to establish genetic relationships, whereas during funerary rites it is generally the relationship recognised by the group that is taken into consideration, which need not be genetic.

A community determines the space that will be assigned to an individual in the cemetery according to its own rules. However, some funerary complexes are dedicated to a particular category of the dead. Examples include the cemeteries of abbeys (with a specialization based on sex), military cemeteries (where the specialization is based on sex and age) and hospice cemeteries (where the specialization is based on age). We have already seen that a particular type of funerary complex concerns children who died in the perinatal period. In Catholicism stillborn babies that had not been baptized were not considered sons of the church and could not be buried in consecrated ground in the cemetery. So called sanctuaries 'à répit' were therefore developed that lasted till the 17th century (Guillon et al. 2001). The corpses of babies were placed under statues of the Virgin Mary or St. Margaret, since popular belief held that they had the power to restore them to life. After a while the corpse of a baby swelled and its limbs moved because of phenomena linked to decomposition. The family believed it to have been revived, baptized it and had it buried in the cemetery.

Finally, large cemeteries give us the opportunity to observe the characteristics of burial deposits across a large sample and thus to distinguish what is ritual from what is not. This can be established thanks to comparisons made within the same site.

9.2 Multiple burials

When several individuals have been buried within the same structure, it is possible to distinguish two categories of funerary complexes, based on the chronology of deposition. The first category is that of multiple burials in which all the individuals have been buried at the same time or within a very short period. These coincide with an event that has caused a serious mortality crisis and for this reason are labelled 'catastrophe' burials.

The first example is a Chalcolithic tomb excavated by Jean Courtin at Roaix (Figure 87), an artificial cave containing a large number of individuals. Excavation in these cases should be extremely meticulous and follow the same principles as for double burials, but the difficulties are obviously multiplied by the presence of so many corpses. By analysing the anatomical connections, it is possible to understand whether the deposition of an individual has disturbed the ligaments of the corpse below, buried previously. In this case scores of corpses were buried simultaneously or within a short period of time (Philippe Chambon has, however, demonstrated that even in this layer deposits were staggered through time). The traumatic event behind this kind of burial was probably warfare. Many flint arrowheads and fragments of arrowheads were found, some of which were embedded in the bones: this may have been a massacre.

A rescue excavation at Sens, south of Paris, has brought to light several pits containing a large number of individuals who were buried at the same time (Figure 88). Since the

Figure 87. Burial chamber from Crottes, Roaix (Vaucluse, France). Eneolithic. Partial view. Excavation by J. Courtin.

Figure 88. Multiple burials from Clos des Cordeliers at Sens (Yonne, France), 5th–6th century AD. General view of one pit. Excavation by D. Maranski.

Figure 89. Multiple burials from Clos des Cordeliers at Sens (Yonne, France), 5th–6th century AD, detail. Excavation by D. Maranski.

bones did not show signs of fracture, it has been assumed that the pits could be related to a plague. Historical sources tell us that a plague decimated the town in about AD 820. Radiocarbon analysis enabled us to date these pits to the fifth -sixth centuries AD, *i.e.* the period of the great epidemic known as the Justinianic plague. Using modern research on DNA it is possible to isolate the bacterium that was responsible for the illness that exterminated the population. Since acute diseases do not leave traces on the skeleton because of their rapid development, it is not possible to carry out this analysis through the usual methods of palaeopathology. In this case, it was *Yersinia pestis*, the plague bacillus (Castex and Drancourt 2005; Drancourt *et al.* 2004). During the decomposition of many corpses which had been heaped together at the same time, the small bones fell into the spaces left by the decomposed soft tissue of the individuals beneath. Each body may also have been constricted through contact with the other corpses. Partial preservation of the thoracic volume was observed in one individual, whose torso was pushed between the lower limbs of the body beneath (Figure 89). These observations are extremely valuable because they enrich our reference corpus for the relatively chronology of the breakdown of joints.

The excavation and interpretation of these complexes requires the same methodology and the same principles which have been outlined for single and double burials. The interlacing of the bodies makes this particularly difficult, as the funerary pits recently excavated during a rescue project at Issoudun illustrate perfectly. These pits are most likely related to one or more epidemics that hit the town between the end of the 17th and beginning of the 18th centuries (Figures 90, 91 and 92).

The excavation of a funerary pit at Saint-Rémi-la-Calonne (Adam *et al.* 1993), in northeast France, provides another example. It contained 21 skeletons of French soldiers and officers killed by the Germans on September 22nd 1914 (Figure 93). Among these was the skeleton of Alain Fournier, author of the famous novel 'Le Grand Meaulnes'. The Minister of Culture decided to excavate in order to find his remains. Since the

9 Funerary complexes (I) 101

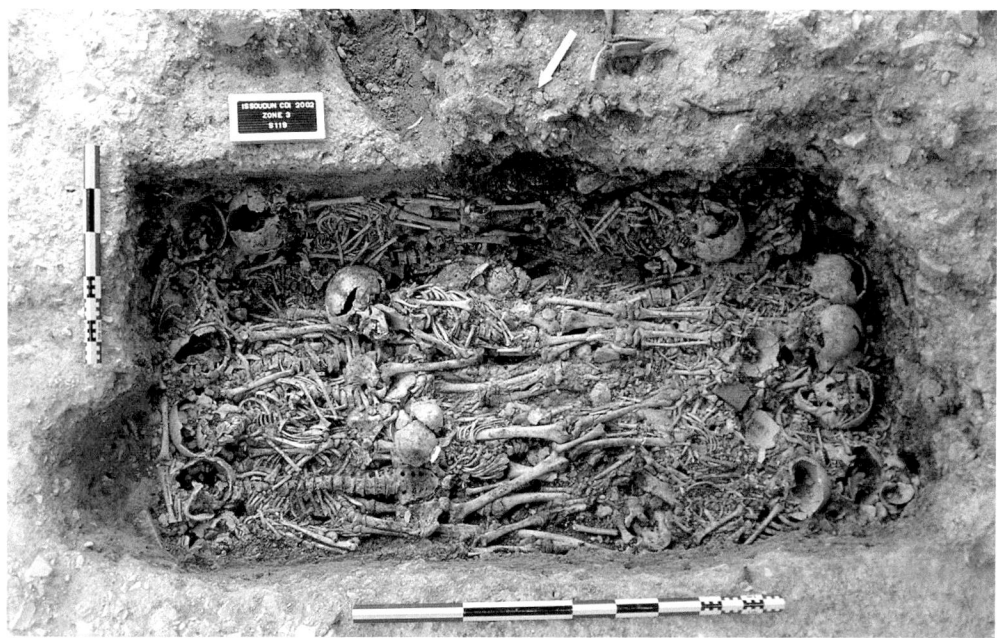

Figure 90. Issoudun (Indre, France). Late 17th–early 18th century. Multiple burial S119, first excavation level. Excavation by Ph. Blanchard, D. Castex, and Y. Leroy.

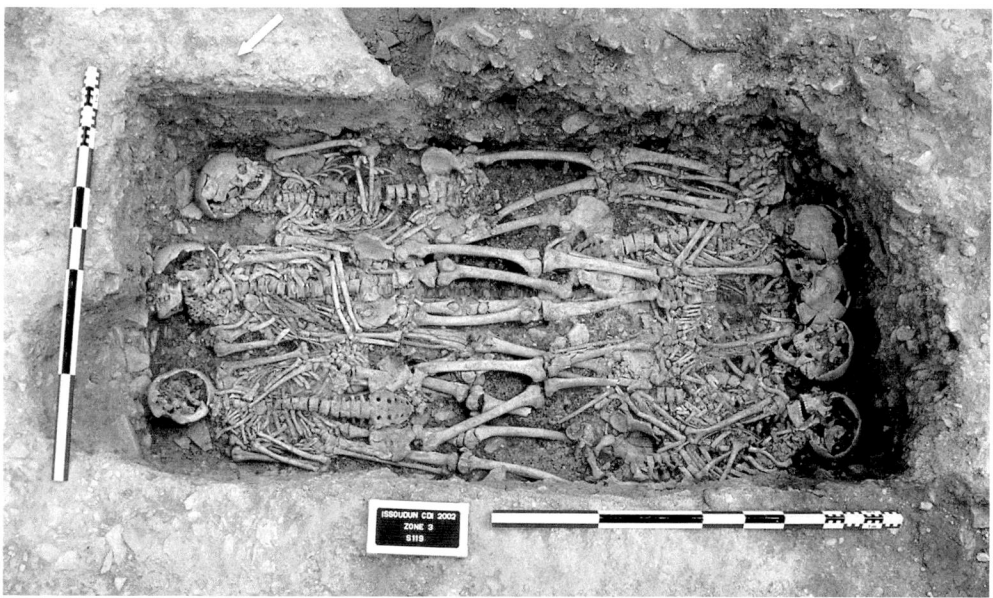

Figure 91. Issoudun (Indre, France). Late 17th–early 18th century. Multiple burial S119, second excavation level. Excavation by Ph. Blanchard, D. Castex, and Y. Leroy.

Figure 92. Issoudun (Indre, France). Late 17th–early 18th century. Multiple burial S119, third excavation level. Excavation by Ph. Blanchard, D. Castex, and Y. Leroy.

French soldier's uniform is well known, it was possible to follow the displacement of different elements during decomposition, such as buttons, belt-buckles and two figure eights in bronze (these men belonged to the 288th infantry) worn on the jacket collar. Some coins were also found near their pockets as well as some officers' stripes. Shoes survived because of the preservation of the leather. The feet were lifted with the shoes after their orientation in the soil had been documented. The shoes were opened and excavated in the laboratory, making it possible to establish the displacement during decomposition of bones in relation to the position of the feet. Inside the shoes a void around the bones was in fact created. These observations allow us to make comparisons with other excavations where the shoes are generally not preserved.

On the same excavation we also obtained, for the first time, the confirmation that the hip joint can be classed among the articulations which break down more rapidly (the 'unstable' or 'labile' articulations). This was not an experiment proper, because it was not possible to vary any of the parameters. However it was possible to compare the original deposit, which is known with certainty, to the form observed at the time of excavation. This has allowed the creation of a set of reference observations which allow taphonomic dynamics to be better understood.

9 *Funerary complexes (I)* 103

Figure 93. Saint-Rémi-la-Calonne (Meuse, France). 22 September 1914. Excavation by F. Adam and F. Boura. Photograph by H. Paitier.

Lecture 10

Funerary complexes (II): collective burials, the karst shaft of La Boucle at Corconne (I)

These cases relate to a single structure, containing a greater or lesser number of individuals whose deposition was staggered over time. Collective burials became much more common during the second half of the Neolithic and we shall therefore discuss this issue taking as examples two sites from southern France, one a cave used for burial, the other a dolmen.

The first collective burial was found inside a karst shaft, a cavity formed by karstic erosion on a limestone massif. The formation of these sinkholes is due to the accumulation of seepage waters at the point of contact with the first impermeable layer. This produces a zone of disintegration of limestone at depth which spreads towards the surface. In the geographical area in question (*i.e.* the Gard), most cavities reach about 60 m. in depth. This site was discovered in 1954 by cavers, looking for underground water for the local village, who noted a very small hole at ground level, *c.* 30 cm. in diameter. They descended for ten metres, at which level they found a bronze belt buckle, dated between the end of the sixth century AD and the seventh, near some human bones. At a lower level was a chamber about 40 m² (Figure 94). Following this discovery, several *sondages* were made which brought to light many ceramic fragments and skeletal remains. These were considered to be of no interest and the site was abandoned until 1973, when Serge Cours undertook a further *sondage*, the results of which led us to undertake an extensive excavation together. This lasted from 1974 to 2002, for four to nine weeks per year and for a total of 36 months. During the excavation many technical problems were encountered, in particular related to safety. It was also necessary to install adequate lighting and build scaffolding on which archaeologists could work without coming into direct contact with the excavated surfaces.

The work began in the large chamber and continued later at a lower level beneath the shaft. There then came to light a relatively recent deposit, dated to *c.* 2000 BC, when the rocky vault had collapsed above the shaft that forms the current means of access. There must have been a different entrance during the Neolithic. The first occupation of the site dates back to the middle Neolithic, by which time the sinkhole was already mainly filled in (the archaeological layers are only ten metres below the surface and overlie almost 50 metres of geological fill). The surface of the clay soil is not horizontal; there is a rather marked slope from its centre towards the western side, caused by the movement of seepage water towards the shaft. The action of gravity means that most of the layers were found in this depression. The surface is less and less steep as the level rises and is horizontal at the end of the occupation. The strata therefore vary in thickness. Near the western side, the fill is about a metre thick, but towards the

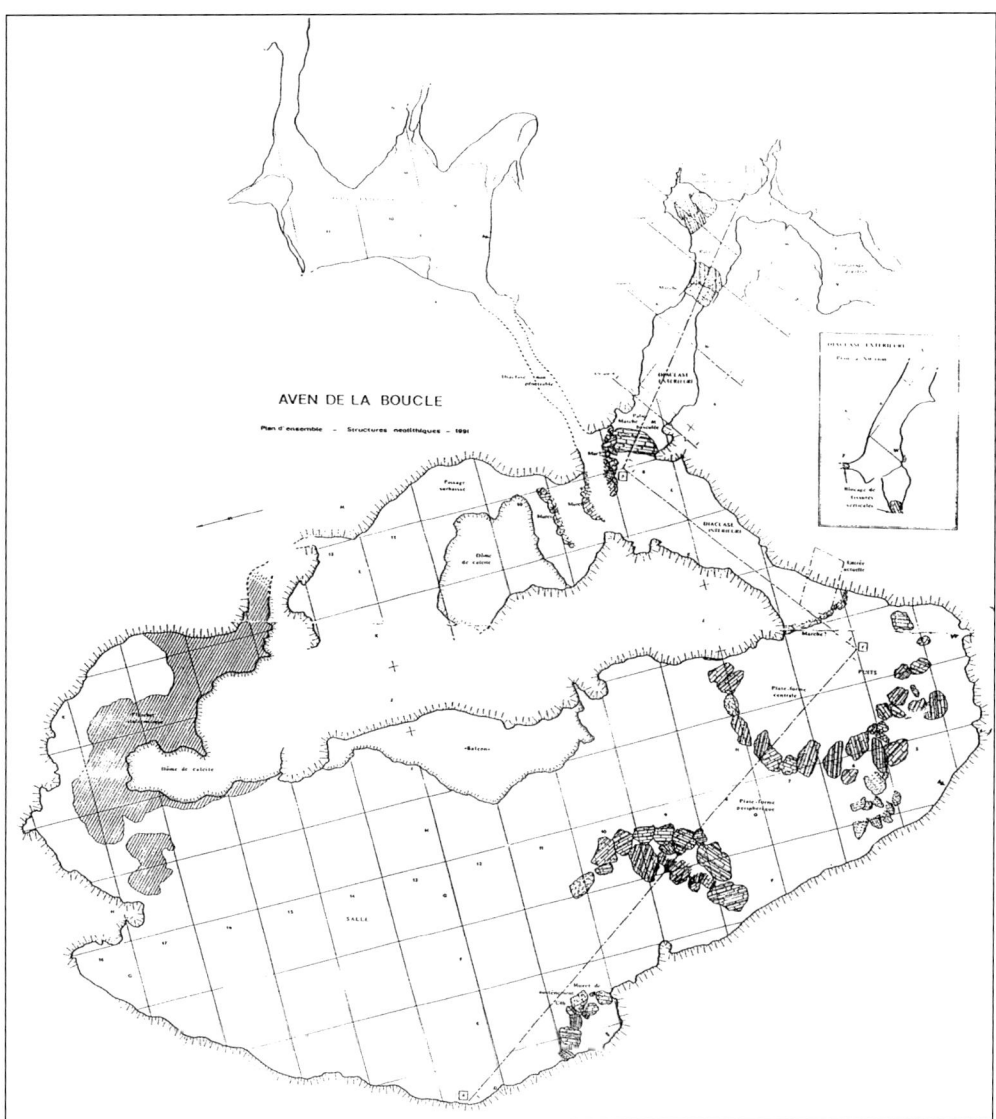

Figure 94. A general plan of the karst shaft at La Boucle, Corconne (Gard, France). Excavation by S. Cours and H. Duday.

centre they become thinner and discontinuous and are sometimes not more than five centimetres thick. It is impossible therefore to attribute the human remains to a well-defined layer. A lumbar vertebra for example is similar in height to the total thickness of the layers referred to above. The bones can moreover be displaced because of the plasticity of the clay, in which cracks sometimes form into which small bones may fall.

Finally the action of burrowing animals may cause disturbance through the collapse of galleries and burrows, mostly excavated into the sterile clay immediately under the base funerary layer. These phenomena are related to the history of the site and must always be taken into consideration when excavating a collective burial in a cave. Part of the skeletal material can only be dated by archaeological observations and we should consider what means could allow us to make up for the lack of excavation data.

The frequenting of the cave began late in the middle Neolithic, around 3500–3300 BC, a period of transition between the Chasséen (middle Neolithic) and the Ferriéres (late Neolithic) cultures. The second stage of occupation dates back to the late Neolithic, about 3100–3000 BC. It was not possible to establish whether there was an interruption in use between the two phases. For the entire period the site was used only for funerary purposes. Later the cave was deliberately closed, marking the end of its funerary use. In the Eneolithic, many centuries later, the rocks above collapsed and opened the current entrance. It was again possible to enter the cave, but by a shaft rather than the Neolithic access. A new phase of temporary, occasional occupation started. Given the difficulty of access the cavity was used only as a temporary shelter. Traces of fire, ceramics, flint weapons and animal remains date back to *c.* 2000 BC A later frequentation occurred also around 900 BC (Bronze Age Final II), with the deposition of a child at the top level of the sinkhole, where traces of fire, carbonized wheat and thirteen vessels were found. The cavity was then again abandoned for about 1500 years until the sixth–seventh centuries AD, to which period further human remains and two belt-buckles should be attributed. It is not possible to know whether this is a funerary deposit or an individual who fell in the shaft by accident, since the bones were disturbed by the discoverers. From then until its exploration by cavers in 1954 the cavity was not visited again. In summary, collective burial of the middle Neolithic was followed by a collective burial of the late Neolithic and a reduced funerary use in the late Bronze Age. We shall examine the Neolithic deposit, in particular the oldest layer.

The natural substratum is formed by a reddish clay sediment, the so-called 'decalcification' clay. In the funerary layer, substantial stone blocks weighing up to 40 kg. rested directly on the bones, which had not however broken (Figures 95 and 96). These blocks of local limestone were brought here from outside the cave. Some show the characteristic marks of erosion caused by rainwater in a karstic environment. On these stones were also visible small holes, less than one millimetre in diameter, created by lichen that need sunlight to live, confirming the exogenous character of the blocks. Their presence is difficult to explain but must represent a deliberate act accompanying the deposition of human remains. Some stones cover the bones, while some bones were found resting on them.

From the middle part of the chamber to its northern edge the funerary layer is composed of a pale yellow sediment (unit C4b), in which fossil sea-urchin (*cidaris*) needles have been found. Jacques-Elie Brochier (1987) has shown that this sediment belongs to the Hauterivian geological stratum. This sediment was formerly sold because of its capacity to remove or absorb fats and is known as 'terre de Sommières' (a type of fuller's earth) after a small village situated about 15 kilometres from Corconne. It can also be found in Italy and Morocco, where it is still exploited. This sediment too is not part of the cave's natural geology and must have been deliberately brought

Figure 95. Swallow-hole at La Boucle, Corconne (Gard, France). View of the limestone blocks and yellow sediment which characterise the oldest funerary layer. Photograph by A. Colomer.

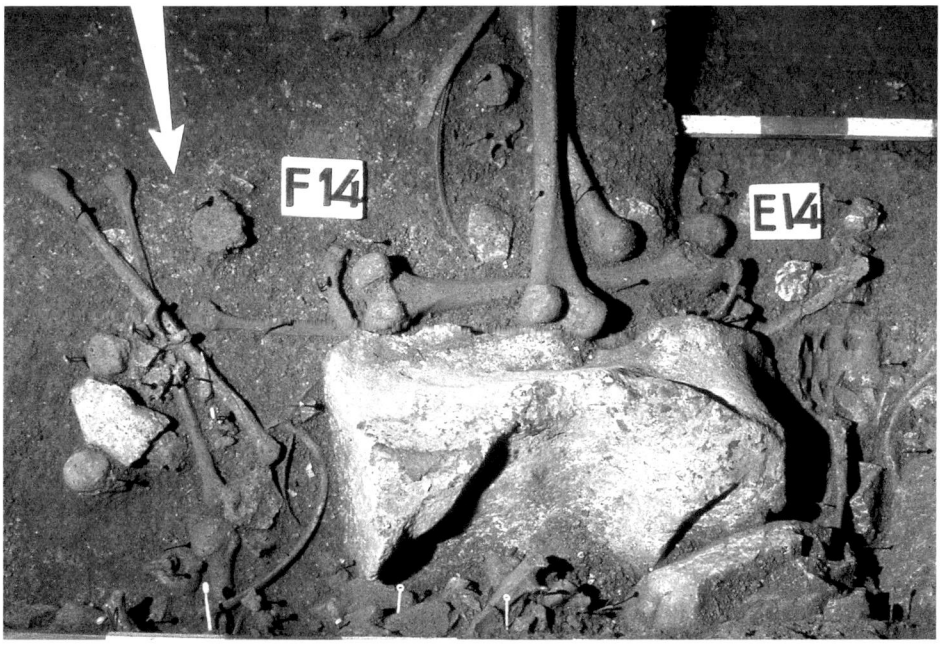

Figure 96. Swallow-hole at La Boucle, Corconne (Gard, France). View of a limestone block in contact with human bones in 'disorder'. Photograph by A. Colomer.

there during the Neolithic. It has been enriched with phosphates deriving from the decomposition liquids of the corpses, showing it to be directly related to the funerary deposits. Within it was found an egg of *Trichuris trichura*, or whipworm, an intestinal parasite of a Neolithic individual (Figure 97).

Among the bones were fragments of stalactites and calcspars which had been deliberately broken off in the Neolithic and carefully laid flat at the base of the funerary layer, sometimes more than six metres from the western wall of the cave from which they had been removed. It has been possible to find their original position because the points where they were broken off are sometimes visible and especially because the development of these concretions has been interrupted.

The human bones are generally well preserved, although most are not anatomically connected. In the Neolithic layers the minimum number of individuals is about 70. More than 12,000 human bones and 30,000 ceramic fragments have been documented and inventoried.

Near the western wall the yellow sediment deposit ends and the reddish clay begins, greyer in places because of the presence of carbon (unit C4b1). In all this area, characterized by a high density of bones, was found a significant quantity of small pointed fragments of local limestone 0.5 to three cm. long (Figure 98). Some have percussion bulbs and on some flakes from the original surface of the block were the small holes produced by lichen action. Large limestone blocks were not only carried into the grave but some were also worked there to make gravel to mix with the human bones.

In some zones were piles of bones *c.* 40 cm. thick from the middle Neolithic alone, lacking any indicators to differentiate between individual layers. This made the stratification difficult and slow to document and interpret. The complex had to be dismantled like a Mikado ('pick up sticks') game, since the bones were tightly interconnected and it was very difficult to determine the order of deposition of the human burials and the starting point from which it began. In these zones the large stones were more numerous than in other parts of the site and at some points formed a practically continuous cover over the human bones (Figures 99 and 100). These were arranged in a particular way: the long bones of several individuals were grouped in bundles (Figure 101) and the skulls were lined up against the side of the cave (Figure 102). It was possible to deduce that the dead were first placed on the yellow sediment and later, at an advanced stage of decomposition, the dry bones were handled to create these deposits which are undeniably secondary. Even if the anatomical connections are almost completely absent, we are not faced with disorder (the inappropriate though commonly used expression to describe such burials), but of a 'secondary' order, a re-arrangement of this space.

Figure 97. Karst shaft at La Boucle, Corconne (Gard, France). Whipworm egg (55μ long). Photograph by A. Cabannes and G. Cliquet.

10 *Funerary complexes (II)* 109

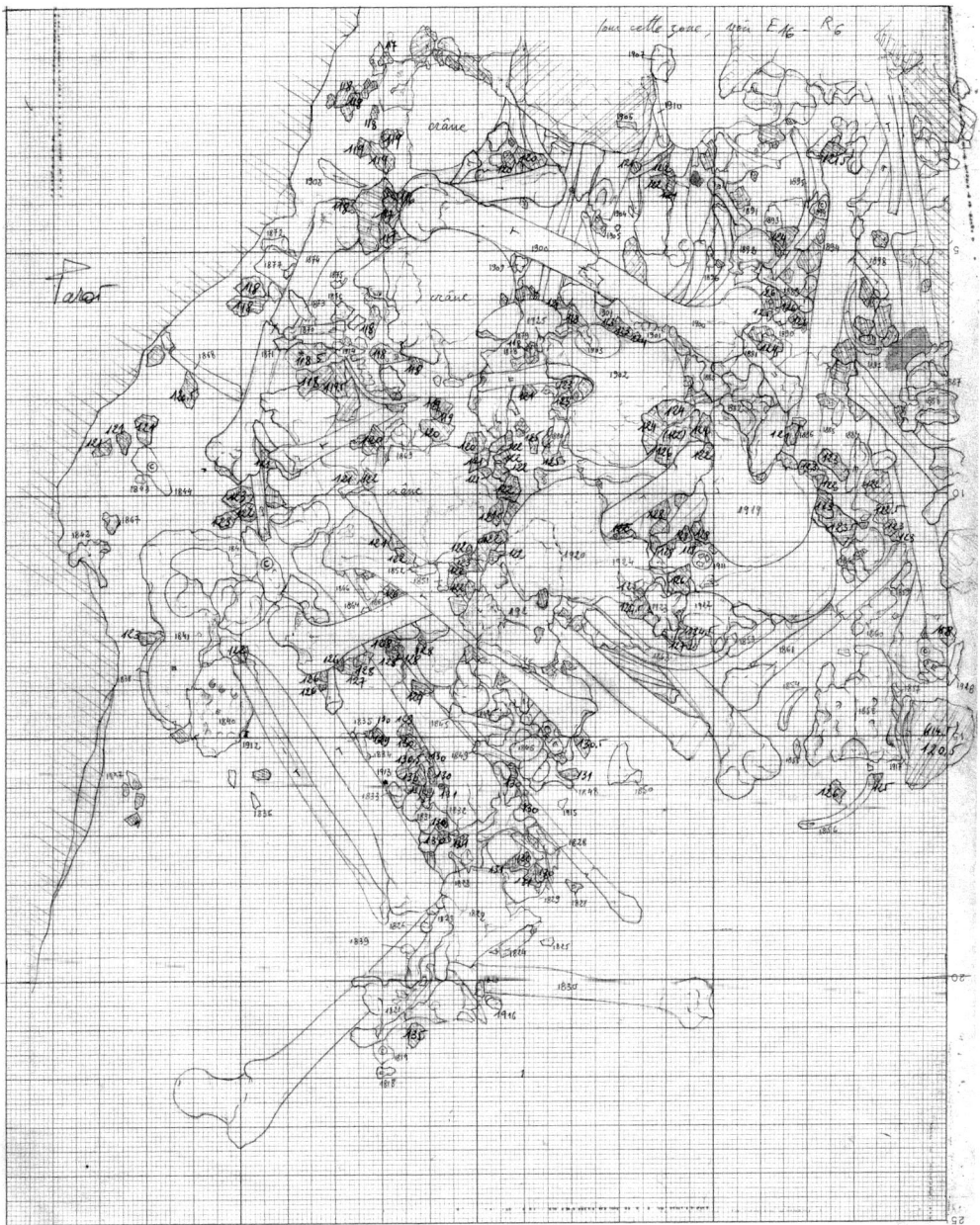

Figure 98. Swallow-hole at La Boucle, Corconne (Gard, France). Plan 23 (by H. Duday) in square E15 against the western wall of the cave. There are very many small stones, the levels of which are written in ink (the inventory numbers for the bones and other archaeological remains are in pencil).

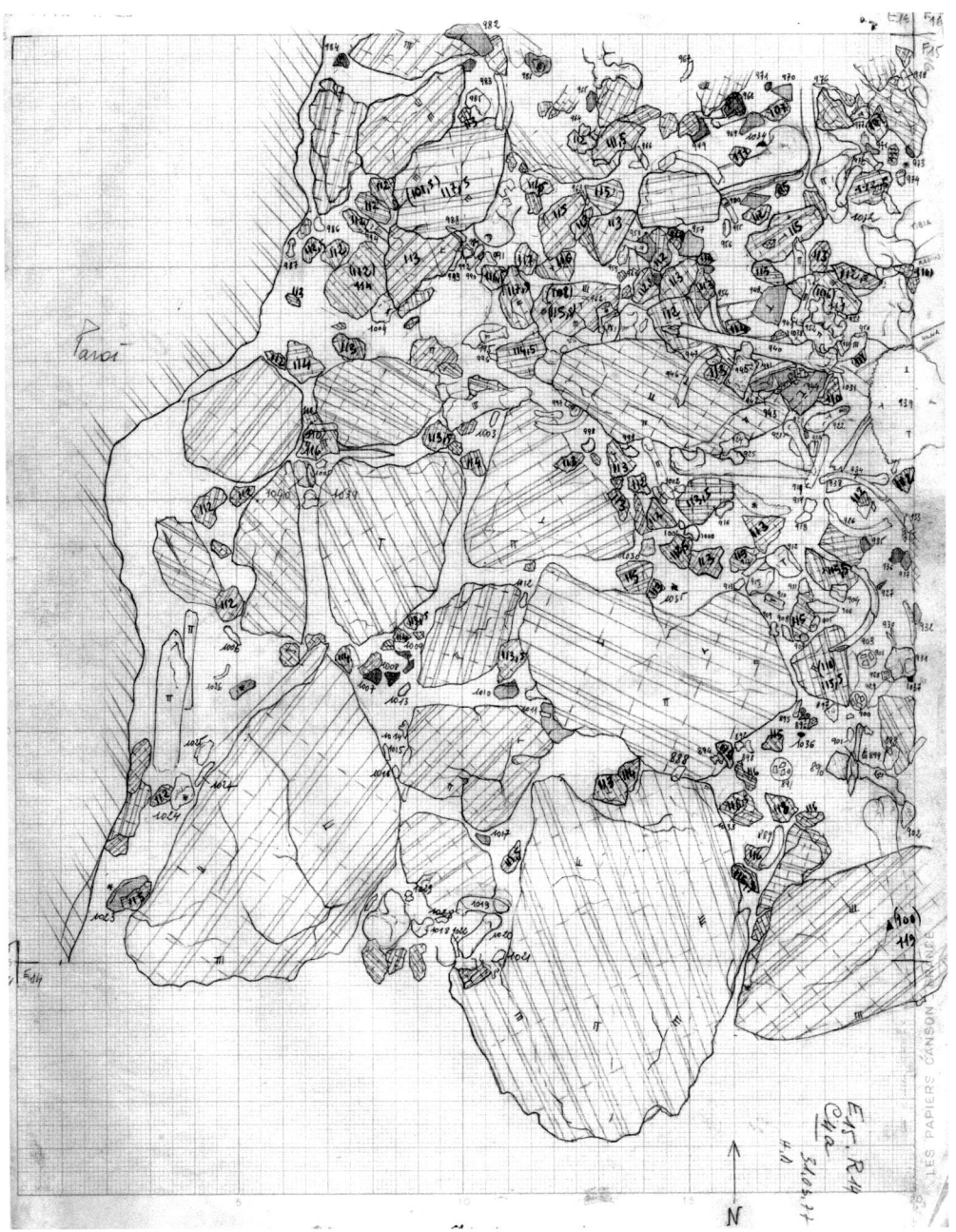

Figure 99. Swallow-hole at La Boucle, Corconne (Gard, France). Plan 14 (by H. Duday) in square E15 shows the accumulation of large limestone blocks over the human bones.

Figure 100. Karst shaft at La Boucle, Corconne (Gard, France). A group of long bones in bundles (five femora are visible) with coxal bones against the western wall of the cave. Photograph by A. Colomer.

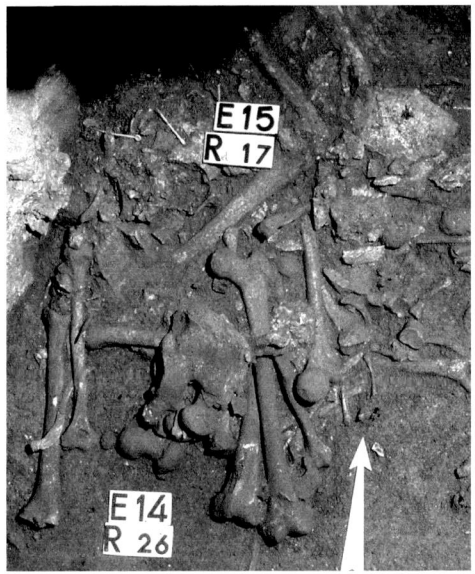

Figure 101. Karst shaft at La Boucle, Corconne (Gard, France). Bundles of long bones near the western wall. On the left a first set is composed of a tibia and a clavicle, while a second in the middle contains five femora, a tibia and a humerus. Photograph by A. Colomer.

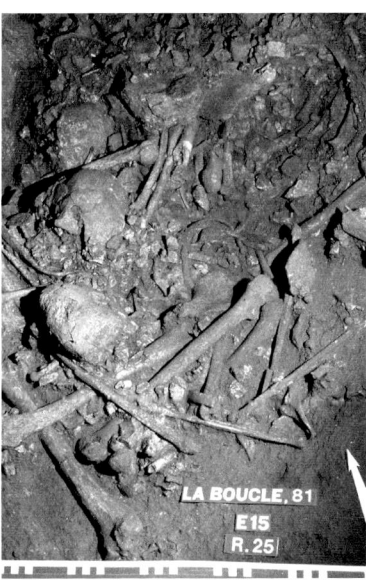

Figure 102. Karst shaft at La Boucle, Corconne (Gard, France). Skulls lined up along the western wall. Photograph by H. Duday.

Figure 103. Karst shaft at La Boucle, Corconne (Gard, France). The bones of a child are grouped together in a limited area. The humerus (top) and the fibula (at an angle and approximately at the centre of the photo) belong to adults. Photograph by A. Colomer.

It was possible to carry out these actions after the decomposition of the corpses because the bones were accessible on the surface; the yellow sediment carried inside the cave was not enough to cover them. The corpses were protected by a structure built to shut the cave entrance. These observations prompt us to reflect on the meaning of two terms that are commonly used in archaeology, cremation and inhumation. Archaeologists often define as 'inhumed' a corpse that has not been burnt, but from an etymological point of view, inhumation means to cover a corpse with soil and so to bury it. In the case of the collective burial at Corconne the bones were not buried but lay on the surface: strictly speaking the term inhumation is not appropriate. In the middle of the chamber there were only small bones, whereas the long bones and skulls were found in the natural depression near the side of the cave. The central part of the cave therefore functioned as a *pourrissoir* while the edges accommodated the secondary deposits, clearly created by human action.

In a sector which produced adult bones the pubis of a child (with a centre of secondary ossification in the acetabulum that was in the process of fusing), an infantile calcaneus and a set of immature vertebral bodies (recognisable from the small furrows arranged radially on the edge of the vertebral discs) were also recognised (Figure 103).

Figure 104. A view of the same deposit at a more advanced stage of excavation. Photograph by A. Colomer.

The maturation characteristics for this group of bones suggest that they belonged to a 12–15 year old individual. Since no part of the skeleton is represented by more than one element, we may be led to think that they all belonged to the same individual, a young boy. Once the sediment was removed, further bones belonging to the same boy were found associated with a perforated *cardium* shell and a bone awl carved from a rabbit's tibia. The remaining bones of the same individual were found lower down beneath two large limestone stone blocks (Figure 104). Also found were very small skeletal elements, for example the ossification centres of the base of the phalanx, small discs about five millimetres wide and less than one millimetre thick. There was no anatomical connection amongst these; the bones were so entangled that a rib was inserted in the vertebral channel of a thoracic vertebra. The femora, tibiae, cranium and mandible were missing here but were identified at the side of the cave in the area of secondary deposition. At this point in the investigation, it seemed difficult to assume that this is a primary deposit. If this were the case, the bones would have to have been manipulated after decomposition, and this manipulation would have to have happened in the same place (because the smallest ossification centres were found here), the stones would have been included in the displacement, since the boy's bones were both under and

114   *The Archaeology of the Dead*

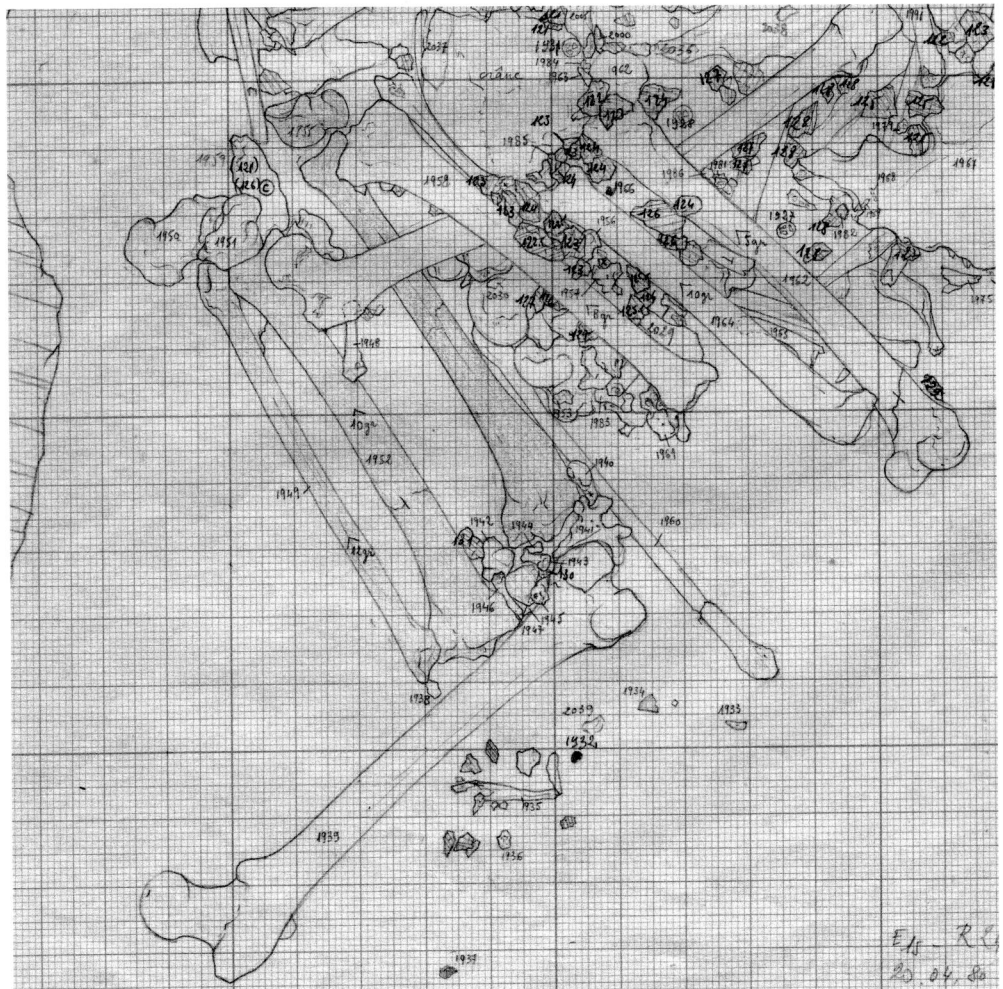

Figure 105. Karst shaft at La Boucle, Corconne (Gard, France). Plan (by H. Duday) of funerary deposits at the base of the Neolithic layer. At centre left there are two legs still connected.

above the stones and all this would have happened without breaking any of the bones. By elimination, the interpretative hypothesis seems to be directed towards secondary deposition or a secondary burial.

Against the western wall of the cave in a pile of bones were a fibula, tibia, talus (the name for the astragalus in international anatomical vocabulary) and a right calcaneus, all anatomically connected, as well as another tibia and a left talus, also connected (Figure 105). These bones belonged to the same individual and the burial could *a priori* be considered as a primary deposit. However these joints are persistent, suggesting

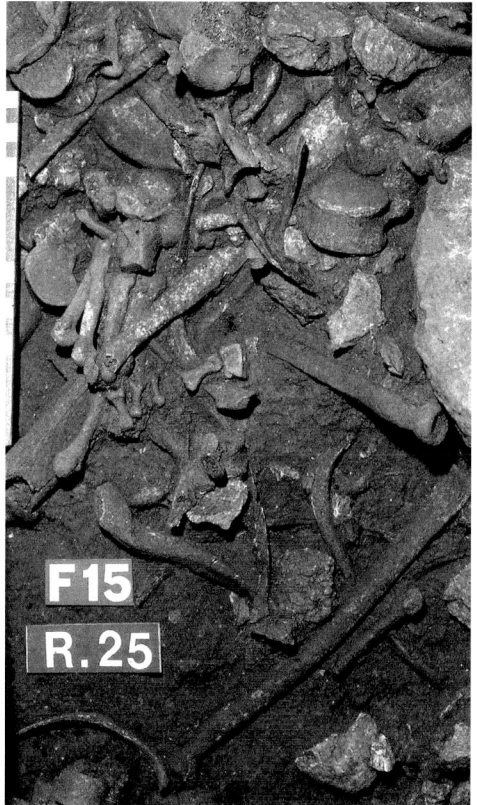 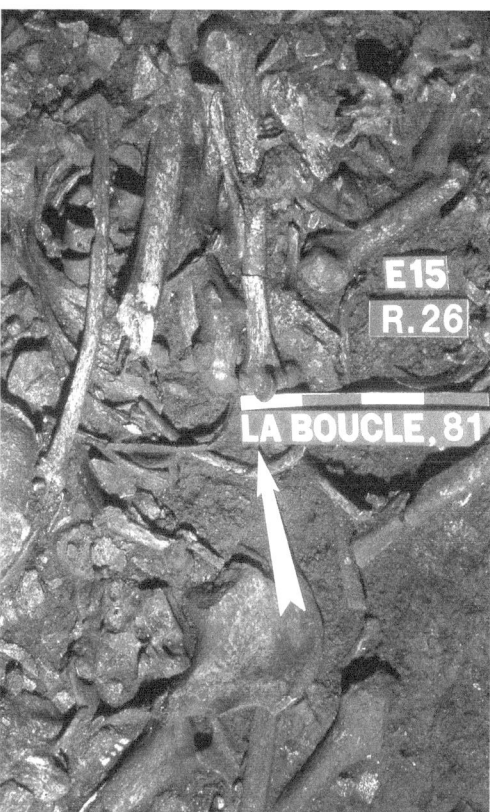

Figure 106. Karst shaft at La Boucle, Corconne (Gard, France). Bones of a partially connected foot at the base of the Neolithic layer. Photograph by A. Colomer.

Figure 107. Karst shaft at La Boucle, Corconne (Gard, France). Torso of an adult in anatomical connection. Photograph by H. Duday.

that this may be a case of secondary deposition of a corpse that had not completely decomposed. Nevertheless, the fact that both legs were found at the same level suggests the original presence of thighs and pelvis as well. It would seem however that the position of the bones of this individual served as a reference point for those piled above it that were no longer in anatomical connection. In an adjacent area, another tibia, talus and calcaneus were found still connected.

Another group comprising various tarsal bones, metatarsals and phalanges was also found in anatomical connection (Figure 106). In this case, however, some of the joints break down more rapidly: the foot decomposed *in situ*. Against the cave wall the torso of an adult was also found in anatomical connection, with its right ribs, vertebrae, a rotated sacrum, left coxal bone, right scapula and left humerus (Figure 107). The scapulo-thoracic joints break down particularly rapidly and this is clearly a primary deposit.

For the same funerary context therefore, some observations prompt interpretation as secondary burials, while some traces of re-working suggest secondary depositions similar to 'reductions' (Chapter 7). But others are certainly primary deposits. How is it possible to explain this apparently heterogeneous funerary behaviour in the same human group?

One possible interpretation is that funerary treatment differed according to age. In all the cases examined, the bones belonged to adults, and only in the case of the young boy was deposition secondary. Another possible interpretation is that funerary practices changed during the period in which the lower burial layer accumulated, in which about 70 individuals have been found. In the south of France, the end of the Neolithic is a period of change in funerary behaviour and marks the appearance of large collective burials. It is possible in fact to establish a chronological succession between the bones that are still in connection, found only at the bottom of the pit in its deepest part and those with traces of later manipulation, visible in the upper and therefore more recent layers. But the bones of the young boy, initially interpreted as a secondary deposit, were lying at the base of the layer. A third possible interpretation is that it is wrong to consider the arrangement of the boy's bones as evidence of a secondary burial. The argument followed has been based on the principle of 'economy of deposit' or 'least-cost hypothesis', and it is not certain that this applies to the funerary context. It is possible that the boy's corpse was buried in the cave, decomposed there, and was disturbed much later in the Neolithic. It may represent a particular instance of disposing of the bones of an individual after its decomposition.

Another possible interpretation relates to the way in which we order the parameters on which the classification of funerary rites is based, whether a burial contains the remains of a single or several individuals, whether an individual is cremated or not (following objective criteria) and whether burials are primary or secondary. We have seen that it is necessary to distinguish between secondary deposits and secondary burials, which is clearly more difficult. In reality it is easy to misrepresent the situation and make terminological errors.

An excellent demonstration of this was given by D. Ubelaker (1974), who has excavated funerary pits of 17th–18th century AD native Americans in the Potomac region in North America. Thanks to the reports of early European settlers in contact with these groups, we know their funerary rites and burials, which are generally secondary. The corpse usually decomposed on a wooden platform, an individual *pourrissoir*, and its bones were later placed in sacks. The excavation of these burials can be compared to an experiment, since the funerary rite is already known and was not deduced from the observed remains. Some deposits give the expected impression of 'sacks of bones', but some bones were still in partial anatomical connection (including the interphalangeal joints). This evidence would suggest that the burials were primary and would seem to contradict the information from the written sources. In reality however a close reading of the texts allows us to explain this apparent discrepancy. This shows that after an interval of some years, the group excavated a pit where it placed the remains of all those who had died since the closing of the last pit. The bones of individuals who had been dead for some years (with skeletons in total disconnection) were therefore mixed with those who had died only a short time before (with skeletons still in close connection) and all those in between. Interpretations based on the archaeological observations alone would lead towards false conclusions, since they give an impression of significant differences in burial treatment. In reality it was possible to take into account the degree of decomposition of a corpse, where the remains of the dead were handled, which joints were still present at the time of deposition and which were not, and so on. However we cannot infer the meaning that the ancient populations gave to the more or less advanced state of decomposition of a corpse from any archaeological data. Among the great majority of human settlements, this certainly affects funerary behaviour, but not always. In this case the precise dynamic of funerary operations was determined by the moment in which a new pit was dug: the changes undergone by the corpse depended only on the time which had elapsed between death and this moment.

In the Corconne case the evidence does not allow us to choose between the different hypotheses. But it is important to underline once more that with the help of texts it is possible for us to understand rites and that without them our study is limited to behaviour and burial practices. Later it was necessary to understand whether, when a corpse was buried, the bones belonging to a previous individual were moved or if, in some periods, the deceased were relocated on a larger scale.

Lecture 11

Funerary complexes (III): collective burials, the karst shaft of La Boucle at Corconne (II)

We have already seen that burrows were found inside this cave, appearing immediately beneath the funerary layer, whose collapse had caused the displacement of some bones and grave goods. In one of these burrows, three metatarsal bones were found in a line that followed the direction in which the animal dug (Figure 108). The movement of the bones in this case is taphonomic, linked to animal rather than human activity. The proof is provided by the traces of the burrow, perfectly visible thanks to their colour and the different appearance of their fill. The activity of small rodents is also revealed by tooth marks on the bones: the diaphysis of a third human metacarpal is cut in two (Figure 109) and several phalanges have been gnawed. All these bones came from the same stratigraphic unit. They slipped into the cracks in the drying clay and were later disturbed by an animal as it dug its burrow.

The grave goods accompanying the deposits comprised ceramic vessels, personal

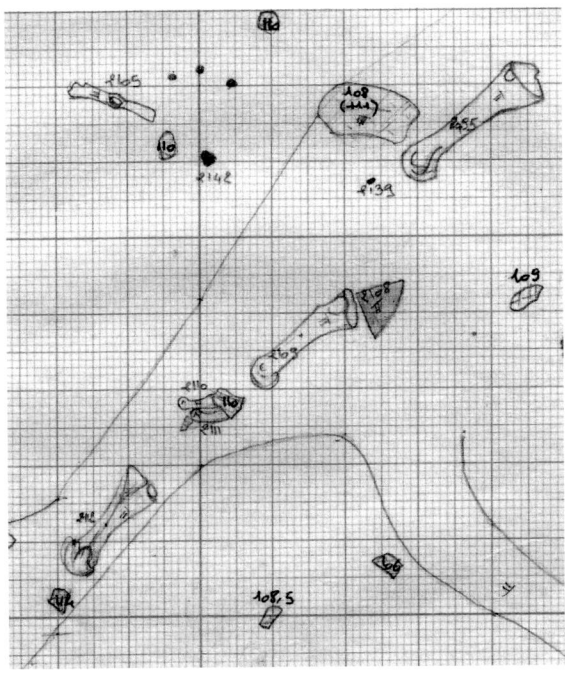

Figure 108. Karst shaft at La Boucle, Corconne (Gard, France). A line of human metatarsals in a small animal's burrow. Plan by A. Colomer.

ornaments and flint blades and arrowheads. Many bone awls were also found (Figure 110), their number corresponding approximately to that of the individuals deposited into the cavity. These objects might have been offerings, or more likely, had a function for closing a garment or wrapping (a mat, cloth or hide) for the corpse.

Child bones were few. Archaeologists generally explain their absence by differential preservation, but on this site bones are very well-preserved, to the extent that hyoid bones and ossified thyroid cartilages survive. These are generally very fragile and much less mineralized than the femur of a neonate, for example. This explanation cannot therefore be valid here. Of the 70 individuals buried here fewer than fifteen are of immature subjects, including three to five teenagers who are immature from a biological point of view but who may be considered mature from a social point of view. In most modern societies, young people acquire civil rights and can marry long before all the growth surfaces of the bones have fused. Only two or three children are less than five years old. This picture is not compatible with a natural mortality rate, especially for a population living in difficult conditions. It is not possible that a Neolithic population had such a demographic profile. A selection has been made for burial in the cave that excluded the majority of dead children. The collection procedures for this funerary complex therefore reflect a specialization based on age at death.

This specialization was first thought to be by area, with some reserved for adults

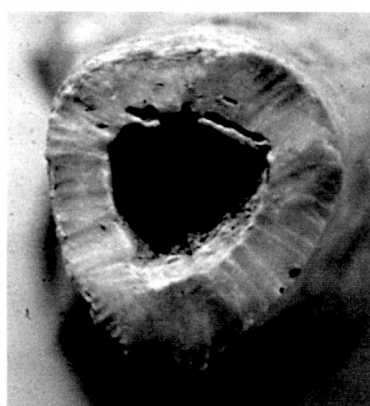

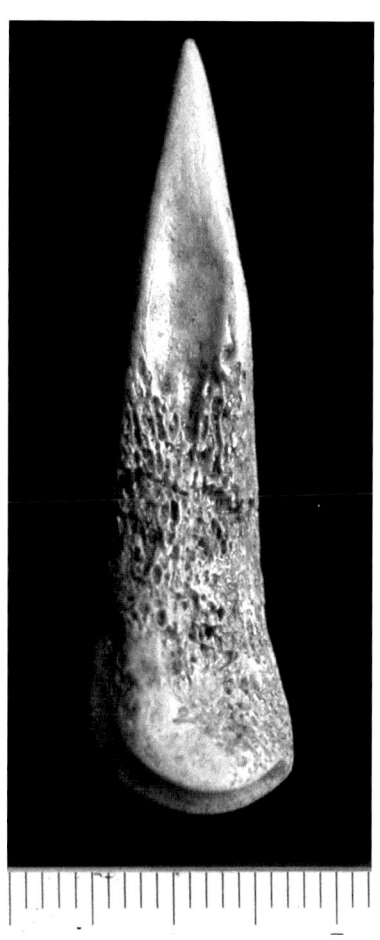

Figure 109. Karst shaft at La Boucle, Corconne (Gard, France). A human third metacarpal cut through by a small rodent. Photograph by H. Duday.

Figure 110. Karst shaft at La Boucle, Corconne (Gard, France). Awl made from an ovine metapodial. Photograph by H. Duday.

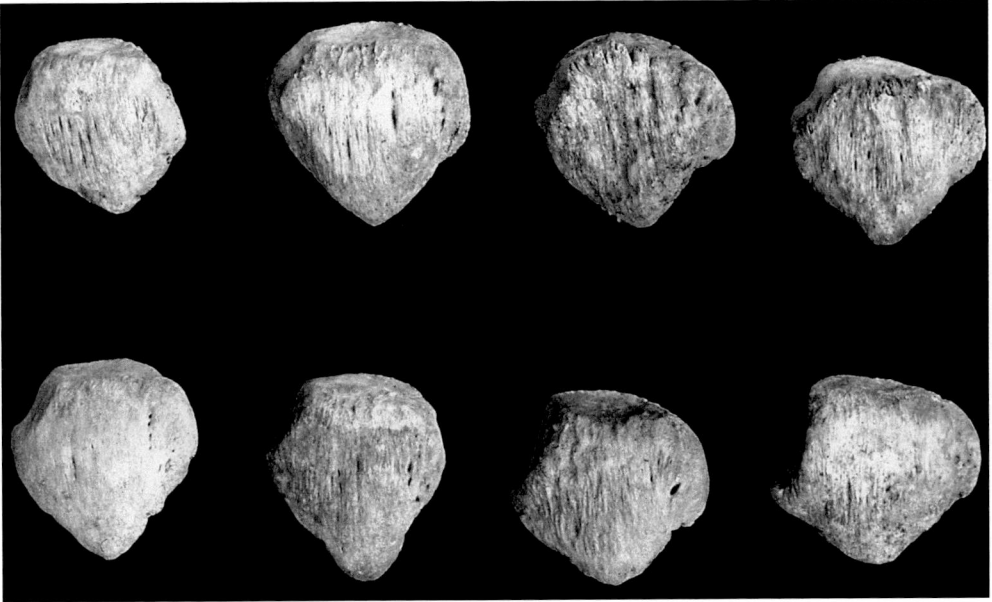

Figure 111. Swallow-hole at La Boucle, Corconne (Gard, France). Sample of right patellae from the lower Neolithic layer. The different degrees of expression of patella emarginata should be noted. Photograph by H. Duday.

and others for children, but at the end of the excavation, after the entire cavity had been examined, the lack of immature individuals remained significant. The remains of children were found in the northern part of the cave, near the wall where the rock roof is lower. There is then a double selection by age, for the cave in general and then within it.

Some morphological characteristics also give us information on the composition of the sample. It has been observed that the patellae generally lack a segment on the upper-medial edge. This is not a pathological characteristic but a variant type of ossification known as *patella emarginata* (Figure 111). We do not know any functional or environmental reasons for this variant, which has a frequency between four percent and ten percent among present-day populations but at Corconne is more than 60% (Duday 1987a). According to the interpretation suggested, this level of variation is genetic and happens in cases of endogamous relationships in a group. In the native population of the far north of Canada (Saunders 1978), higher frequencies have been observed in small groups separated by great distances that were difficult to travel in winter. At Corconne the individuals have therefore been probably selected according to their belonging to the same genetic pool. This may have been as the result of a regular exchange of relatives between two small communities that lived adjacent to one other for some generations, or the selection of a branch of individuals that were related by marriage (for example a family tomb) within a group whose marriage strategies were based on the exchange

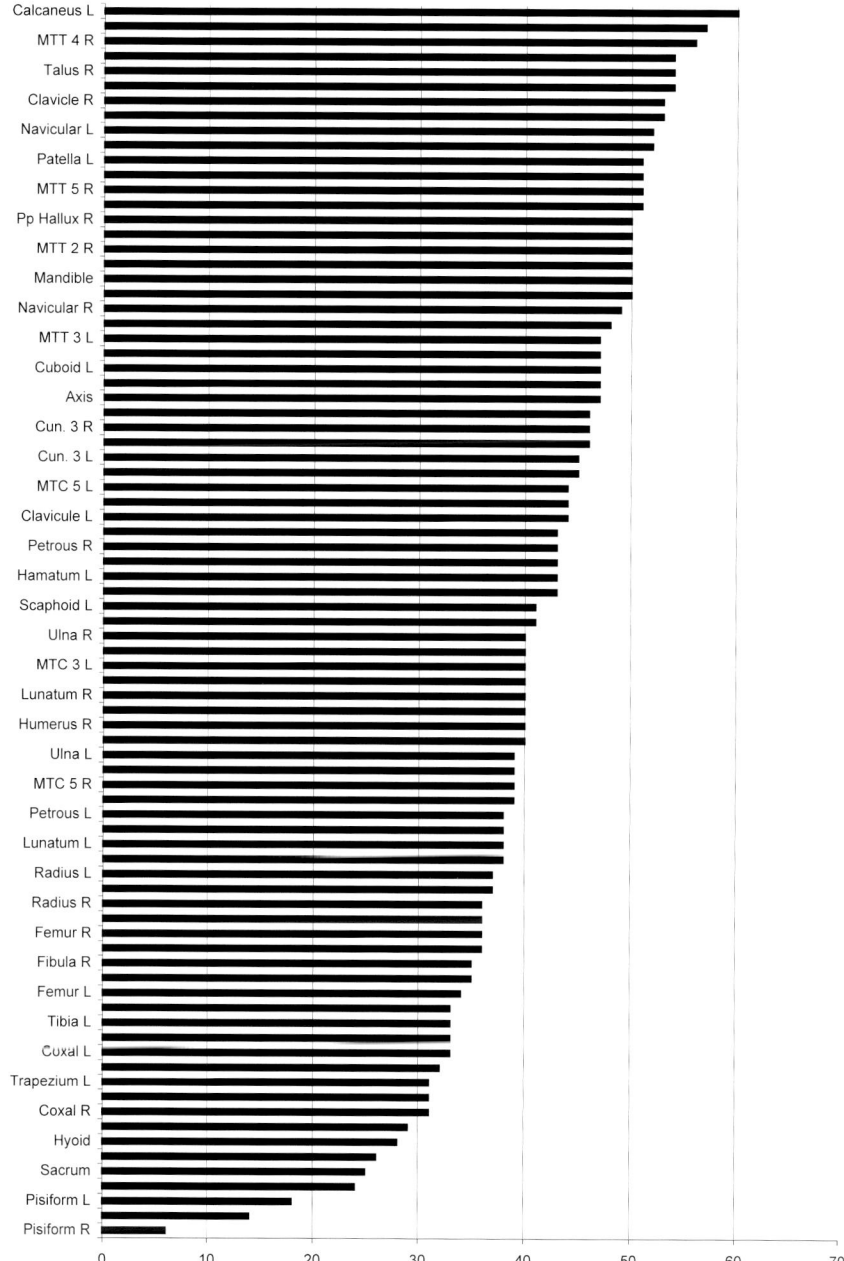

Figure 112. Karst shaft at la Boucle at Corconne (Gard, France). Minimum number of individuals (frequency MNI) based on the different types of bones found in the Neolithic funerary layer. Illustration by S. Hérouin.

of relatives with nearby groups. We cannot decide which interpretation is correct, but we can record the strict selection of the individuals to be deposited within the cave.

The table for determining the minimum number of individuals (M.N.I.) shows that the best represented bones are the left calcaneus and the tarsal bones in general, whereas the large long bones of the upper and especially the lower limbs were not found in such great numbers, only 50% of the estimated original number (Figure 112). The bulkiest bones of the skeleton are under-represented (cranium, scapulae, coxal bones, sacrum and long bones, as already noted), whereas the smaller bones (clavicle, mandible, vertebrae, metacarpals, metatarsals and tarsals) are better represented. This cannot be explained by differential preservation since bones like the femur are more resistant than metatarsals.

Crania are thought to have been originally more numerous in the cavity. The upper incisors, with very conical roots, were found in normal numbers. They therefore remained in the cave after their detachment during decomposition, before the crania were removed. These observations lead us to assume a later interference with the bones that accumulated in the cavity, including the taking of some material outside the cave. This would be deliberate funerary behaviour by the population under study.

The Corconne bones are therefore quite anomalous, with a threefold bias in the selection of individuals related to age at death, genetic origin and type of bone. The sample from the site is therefore not representative of the population from which it derives. This is due to cultural phenomena of great importance which show the 'functioning' of Neolithic collective burial in a completely new way.

We have already seen the different stratigraphic units that characterize the first activity in the cavity. They are the yellow soil (unit C4b), the re-worked zones near the side of the cavity with grey-brown clay and small stones (unit C4b1) and a small pit (unit C4b4) whose fill is characterized by the presence of many small exogenous broken stones with percussion bulbs and occasional small human bones, phalanges, metatarsals and cervical vertebrae. All these stratigraphic units were found at the same level, on the sterile clay surface, without relationships between them. The problem is to know whether these units relate to the same funerary use of the cavity or different activities and separate funerary episodes.

If the bones of the same individual are spread over several stratigraphic units then these are complementary, whereas if each individual is found in a single unit, then we can conclude that each unit corresponds to a separate funerary 'episode'. In order to understand the internal dynamics of deposit formation, it is important to recognise the bones belonging to the same individual (which are strictly contemporary), and to study their spatial division which reflects the way in which they are distributed on the surface. I have called this process the method of 'osteological linkage' (Duday 1987b).

Two types of linkage can be distinguished, first and second order. First order linkages are those seen on the ground at the time of excavation, above all the anatomical connections which we have discussed at length: a connection can only occur between two or more bones of the same individual. For example a tibia can only be connected to the femur of the same individual and connection must always be distinguished from spatial proximity. At Corconne only five groups of bones in anatomical connection were identified, a small number considering the substantial quantity of bones excavated.

There is another kind of first order linkage, which concerns the recording procedure for the different pieces of the same bone (e.g. a cranium) that is broken *in situ* and is taken apart piece by piece during excavation. It is important to note whether these remains are complementary in order to facilitate their later reconstruction, but this does not give information on the formation of the deposit.

Second order osteological linkages are based on laboratory study. The first concerns the joining of bone fragments that fit: if two fragments of femur can be joined, for example, they must certainly belong to the same bone and therefore to the same individual. Other linkages are also sought based on articular contiguity. From an anatomical point of view, cranial sutures are joints. The great variety among human beings means that when two parietal bones fit perfectly they derive from the same cranium and therefore from the same individual. The archaeologist may think of this as a connection of the previous type, analogous to reconstructing a vessel. In this case, however, it is a matter of articular relationships rather than of broken fragments.

In his doctorate under my supervision Nuria Villena i Mota (1996: 317; 1997) has tested the validity of this type of linkage for several joints. If a coxal bone and a sacrum fit together, they certainly belong to the same person, either because this joint has a variable morphology among individuals or because the various surfaces join perfectly. Other joints do not however allow us to reach definitive conclusions, for example between the atlas and axis and between the tibia and femur, because the correspondence between the articular surfaces is rather less precise. The meniscus is necessary to establish an elastic connection between the femoral condyle and the glenoid cavities of the tibia. After deposition the meniscus breaks down, explaining why at excavation the patellae generally seem displaced.

Connections between bones can also be investigated from shared pathology, for example at Corconne between a talus and calcaneus which both had traces of joint inflammation (Figure 113). An ulna with a pseudarthrosis, a consequence of an unfused fracture, was also found (Figure 114): inside the diaphysis the medullary canal was closed with bony irregularities. Generally, a fracture knits through formation of a callus, but when the displacement is too wide, the two bone margins may remain mobile in relation to each another. Therefore, the pseudarthrosis gives rises to a false joint. The distal part of this ulna was found more than three metres from the proximal. 60 fragmentary or whole bones belonging to another individual (the cranium, vertebrae, sacrum, sternum, coxal bones, femora and very many rib fragments) were found with lesions characteristic of Paget's disease, as Jean-Pierre Arnautou has shown.

The stage of maturation and robusticity of the bones are also frequently used criteria. We have already seen how these enabled us to identify the secondary deposit of an immature individual at Corconne. However the possibility of taking these characteristics into consideration depends on the composition of the sample examined. If the series includes only a tall robust man, a short thin woman and a two-year old child it will be easy to attribute each piece to an individual. This operation becomes much less certain if there are many children with a similar age at death as well as many adults.

The association of bones with individuals can also be made from symmetry or pairing. In our body there are unpaired bones along the median line and paired bones on either side. In the latter there is symmetry specific to an individual, which is

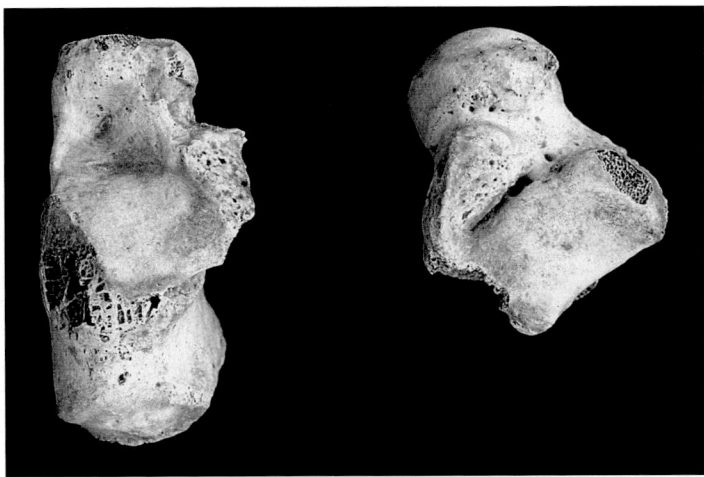

Figure 113. Karst shaft at La Boucle, Corconne (Gard, France). Pathological right talus and calcaneus. Photograph by H. Duday.

Figure 114. Karst shaft at La Boucle, Corconne (Gard, France). Distal extremity of an ulna which shows signs of pseudarthrosis. Photograph by A. Colomer.

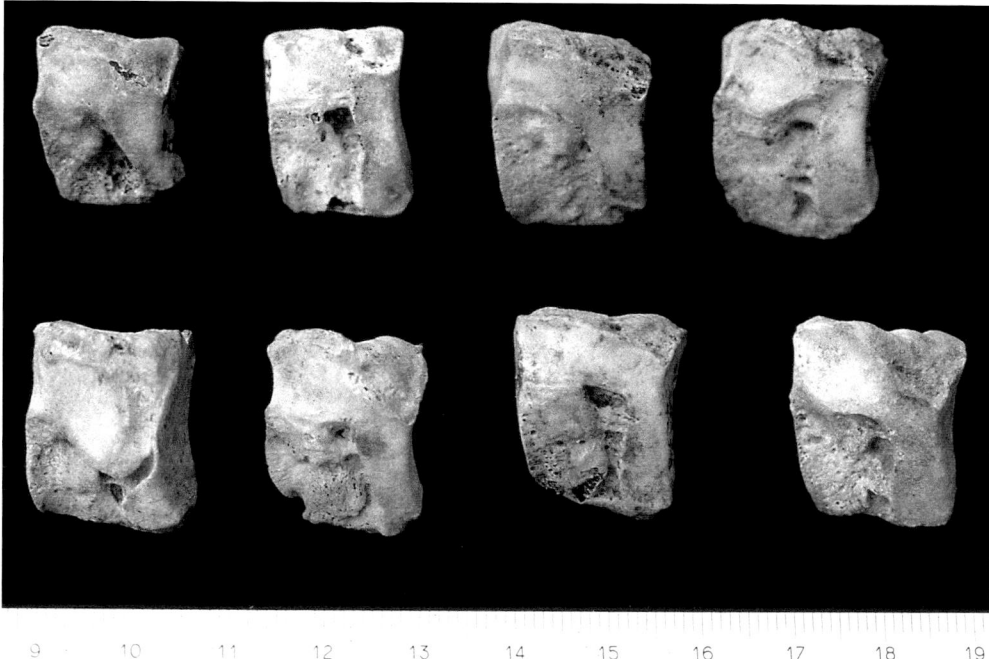

Figure 115. Karst shaft at La Boucle, Corconne (Gard, France). A sample of intermediate right cuneiforms from Neolithic layers. Photos by H. Duday.

imperfect because we are all more or less right- or left-sided, but recognizable from bone consistency and small anatomical variations related to the joint surfaces and the muscle or ligament insertions. In his thesis Nuria Villena i Mota has shown that the bones with the best guarantees for pairing are the patellae and the carpals, tarsals, metacarpals and metatarsals, *i.e.* smaller bones. For the Corconne sample Figure 115 shows the enormous variety on the medial aspect of a tarsal bone, the right intermediate cuneiform, one of the bones which have provided us with the greatest number of symmetrical connections. The best results are given by bones that are often considered by archaeologists and also by many anthropologists as less interesting than the cranium, mandible or long bones. It is therefore important to record their position precisely during excavation in order to understand their distribution on the site after laboratory study.

Using the methods based on articular contiguity and symmetry, 200 second order connections were identified at Corconne, some of them within the same stratigraphic unit and others between bones found in two different stratigraphic units (C4b yellow sediment; C4b1 brown-grey clay; C4b2 against the wall of the cave and the rocky pit fill). These different units are therefore to be related to the same episodes of activity. Osteological connections also enabled us to attribute *a posteriori* the bones found in the middle of the large chamber (where the layers are thinner and discontinuous) to one or other of the occupation phases.

 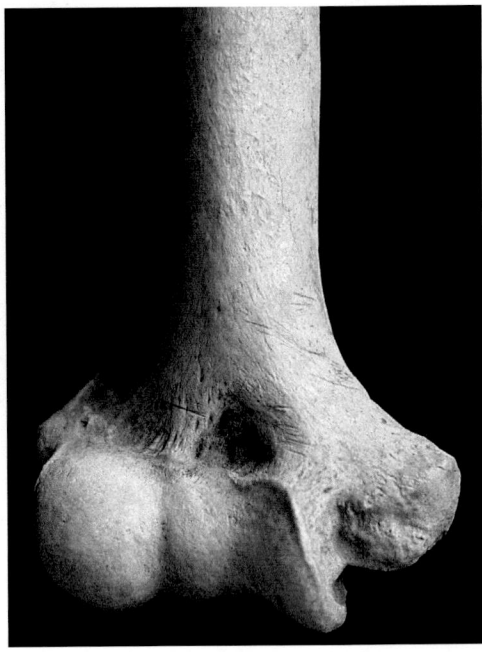

Figure 116. Karst shaft at La Boucle, Corconne (Gard, France). A pathological human humerus in situ in the Neolithic funerary layer. Photograph by A. Colomer.

Figure 117. Karst shaft at La Boucle, Corconne (Gard, France). Flint cut-marks on the same humerus. Photograph by H. Duday.

If the interpretation of an individual burial, a cemetery or burials related to mortality crises is based on the study of anatomical connections, in large collective burials it is instead based on analyses of second order osteological linkages. When defining excavation strategies at the beginning of a project, it is therefore necessary to consider the information which may be related to every single bone. In the future, research on molecular palaeo-chemistry (e.g. ancient DNA) may enable us to identify bones belonging to the same individual, but for the moment, besides being a destructive technique, its costs are very high.

Near the cave wall the humerus of an adult was found which was very short, measuring 208 mm. in length (an adult 1.40 m. tall on average has a humerus 240 mm. in length), and peculiarly shaped (Figure 116). We may infer that it belongs to a dwarf or to an individual with an atrophied right arm. The morphological anomalies that characterize the upper part of the humerus in particular show the destruction of the growth cartilage between its head and diaphysis. On the anterior aspect of its distal extremity, which corresponds

Figure 118. Karst shaft at La Boucle, Corconne (Gard, France). The platform built under the shaft which forms the present-day access. Photograph by H. Duday.

to the elbow, some small incisions are visible (Figure 117). Their study under scanning electronic microscope by Françoise Le Mort (1987) has shown that they have been made using a flint blade, traces of an activity often cited to prove the secondary character of a deposit. However this is the only bone among the 12,000 human remains found on the site that shows cut marks. It is surprising to observe that this was the bone of which the pathology was more visible from its exterior morphology. It is therefore logical to assume an autopsy or some anatomical examination performed after death. It is worthwhile remembering that in this period the practice of trepanning was widespread.

Beneath the entrance of the cave shaft was found a large platform, about three metres in diameter and built with massive blocks (Figure 118) which was covered by stones which fell when the ceiling collapsed. Human remains, elements of personal ornament and ceramics of the late Neolithic were also found on it. This platform therefore dates to the period in which the cave was used for collective burial. The Neolithic entrance was then sought. In a diaclasis (fissure) leading to the platform were found some large flat stones which originally had been deliberately laid horizontally, certainly corresponding to a partially collapsed wall (Figure 119). The Neolithic people had therefore walled up the access with large stone slabs when they decided to no longer use the cave for burial. This closure is not unique, since similar examples are known in many caves used for burial in the Neolithic in the same region, such as the Grotte du Bois de Clastres (Figure 120)

Figure 119. Karst shaft at La Boucle, Corconne (Gard, France). Filling of the diaclasis. Photograph by H. Duday.

Figure 120. The closing deposit of a Neolithic funerary cave at Bois de Clastres, Saint-Mathieu-de-Tréviers (Hérault, France), photograph taken from inside the cave by H. Duday.

Figure 121. Closing deposit installed at the abandonment of a funerary cave at the swallow-hole of La Tourette (Causse de l'Hortus, Hérault, France). Photograph by H. Duday.

or the karst shaft of La Tourette (Figure 121), less than 20 km. from Corconne (Colmera 1980). Exploration allowed us to find the original access passage on the surface. It was covered by massive stones, laid horizontally like the cover slabs for the corridor in a

Figure 122. Karst shaft at La Boucle, Corconne (Gard, France). View of the external diaclasis at the level of the original entrance. A wall above retains the fill of a crack in the rock. Below and to the left are the first steps of the access built during the Neolithic. Photograph by H. Duday.

dolmen, with steps along the descent in order to deposit corpses which could be identified from their worn surfaces and structures made to stabilise the sides (Figure 122). When the site was abandoned, everything was destroyed. The covering slabs were pushed into the diaclasis which was completely closed with a mass of stones. The excavation of this passage has unearthed some human remains, personal ornaments and ceramics (some belonging to vessels in the cave), confirming the complexity of the process of funerary deposition. The story of the excavation of the cavity shows how tightly the anthropological and archaeological contributions are linked to one another.

Lecture 12

Funerary complexes (IV): collective burials, the dolmen of Les Peirières at Villedubert

This dolmen lies on a small hill, below which flow the river Aude and the Canal du Midi, built during the reign of Louis XIV. It was not possible to identify the settlement related to the burial place, since this zone has been highly modified by widespread viticulture, by terraces for the canal excavation and the stone quarries for extracting material to build bridges and other structures during the construction of the canal (Figure 123). A large quarry for sandstone extraction was opened about 50 m. south of the dolmen, radically changing the profile of the slope and starting new soil erosion. When it was discovered in 1972 this monument was hardly visible. From a small heap of earth, covered with large pebbles and vegetation emerged a vertical slab – an orthostat

Figure 123. Dolmen of Les Peirières, Villedubert (Aude, France), aerial view. At the bottom the alluvial plain of the river Aude and the Canal du Midi, at the centre the monument and at the top (to the north) the vineyards of Languedoc. Photograph by P. Carné.

Figure 124. Dolmen of Les Peirières at Villedubert (Aude, France). View of the site at the time of discovery. Photograph by R. Aymé.

(Figure 124). On the surface were found some fragments of human bone and a small discoidal pearl from a shell.

A dolmen is a monument formed by two parallel rows of vertical slabs (orthostats) closed at one end by another vertical slab and covered by large horizontal slabs laid on the orthostats on either side. The monument was covered with a tumulus of earth or stone. The funerary deposits were found within the chamber, generally under the outer part of the dolmen. In this case the few remains on the surface were found in the upper part of the mound above, which *a priori* seems somewhat surprising.

The pebbles documented at the beginning of the excavation are considered to postdate the destruction of the monument, since they cover both the internal surface and the peripheral zone. They were first considered to have been brought there by farmers piling up the stones after field clearance. In reality the pebbles formed a single layer (not a pile), which directly overlay the prehistoric human remains. They could not therefore be related to agricultural activity.

The pebble layer sealed the base of two other orthostats broken at ground level, as it seemed at the time of discovery, and the incomplete remnants of two others, which formed the southern limit of the funerary chamber, which was 4.2 m. long and 2.2 m. wide (Figure 125). For this part of southern France a particular type of megalithic dolmen with wide corridors is known. These may differ in size but their proportions are fairly constant. A monument two metres wide is generally nine to ten metres long. The Peirières dolmen is either too wide or too short.

The bones, found over an area of *c.* eight square metres, were not only in great numbers but were also extremely fragmented (Figure 126). The alteration is mechanical

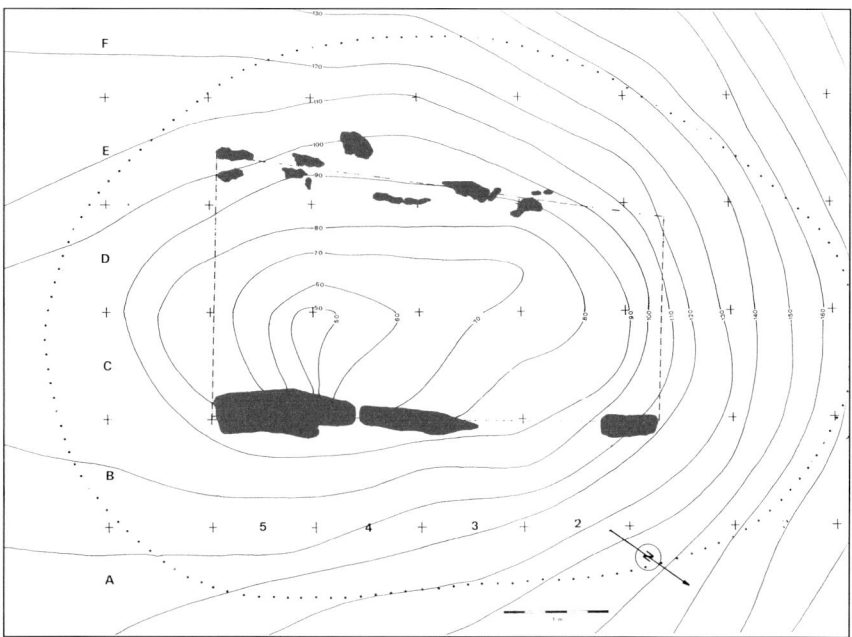

Figure 125. Dolmen of Les Peirières, Villedubert (Aude, France). Contour plan (10 cm. intervals: the lower values correspond to the higher points) and location of architectural elements visible on the surface. Plan by H. Duday.

Figure 126. Dolmen of Les Peirières, Villedubert (Aude, France). A view of the Eneolithic funerary layer. Photograph by H. Duday.

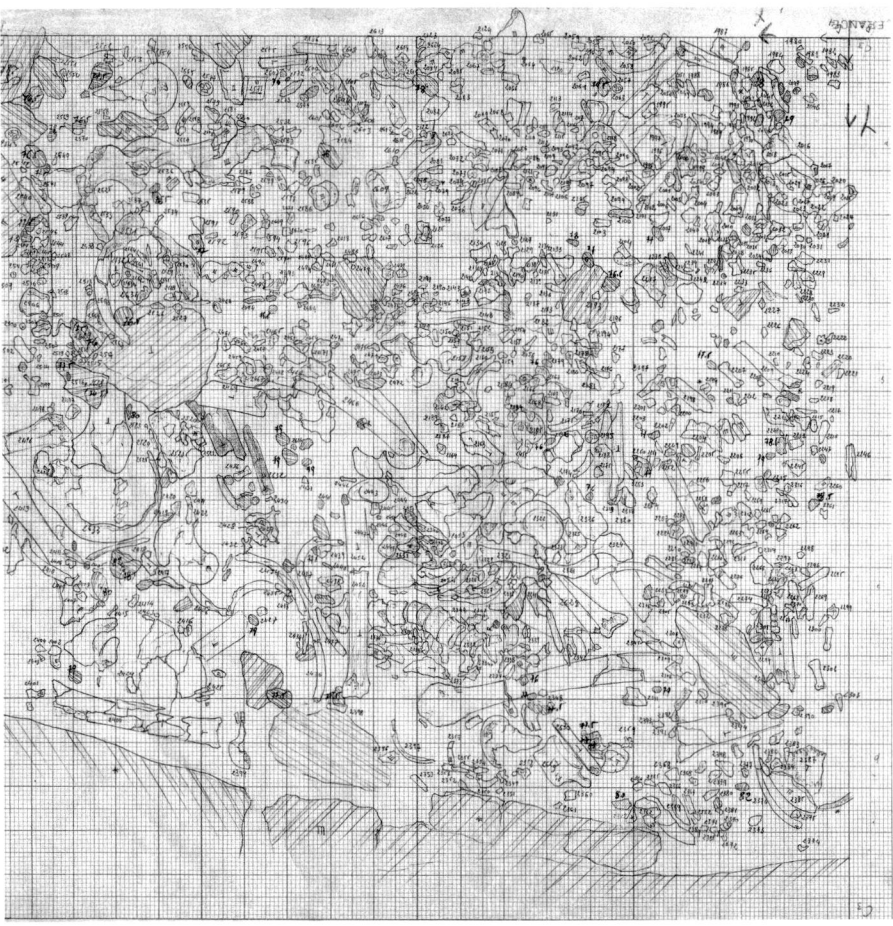

Figure 127. Dolmen of Les Peirières, Villedubert (Aude, France). Plan (19) at 1:5 scale of the Eneolithic funerary layer in square metre C4. Plan by H. Duday.

rather than chemical, the breaks are clean and the bone is well preserved. The associated archaeological material dates back exclusively to the Chalcolithic, in particular to the 'Campaniform' period (2500–2200 B.C.). This raises problems since in this region dolmens were generally used continuously from the later Neolithic to the beginning of the middle Bronze Age, *i.e.* for over one and a half thousand years. As well as ceramics, other objects also date back to the same period, such as flint arrowheads, bone buttons with V-shaped perforations, hemispherical or turtle-shaped, a small blue glass bead and small steatite discoidal beads that are sometimes less than two millimetres in diameter. The history of the Peirières dolmen seems to begin too soon and to end too soon.

In all 120,000 fragments of human bones (Figure 127) were numbered and documented, along with more than 90 bone groups still in anatomical connection. The most difficult task was to isolate the bones that were still in connection within the huge pile (Figure 128). Unlike the Corconne collective burial, the connections in this case are relatively numerous. Many are joints that break down more rapidly, proving that there are primary deposits, but it is essential to check the reality of these connections while excavating. In one sector of the site, for example, five adjacent bones were found, drawn, numbered and levelled (Figure 129). These were the fourth, third, second and first metacarpals and the first proximal phalanx of a right thumb, but only the fourth, third and second metacarpals were still in anatomical connection showing their palmar face. The first metacarpal was in dorsal view and was in contact with the head of the second metacarpal (metacarpal-phalangeal joint) and not its base. The proximal thumb phalanx was not in contact with the head of the first metacarpal but with its base, so that the hypothesis of connection can be discarded. Here there is only spatial proximity between the bones, perfectly normal if the number of individuals is considered whose remains were piled on a small surface (more than 90 over *c.* eight square metres). If, for example, we placed 90 right tali, 90 left tali, 90 right calcanei and 90 left calcanei in a bag, shook them and poured out the contents over a surface of eight square metres, simple probability suggests that we would find a right talus near a right calcaneus. In such contexts spatial proximity does not mean that the bones are connected.

Figure 128a. Dolmen of Les Peirières, Villedubert (Aude, France). An anatomically connected group of bones in the Eneolithic funerary layer. The picture shows a right coxal bone and the right femoral head (immediately beneath the NO marker), the sacrum and the last two lumbar vertebrae (L4 and L5, in rear view), the left coxal bone (partially hidden by the calcaneus of another individual). At the centre of the photo is the whole left lower limb: the femur next to the tibia and fibula, along with the left talus and calcaneus. Photograph by H. Duday.

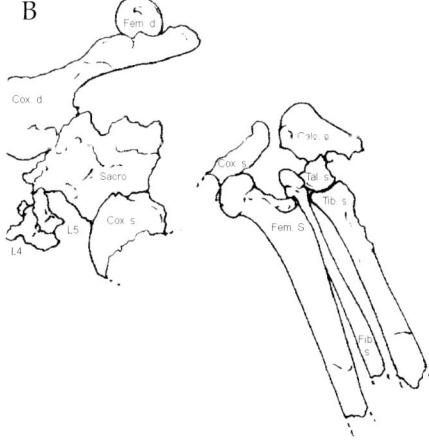

Figure 128b. Simplified representation of Figure 128.

Figure 129. Dolmen of Les Peirières, Villedubert (Aude, France). A partial connection (three right metacarpal bones) and a false connection (first right metacarpal and proximal phalanx of the right thumb).

In order to demonstrate any connection, it is necessary to verify that the related articular surfaces are in contact. This requires the presence on site of people trained in osteological anatomy.

As the excavation proceeded, the 'Campaniform' period layer turned out to be lying on a pavement of large sandstone slabs (Figure 130), which were partly composed of fragments of one of the orthostats from the southern side of the chamber. The funerary deposit is not therefore the fill of the dolmen, but lies above a ruined and reworked monument. In the Chalcolithic period the dolmen was destroyed and most of the orthostats were broken at ground level (only one has been partially preserved), which implies that there could have been no covering slabs. The people responsible created an entrance on the southern side of the chamber, laid the pavement from fragments of orthostats from the earlier monument and built two drystone stacks (the base of one was found in its original place, while the other was disturbed), which probably supported a cross beam. This new construction would have looked like a real 'house of the dead', quite different from a dolmen. The tumulus was completely removed so that the funerary area was in a higher position with respect to the peripheral part of the tomb.

The pebbles on the surface can now be interpreted as the abandonment layer, marking the end of the funerary use of the structure. After a relatively short period of use (the history of the monument therefore ends earlier than that of other dolmens), the community decided to use the tomb no more. They dismantled the superstructure of the 'house of the dead' and covered the funerary deposits and the peripheral area with a layer of large pebbles, forming a closing structure.

As for the internal dynamics of the deposit, some vertical connections were found, from which it can be inferred that some individuals were deposited in a sitting position:

Figure 130. Dolmen of Les Peirières, Villedubert (Aude, France). The legs and feet of an adult lying directly on the slabs at the base of the monument. Photograph by H. Duday.

others rested on their stomach. The deposits were made at different times. It was observed that the burial of some individuals displaced corpses which had been buried before and had already decomposed. In one area of the chamber, evidence was found of 11 consecutive depositions which were sometimes separated by relatively long intervals. The remains of an overlying forearm (individual A) have caused the rotation of the last two lumbar vertebrae of another corpse (individual B) in relation to its sacrum (Figures 131 and 132). Since the lumbar-sacral joints are much more persistent than those of the elbow and wrist, it can be assumed that individual B had been there for a long time and was in an advanced state of decomposition when individual A was deposited.

The fact that deposits were staggered does not contradict the homogeneity of the associated archaeological material (of the 'Campaniform' period), since different time scales are concerned in these two observations: the time required for ligaments to dissolve is measured in months, while archaeological dating, whatever the method used (excluding dendrochronology, which is not applicable in this case) does not refer to a period shorter than a century.

Figure 131. Dolmen of Les Peirières, Villedubert (Aude, France). In the background the cranio-facial region and mandible still in anatomical connection, with various thoracic vertebrae and a clavicle belonging to the same individual (C). A radius and ulna in connection are also visible (individual A) which lie on two lumbar vertebrae (L4 and L5), in vertical connection (individual B), above the sacrum. Photograph by H. Duday.

It is particularly interesting to observe the position of the crania, originally complete and broken *in situ*, which were found in a restricted area along the north wall. *A priori* this could be explained in two possible ways. First, since these are primary deposits, the bodies might always have been buried with their heads in this area. It is also possible that after decomposition, the crania were taken and gathered together. The latter hypothesis was confirmed since the cervical vertebrae, unlike the crania, were uniformly distributed over the whole surface, except for the atlas which was generally in connection with the cranium. The heads were gathered when some organic material was still present (certainly, some fragments of ligaments) between the atlas and the occipital, a joint which as we know is persistent. Other signs of reorganization can be found among the long bones, sometimes grouped in bundles (Figure 133). These observations enable us to infer that the surrounding space was empty, since the bones were easily accessible.

The Chalcolithic layer also produced some animal remains. Except for occasional teeth of large mammals, the presence of which remains unexplained, these were not brought by people. In this environment there were insectivorous animals, such as shrews, moles, batrachians (toads, frogs and newts) and reptiles, attracted by the presence of worms, larvae and necrophagous beetles. These are indirect but relevant clues to the primary character of deposits. Finally there were rodents (which must continually use their

Figure 132. Dolmen of Les Peirières, Villedubert (Aude, France). The same group at a later phase of excavation. The right ribs of individual C can be seen in anatomical connection to the vertebral column, as well as the right clavicle and scapula. The fifth lumbar vertebra has rotated 90° in relation to the sacrum. Photograph by H. Duday.

incisors, the growth of which never stops), as gnawed diaphyses of some bones show. These traces are very different from those observed at Corconne: here the gnawing affects compact zones with relatively thin edges, such as bone crests and the upper edges of the vertebral laminae. As these traces are visible all along the diaphysis, we may assume that the animal has been free to move around the bone, thus suggesting the presence of a free space. Some animals must have been the prey of others, brought to a sheltered place to be eaten. This probably explains the presence of a rabbit's leg which was still in perfect connection (Figure 134). If this animal had excavated a burrow, it would have inevitably modified the arrangement of the human remains.

Other problems relate to the varying degree of bone fragmentation, which is particularly marked in an L-shaped area which begins at the threshold and then turns

Figure 133. Dolmen of Les Peirières, Villedubert (Aude, France). A mass of long bones gathered in a bundle in the Eneolithic burial layer. Photograph by H. Duday.

at right angles, immediately in front of the place where the cross beam presumably was. This fragmentation is therefore also to be related to the circulation area. The breakages have produced elongated fragments of long bones, the main axis of which is parallel to the longitudinal axis of the diaphysis and whose traces of fragmentation are transversal but irregular (what Claude Masset has called 'match-like' fragmentation), different from the fragmentation of fresh bones (ogival extremities, spiroid edges). From this we can see that dry bones were being walked over, confirming the relatively long period of funerary use in the Chalcolithic and suggesting that the bones were not covered by earth. A malacological observation proves the absence of earth. Inside one cranium were 1108 shells of small snails. The largest measured only 3.5 mm. long and the larger species were represented only by immature individuals in the form of embryonic coils. Comparing their density to the surface area of the cranium gives a ratio of 10:1. The shells could not therefore have slipped inside the cranium when the soil filled it: the snails therefore entered by themselves while living. The size of the shells depends on

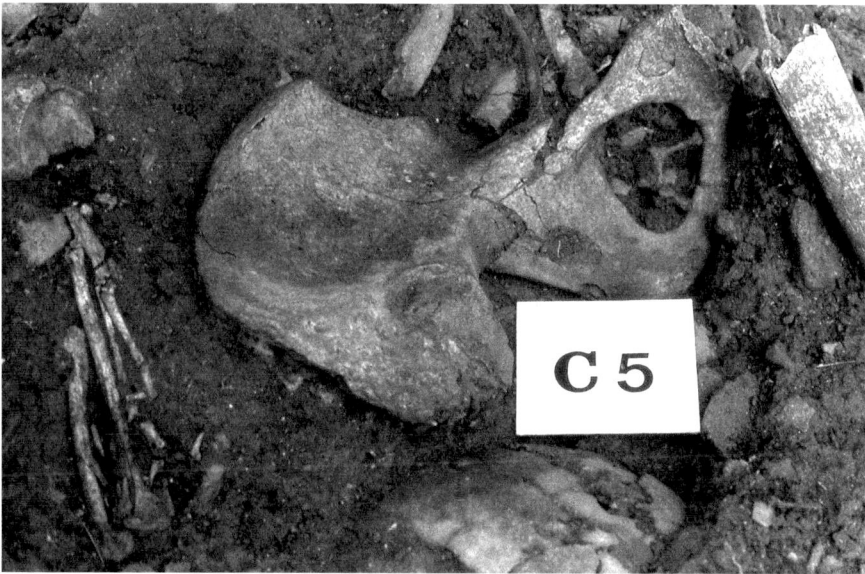

Figure 134. Dolmen of Les Peirières, Villedubert (Aude, France). A rabbit's paw in anatomical connection next to a complete coxal bone. Photograph by H. Duday.

the *foramen magnum* being closed as the occipital was tightly connected to the vertebral column. The snails therefore entered via the small holes in the face or base of the cranium. A concentration of shells was also found in other crania and in the medullary canal of broken long bones. Joël André (1986) has shown that they mostly belong to aerobic species that do not bury themselves. The cranium must have been empty to allow such an accumulation to form, further evidence that sediment only entered later.

We wondered how the soil could have entered. According to Jacques-Elie Brochier, earthworms attracted by the decomposition fluids from the corpses introduced the sediment that progressively filled the 40 cm. thick burial layer. His studies have also demonstrated that small stones up to a maximum of three millimetres in diameter can pass along the digestive tube of an earthworm. More than half of the 450 steatite beads have a smaller diameter than this, which might explain their distribution in the burial layer.

At the northwest edge of the monument completely disconnected bones were found in one area, among which were many shells or fragments belonging to a very common species, *helix aspera*. This first appeared in Gaul during the period of the Roman conquest and must relate to more recent disturbance which could be attributed to the activity of poachers (a ferret ring was also found).

Beneath the floor we also sought to find a pre-Chalcolithic burial deposit from the period before the dolmen was destroyed and transformed into a 'house of the dead'. This lower layer exists, but is discontinuous: only a few bones remain in some depressions in

Figure 135. Dolmen of Les Peirières, Villedubert (Aude, France). Traces of the Neolithic funerary layer visible after partial dismantling of the paving below the "Campaniform" period layer. On the right are many shells of snails which infiltrated beneath this paving, in contact with the alluvial terrace pebbles. On the left are human bones flattened by the paving stones. Photograph by H. Duday.

the geological substratum formed by a fluvial terrace of pebbles (Figure 135), in which the orthostats were erected and on which the slabs were laid where the Chalcolithic deposit was created. The dolmen had therefore been used for burial, but before its destruction people in the Chalcolithic took away most of the human remains leaving the funerary chamber empty.

The destruction of the monument in antiquity allowed us to excavate some of its foundation trenches completely. When *in situ* on the alluvial terrace the pebbles show a calcite layer on their lower faces. In order to build this structure, some pits were dug into this terrace in which the orthostats were set up and which were then filled in with pebbles coming from the excavation of the trench. The parts of these pebbles with calcite encrustations could obviously also be found on their upper face or sides. Within the fill, flakes of pebbles with sharp edges, small sandstone blocks and numerous snail shells were also found (which were not found on *in situ* on the terrace). The systematic recording of this data has made it possible to identify the division between the undisturbed alluvial terrace and the cut features.

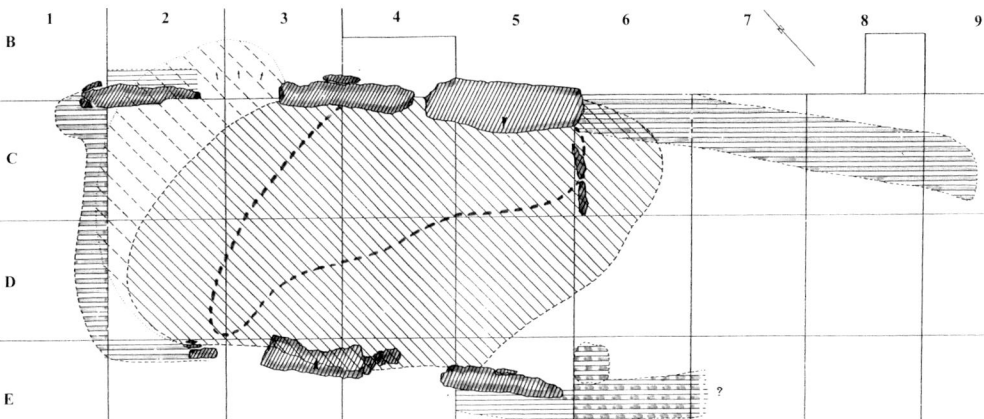

Figure 136. Dolmen of Les Peirières, Villedubert (Aude, France). General plan of the structures.

Widening the excavation allowed the discovery of the foundation trench of the corridor. The original monument can be placed within the architectural typology of dolmens in the region, since it comprises a funerary chamber, anteroom and corridor with a total length of c.10.5 m. and width of 2.2 m. in the chamber (Figure 136). When the structure was modified in the Chalcolithic, not only were the covering slabs removed and the orthostats of the chamber broken up, but the slabs in the corridor and anteroom were pulled up, creating empty spaces in the axial part of the foundation trench. These were filled with the remains derived from cleaning the chamber, including human bones and objects of Neolithic date removed to make room for the slabs. The area of the entrance has entirely disappeared.

Among the bones found in the voids left by the removal of the orthostats were part of three vertebrae and two ribs still in anatomical connection and a middle phalanx of a child's hand. The base of this phalanx had not yet fused (growth cartilage was therefore present at this point when this individual died) and was found still connected with the diaphysis. The transformation of the dolmen therefore happened when some corpses were decomposing and organic matter still survived. Only a short time had elapsed (a few months at most) between the last Neolithic deposit in the dolmen chamber and the architectural change made in the Chalcolithic, with no phases of abandonment or interruption in use.

The funerary layer at the base of the structure lay on an alluvial pebble terrace. Some of them show a concentric alteration that post-dates their formation under the action of the river (Figure 137). The biggest pebbles have been altered in their upper part, whereas the smallest ones have been across their entire surface. On the surfaces of cracks in these stones a mineral deposit has also formed. This is hydroxyapatite, a calcium phosphate, which is also the mineral constituent of human bone. Its formation is due to the union between phosphoric acid produced by the decomposition of corpses

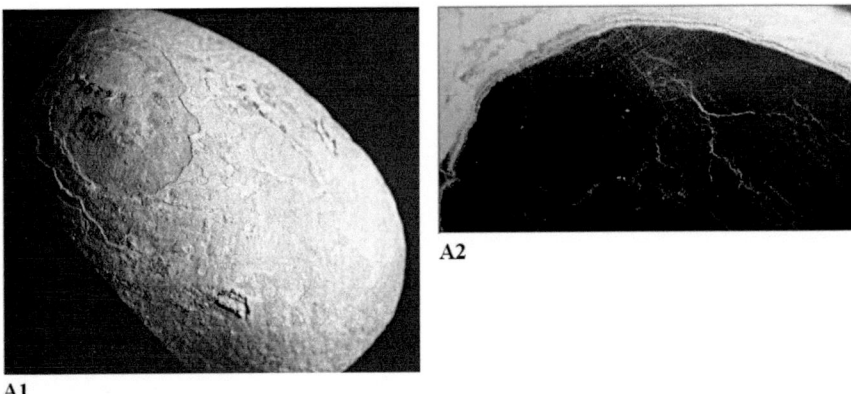

Figure 137. Dolmen of Les Peirières, Villedubert (Aude, France). Limestone pebble from the river terrace altered by the decomposition fluids of the corpses. Illustration by F. Bechtel, N. Platel, and C. Raffaillac.

and the calcium in the limestone pebbles (the presence of phosphoric acid is linked to decomposition fluids). This chemical reaction is characteristic of primary deposits. From the discovery of further altered pebbles inside the anteroom and in the corridor of the original monument we can infer that the corpses were first laid there and were brought into the chamber when decomposition was advanced.

These observations highlight what might be directions for research in funerary archaeology today. To show the primary character of a burial, we first mentioned anatomical connections, underlining that these must concern joints that break down more rapidly. We then referred to the information that insectivorous animals preying on necrophagous insects can provide, as well as predators on worms, especially the *testacella*, a particular type of carnivorous snail that usually lays calcified eggs which are often found during burial excavations. Finally, we drew attention to the chemical reactions that can be produced between the products of decomposition of the body and mineral elements of the geological substratum. In this perspective it is obvious how much our research must be open to interdisciplinarity. The aim is, and must always be, the analysis of human behaviour in relation to death, the reconstruction of burial structures and their history. The means for arriving at this are those of traditional archaeology, as well as anthropology, biology, geology, physics and organic chemistry. However the direction that we follow is archaeological and, because of this, the analysis becomes part of historical reflection.

Lecture 13

Cremation

By cremation or incineration we mean the treatment of corpses with fire. To carry out this process it is necessary to use an external source of heat, a fire, in the immediate vicinity of the body, for example underneath it. The significant increase in temperature causes the corpse to lose water and the cephalo-rachidian liquid in the cranium, around the brain, to boil. In order to avoid the explosion of the cranium, many populations which practise open air cremation split it with an instrument, for example a stick, to allow the gases to escape.

At a certain stage the subject begins spontaneous combustion (*i.e.* the process in which organic matter burns by itself). Eventually large fragments of bones are produced which can be reduced to powder to obtain ash. By pouring cold water on the combustion products thermal shock can produce small fragments or the bones can be broken down mechanically, as in present-day crematoria.

13.1 Secondary cremation deposits

In most cases cremation burials are secondary deposits. In general there is a structure on which the combustion takes place, for example a pyre, and the bones are later recovered and deposited in a container which is eventually placed in the final tomb. There are therefore usually two stages in the funerary process and the deposit can be considered as secondary.

It is relatively rare to be able to study both the remains of the pyre *in situ* and the contents of the cinerary urn (or more generally the container of the secondary deposit). This happens only when the tomb is found in the immediate vicinity of the cremation area. However at least part of the residue of burning is quite frequently placed in the structure destined to house the secondary deposit. In tomb 16 in the Roman cemetery at Classe, near Ravenna, a pit was excavated in the sand that in its deepest part contained a charcoal-rich layer with burnt material, including human bones, coins and fragments of glass and ceramic balsamaria, on which the urn had been laid, hermetically sealed by a lid. This was protected by an amphora that had been cut at the neck and turned upside down like a bell (Figure 138). It should obviously be checked that all the bones belong to the same individual: in this case from Classe a right lateral cuneiform and the base of a fifth left metatarsal could be restored, in both cases using a fragment contained in the urn and another coming from the material thrown into the pit (Figure 139). Sometimes the two different groups provide us with bones belonging to two different individuals (for example in tomb 50 in the same cemetery at Classe).

Figure 138. The cemetery at Classe, Ravenna (Italy), Podere Minghetti sector, tomb 16. Excavation programme by M. G. Maioli, J. Ortalli, and J. Scheid. Study by H. Duday.

13.2 Anthropological parameters in cremation burials (Duday *et al*. 2000)

The examples given above show that reasoning must be based above all on the most precise identification possible of skeletal remains. It cannot be expected to find by chance all the fragments that are to be assembled (it is as if an archaeologist tried to glue together sherds from a site without first selecting them on the basis of fabric, form, decoration *etc*). The identification is obviously easier if the fragments are large. Cremation causes some deformation and cracking in particular that make the bones extremely fragile. They must be handled with care (one of the worst things we can do is to throw the contents of the urn in a sieve and clean everything under a tap!) and it is highly recommended that the laboratory excavation be done by an anthropologist. It is important to have an adequate anthropological training since the study of cremations requires a particular specialization. The bones must be identified as they are extracted from the urn; otherwise there is a risk of breaking the fragments and making subsequent classification impossible.

The first stage consists of selecting the bones and fragments, distinguishing human from animal. It is common to find the remains of animals burnt on the pyre. Worked bone elements must also be detected, *i.e.* the décor of funerary beds or small boxes or toilet objects made of bone or ivory.

The number of individuals is then estimated. Generally these are individual burials, but it is not rare to find two or more bodies deposited together. These can be distinguished by detecting duplication among the bones, and here again the determination of the anatomical origin of the fragments plays a key role, especially in

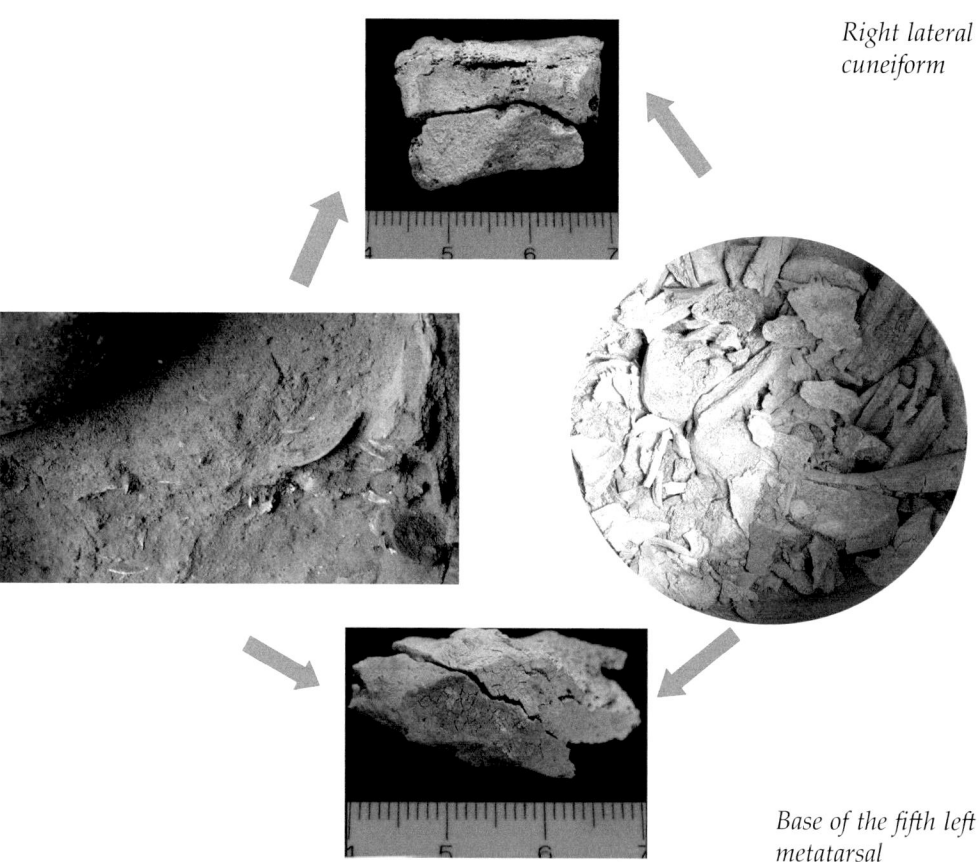

Figure 139. The cemetery at Classe, Ravenna (Italy), Podere Minghetti sector, tomb 16. Reassembly of human bone fragments from the urn with those deposited in the pit. Illustration by H. Duday.

relation to the side of the body from which they derive. If, for example, two mandibular condyles are present, they may belong to a single individual, but if there are two left mandibular condyles then these obviously belong to two different individuals.

Similarly, age incompatibility may be noted, if, for example, a child vertebra and adult femur are found in the same burial, although it is necessary to be attentive to the different degrees of maturing in bones. An adolescent or young adult may have at the same time both fused secondary ossification centres (as in adults) and others where the growth of cartilage is still present (the medial epiphysis of the clavicle may still have its immature aspect until the age of 30). Finally the total mass of burnt bones may also provide useful information. From personal experience I do not remember any individual cremation burial in which this parameter is higher than 2300 grams. This is true if the bones have been accurately cleaned (the earth must also be removed from the medullary canal of the diaphysis), but this operation must be carried out carefully. It is better to have large fragments with some earth rather than perfectly cleaned small flakes (cleaning in an ultrasonic tank, which is often advised, produces catastrophic results from this point of view).

Where the remains belong to more than one individual, it is necessary to understand whether these have been buried together intentionally or whether it is accidental. If the pyre is always built in the same place, some remains of an individual might have been left behind and have been placed in an urn with those of an individual who was later burnt in the same place. The answer is determined by the representation of each individual: if both are represented by a significant quantity of fragments (several instances of duplication or incompatibility, too high a mass of bones), it is evidently a double burial. If there is instead only one indicator of the presence of two individuals, we must be more prudent in our interpretation. Here, the comparison with the archaeological material is of particular importance. In the Peyrou cemetery at Agde (Duday 1989), almost all the tombs for which the anthropological analysis indicated the presence of two individuals also revealed an anomaly in the grave goods (a double set of offerings, in particular a double set of ceramics, as well as the presence of both 'female' and 'male' objects).

Once the presence of two individuals has been established it is necessary to examine the relative chronology of deposits. We shall take as a first example tomb 15 from enclosure 23 at the Porta Nocera cemetery in Pompeii. The container for the burnt bones was an amphora cut at its shoulder and base. The amphora was placed upside down in a relatively deep pit and through its base the remains of the burnt corpse of a 15–20 year old man were inserted with a burnt bronze coin. Some burnt bone fragments of the same individual were thrown into the fill of the pit, with burnt fragments of a lamp and a glass unguent vessel. The hole was then closed with the base of another amphora. Later, this plug was removed in order to deposit the remains of a second person inside the amphora (an adult male whose skeleton showed several degenerative lesions) with a coin of Nero and some burnt fragments of a lamp. The bones of the two corpses touched without mixing. The boundary between the two levels is dotted with little white splinters, tiny fragments of spongy bone that have slipped through the mass of bone belonging to the upper individual and come to rest above the bones of the young woman which were already covered with earth (Figure 140). The two deposits had obviously been placed at different times; unlike other cremation tombs in the enclosure, it must have been planned to re-use this structure.

In other cases it is clear that the remains of the two deceased were placed simultaneously in the container. In a tomb of the archaic Greek necropolis at Megara Hyblaea, for example, a Laconian crater of the 6th century BC contained *c.* 3200g of burnt bones belonging to a man and an old woman. A photograph taken at the time of discovery shows bones that undoubtedly derive from two different individuals (including large fragments of the coxal bone and femoral heads). It is possible that the two corpses were burnt at the same time, but contrary to what was said about double inhumation burials, in this case simultaneity of deposit does not necessarily imply simultaneity of death. It is possible that the man died and was cremated first, his bones being preserved in a temporary

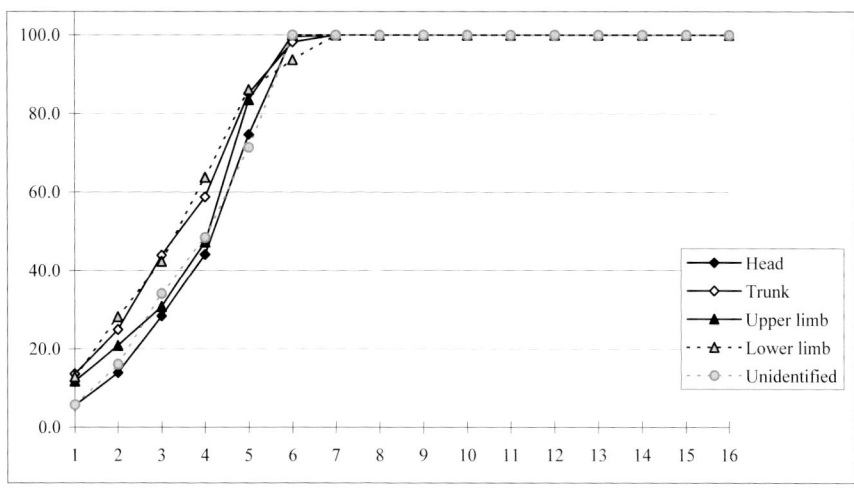

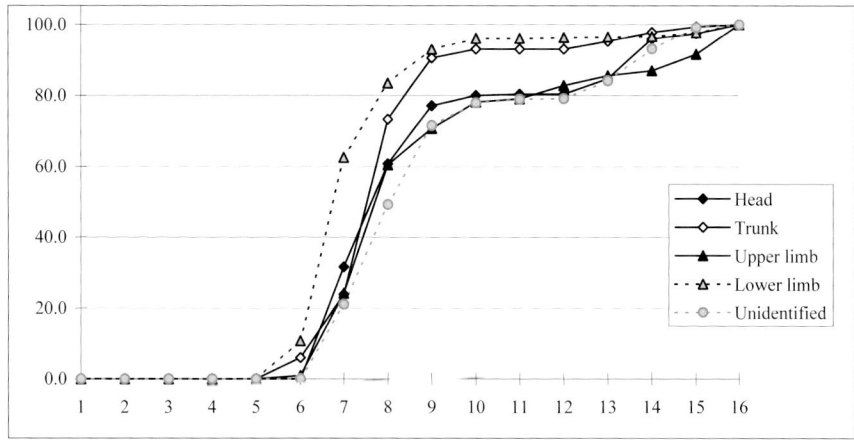

Figure 140. The cemetery of Porta Nocera in Pompeii. Enclosure 23, tomb 15. Cumulative frequency diagrams (by percentage) of the distribution by anatomical area of the remains of a young 'man' (A) and an older adult man (B) at the different stages of excavation of the cinerary container from 1 (upper part of the fill) to 16 (the bottom of the amphora). Where the two deposits meet (phases 6 and 7) there are many very small bone particles. Excavation programme by W. van Andringa and S. Lepetz. Study by H. Duday and D. Joly.

container which were only subsequently mixed with those of the woman who died later. The burning does not allow us to observe phenomena related to decomposition of the corpse and derive chronological information from this.

Temperature is a fundamental problem we face when studying cremation burials. In a laboratory, using the methodology of physics, it is possible to trace the heat reached when the bones were burnt. For simplicity and cost, a scale of chromatic variation is often used (Bonucci and Graziani 1975). Bones pass from white-yellow to brown, intense black, blue, grey-blue, grey, grey-white and white. They increase in density and at the final stage have a 'metallic' resonance. It seems that the same effect can be obtained both by quickly reaching a high temperature and by slower burning at a lower temperature. It is therefore better to speak of more or less intense rather than high or low temperature combustion.

We should also examine whether the degree of cremation was homogeneous or heterogeneous. The anthropologist must analyze how the parts of the skeleton have burnt to see whether there is an anatomical logic in this, in order to understand the way in which the cremation was conducted.

13.3. Quantifying the human remains in the tomb

First it is important to study the total mass of burnt bones because this is an important parameter from an archaeological point of view. In protohistoric cemeteries in the south of France, it has been possible to demonstrate a statistically significant variation in the weight of burnt bones in the tombs of adults and adolescents during the different phases of the first Iron Age that reflects a change in funerary behaviour.

The representation of the different parts of the body must then be analysed to establish if one anatomical region (for example the head) has been privileged or if there is a constant ratio in the collection of bones from different parts of the body. Study of the literature shows that this quantification has been based on varying parameters. Some authors have used weight, others the number of bone fragments while the percentages have been calculated both as a proportion of the remains that have been identified and of the total human remains in the container. Figure 141 shows the results obtained for the same tomb using these four methods: the difference is obvious.

If percentages are calculated from the identified remains there is a systematic overestimation of the anatomical regions that are easily recognizable, such as the head (cranium, mandible and teeth) and trunk. The spongy material of the vertebrae is very characteristic, especially if part of the cortex of the vertebral body is preserved. The ribs are easily identified from the specific arrangement of the trabeculae in the spongy bone. The representation of the thorax generally seems too high, if the relationship is used between the number of these fragments and the total identified (even the smallest fragments of ribs can be identified), but this overestimation tends to diminish when weight is considered. This often results in a discernable drop in the proportion accounted for by this area, because the spongy fraction of the vertebrae comprises many very small particles.

If the number of fragments by anatomical region is considered in relation to the total number of fragments in the deposit (identified or not), the proportion of those

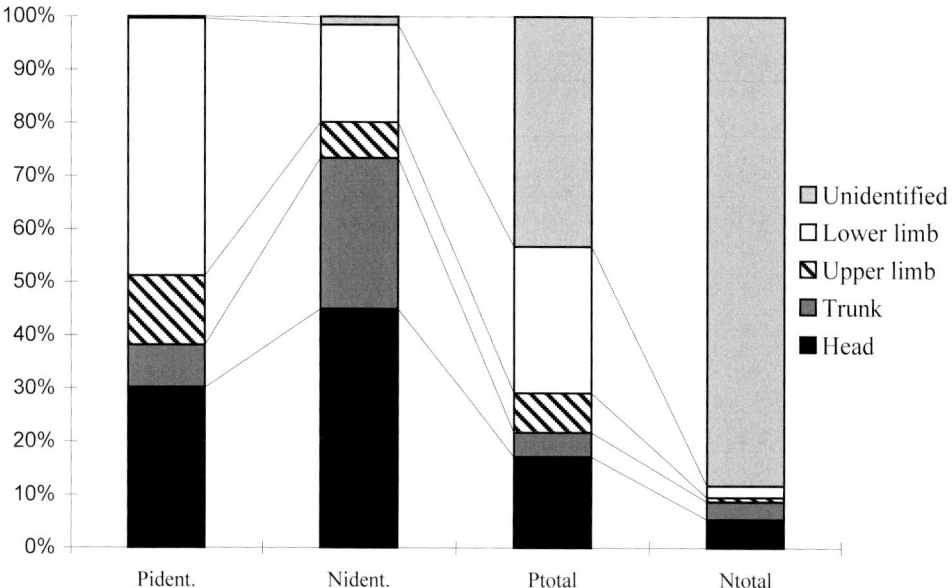

Figure 141. The cemetery at Classe, Ravenna (Italy), Podere Minghetti sector, tomb 4. Representation of different anatomical regions by different quantification methods: Pident = percentage of weight of bone identified by anatomical area only; Nident = percentage of number of fragments of bone identified by anatomical area only; Ptotal = percentage of weight of all bone; Ntotal = percentage of number of all fragments. Study by H. Duday.

of unknown origin is considerable because even the smallest flakes can be considered (which raises the question of the smallest mesh to be used in sieving: many get rid of fragments smaller than 2mm).

In practice the preferred method is to compare the mass of fragments by anatomical region to the total mass of the skeletal remains (animal remains must be previously separated). It is possible then to compare the results with reference values, for example those suggested by Krogmann from data provided by Lowrance and Latimer (meaningful data for child skeletons are not yet available). We can investigate the way in which different anatomical regions are found within the urn. This investigation requires that the urn be excavated as a micro-site, gradually removing layers of a constant thickness (1.5–three cm). If the urn is filled with soil, a small *sondage* can be used to identify the upper level of the mass of skeletal material and to understand the dynamics of the fill after the disappearance of a putative lid. The proportion of bones is calculated for each layer (the weight of fragments by anatomical region compared to the weight of all fragments collected at each stage of the micro-excavation). The distribution of the bones is sometimes random, but it is also possible to find anatomical order respected (Figure 142). For example, the elements of the head can be found mainly in the upper

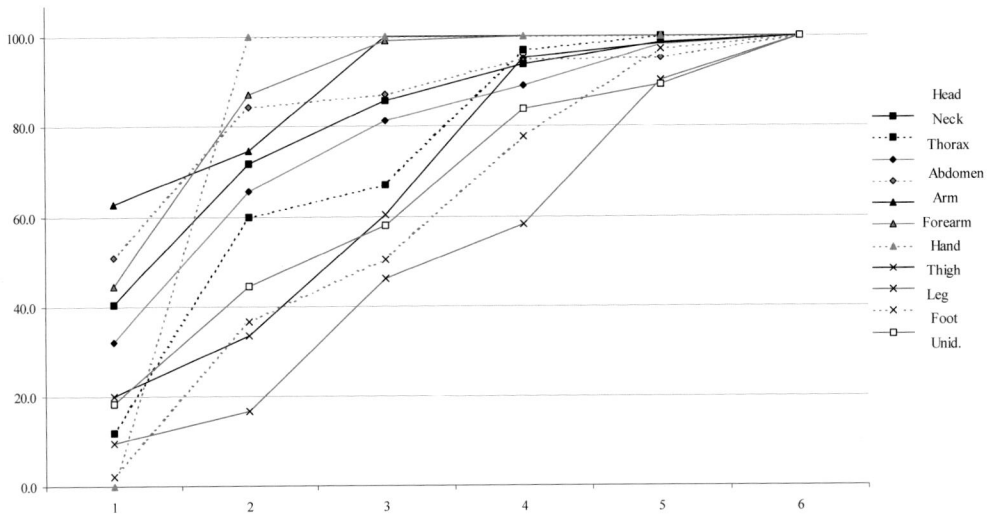

Figure 142. The cemetery at Classe, Ravenna (Italy), Podere Minghetti sector, tomb 16. Cumulative frequency diagram (by percentage) showing the distribution of different anatomical regions in successive excavation levels (numbered 1 to 6, proceeding from the top to the base of the fill). Study by H. Duday.

levels, those of the trunk and upper limbs in the middle, and those of the lower limbs at the bottom of the urn (as if the deceased was 'standing' within it).

The impression is thus given that collecting at the cremation area began at the feet and finished with the head (or the other way round in cases where another container has been used before placing the bones in the urn). It is also possible to infer whether the cremation was 'assisted', *i.e.* if those officiating used sticks, for example, to push the outer parts of the body towards the middle of the pyre where the fire is more intense. When the flames are extinguished, the bone fragments are mixed and anatomical logic will not be respected in their collection.

13.4. Primary cremation deposits

There are also primary cremation deposits. This type of deposit is usually called a *bustum*, but it would be more logical to speak of a 'pyre tomb' or 'pit tomb', if it has been dug out. We shall give a few examples. The first is from Caramany, in the eastern Pyrenees, dating to the early phase of the middle Neolithic. Here there were circular funerary structures with a radius of seven metres, next to which were circles marked by standing stones which often contained stone containers with individual inhumations. Secondary cremation deposits were also identified, for example an individual placed in a perishable container, a bag made of organic material.

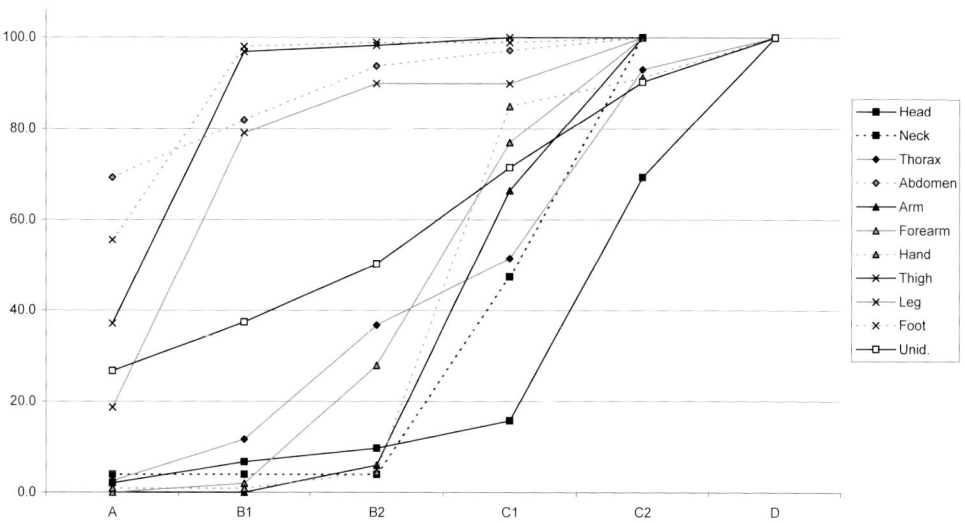

Figure 143. The cemetery at Classe, Ravenna (Italy), Podere Minghetti sector, tomb 7. Cumulative frequency diagram (by percentage) showing the distribution of anatomical regions by excavation sector. The pit was divided into four longitudinal strips from D (west) to A (east), which were each divided into northern and southern halves. Illustration by V. Bel and H. Duday.

One of the stone circles delimits the area where cremation took place, within which were identified burnt bones whose arrangement corresponds to that of an individual laid on his left side in a contracted position. It is a primary deposit with the bones *in situ* on the combustion structure, later covered without being collected up. The corpse was placed on the pyre while still fresh, the fire accelerated decomposition and the bones were not recovered. There was only one stage in the funeral and this is therefore a primary cremation deposit.

In the Roman cemetery at Classe primary cremation deposits were also found. These pits are regularly placed, parallel, equidistant and measure from 0.8 to one m. long. As well as archaeological and organic material such as walnuts or cones, they also contained burnt human bones in anatomical order (Figure 143). The pit was situated beneath the pyre and received the remains as they gradually fell into it.

In the Roman cemetery at Pupput, in Tunisia, there are similar structures, but these contained the remains of individuals buried by different methods, inhumation as well as secondary and primary cremation deposits. Some tombs in particular contained individuals whose bodies were burnt very intensely and evenly but which were still found in anatomical connection. This very close following of anatomical logic allows us to suppose that cremation took place inside some kind of combustion structure like a charcoal pile.

Conclusions and perspectives

'Archaeothanatology' is an essential part of the archaeological analysis of funerary complexes, both for the study of burial practices and for establishing the internal chronology of deposition. It seems today to be one of the most promising approaches in the 'archaeology of death'. In developing its own methods and perspectives, it must specify the nature of the observations necessary to solve the problems raised by the interpretation of the funerary contexts that are discovered. Fieldwork strategies, in particular for rescue excavation, should not be established without taking account of this.

As a biological discipline, the particular status of which derives from the fact that it is deprived of an experimental basis, 'archaeothanatology' is obliged to establish its foundations at the same time as it contributes to the understanding of funerary complexes. Fieldwork replaces laboratory study and excavation replaces experimentation. It is essential that archaeologists who direct excavations are aware of their responsibility. An element that might have little interest for the understanding of the individual site might be of fundamental importance for the global understanding of the decomposition process and thus for making sense of other funerary deposits. The observations previously discussed from the sites of Lattes and Saint-Rémi-la-Calonne give, in my opinion, particularly meaningful examples of this 'experimental' archaeology. The use of the term 'experimental' is not really appropriate here (hence the quotation marks), since an experiment proper presupposes that the experimenter can change each of the key parameters involved in the phenomenon under study. Only by changing one parameter at a time and observing the differences in the results can one attempt to understand the whole process. For ethical reasons this type of experimentation, which is generally applicable in biology, is inconceivable in the case of 'archaeothanatology'. We must therefore be able to take advantage of all the opportunities where it is possible to observe anomalies and particularities in the arrangement of bones and to know precisely the conditions and characteristics of the original funerary deposit, either through oral tradition or written texts or through direct observation of evidence that can be clearly observed at the time of excavation (for example the inhumation of corpses in a sitting position, the preservation of perishable containers *etc*.). This clearly shows how sites of recent periods have great importance for establishing our corpus of reference knowledge.

The objectives and methods of this new discipline are fundamentally independent of chronological and cultural divisions. It is through a multiplication of reflections developed on each site that it will refine its analytical methods and widen the scope of its contribution. It is therefore essential to create everywhere a specific category of researchers who are both trained in general archaeological methods and who also possess a developed knowledge of human osteology. Only thus can the understanding of ancient burials make progress: 'l'anthropologie de terrain', or, rather 'archaeothanatology', is still defining its methods and developing the precision of its methodology. However, its systematic application to large funerary contexts is bearing fruit in the publication of its first syntheses, so that this newly born science can truly acquire its full historical dimension. Thanks to a careful and pro-active policy based on the organization of specialist *stages* like that held in Rome in the autumn of 2004, there are now in France about a hundred archaeologists who have acquired the necessary skills, so that for more than 20 years several thousand tombs have been annually excavated and recorded in the way outlined here. These excavation campaigns, often linked to public works including the re-structuring of urban space and the construction of communication routes, relate mainly to medieval and modern cemeteries: whatever many prehistorians might say, the understanding of Palaeolithic burials depends in large part on scientific progress achieved by emergency excavations on ancient, medieval, and modern sites.

Appendix: Anatomical terminology

Cephalic skeleton (skull)	
	Cranium
	Mandible
	Hyoid
Vertebral column	
	Cervical vertebrae (seven, including atlas (C1) and axis (C2))
	Thoracic vertebrae (12)
	Lumbar vertebrae (5)
	Sacrum
	Coccyx
Rib cage	
	Ribs
	Sternum (including the manubrium)
Upper limbs	
	Scapula
	Humerus
	Radius
	Ulna
	Carpals (scaphoid, lunate, triquetral, pisiform, trapezium, trapezoid, capitate and hamate bones)
	Metacarpals
	Phalanges (proximal, medial and distal phalanges)
Lower limbs	
	Coxal or innominate bones (including ilium, ischium and pubis)
	Femur
	Patella
	Tibia
	Fibula
	Tarsals (calcaneus, talus, navicular, medial, intermediate and lateral cuneiforms, cuboid bone)
	Metatarsals
	Sesamoids
	Phalanges (proximal, medial and distal phalanges) (hallux = 'big toe')

Bibliography

Adam, F., Boura, F. and Duday, H. (1993) La fouille de Saint-Rémi-la-Calonne: une opération d'archéologie funéraire expérimentale, ou l'anthropologie de terrain en quête de ses références. *Les Nouvelles de l'Archéologie* 48/49, 59–61.

André, J. (1986) Contribution de la malacologie à l'étude des sépultures, un exemple: le dolmen des Peirières à Villedubert. In H. Duday and C. Masset (eds), *Anthropologie physique et archéologie,* 289–295. Paris, Editions du CNRS.

Bass, W. M. (1984) Time Interval since Death: A Difficult Decision. In A. T. Rathbun and J. E. Buikstra (eds) *Human identification: Case Studies in Forensic Anthropology,* 136–142, Springfield, C. C. Thomas.

Bass, W. M. (1997) Outdoor Composition Rates in Tennessee. In W.D. Haglund and M.H. Sorg (eds) *Forensic Taphonomy, the Postmortem Fate of Human Remains,* 181–186. CRC Press, Boca Raton, Florida.

Binder, D., Brocher, J.-E., Duday, H., Helmer, D., Marinval, P., Thiebault, S. and Wattez, J. (1993) L'abri Pendimoun (Castellar, Alpe-Maritimes, France): nouvelles données sur le complexe culturel de la céramique imprimée méditerranéenne dans son contexte stratigraphique. *Gallia Préhistoire* 35, 177–251.

Bonucci, E. and Graziani, G. (1975) Comparative Thermogravimetric, X-ray Diffraction and Electron Microscope Investigations of Burnt Bones from Recent, Ancient and Prehistoric Ages. *Accademia Nazionale dei Lincei,* Acta Series 8, 59(5), 518–533.

Boulestin, B. and Duday, H. (2005) Ethnologie et archéologie de la mort: de l'illusion des références à l'emploi d'un vocabulaire. In C. Mordant and G. Depierre (eds) *Les pratiques funéraires à l'Age du Bronze en France* (Proceedings of the round table organized at Sens-en-Bourgogne (Yonne) by the Société Archéologique de Sens, 10–12 June, 1998), 17–35. Paris, Editions du Comité des Travaux Historiques et Scientifiques.

Brochier, J.-E. (1987) Le sédiment jaune de l'Aven de la Boucle à Corconne (Gard). In H. Duday and C. Masset (eds) *Anthropologie physique et archéologie,* 105–108. Paris, Editions du CNRS.

Castex, D. and Drancourt, M. (2005) D'un site funéraire à la détection d'une crise épidémique. Identités biologiques et patrimoine génétique. (Actes du colloque "Epidémies et Sociétés dan le Monde Occidental XIe–XXIe s.", Paris, 12 June 2005). *Revue Sociologie Santé.* Coll. "Les Etudes Hospitalières" 22, 190–209.

Colmera, A. 1980. Les grottes sépulcrales préhistoriques murées en Languedoc oriental. In J. Guilaine (ed.) *Le Groupe de Vèraza et la fin des temps néolithiques dans le Sud de la France e la Catalogne,* 264–265. Paris, Editions du CNRS.

Dedet, B., Duday, H. and Tillier, A.-M. (1991) Inhumation de fœtus, nouveau-nés et nourrissons dans les habitats protohistoriques du Languedoc: l'exemple de Gailhan. *Gallia* 48, 59–108.

Drancourt, M., Roux, V., La-Vu, D., Tran-Hung, L., Castex, D., Chenal-Francisque, V., Ogata, H., Fournier, P.-E., Crubézy, E. and Raoult, D. (2004) Genotyping, Orientalis-like *Yersina pestis* and Plague Pandemics. *Emerging Infectious Disease* 10(9), 1585–1592.

Duday, H. (1979) Les sépultures chasséennes de Saint-Michel-du-Touch (Haute-Garonne) : étude anthropologique. *Bulletin de la Société Préhistorique Française* 76, 404–407.

Duday, H. (1987a) Organisation et fonctionnement d'une sépulture collective néolithique:

l'Aven de la Boucle à Corconne (Gard). In H. Duday and C. Masset (eds) *Anthropologie physique et archéologie*, 89–104. Paris, Editions du CNRS.

Duday, H. (1987b) Contribution des observations ostéologiques à la chronologie interne des sépultures collectives. In H. Duday and C. Masset (eds), *Anthropologie physique et archéologie*, 51–59. Paris, Editions du CNRS.

Duday, H. (1989) La nécropole du Peyrou à Agde (Hérault). Etude anthropologique. In A. Nickels, G. Marchand and M. Schwaller (eds), *Agde, la nécropole du Premier Âge du Fer*, 459–472. Paris, Revue archéologique de Narbonnaise, Supplément 19.

Duday, H. (2005) L'Archéothanatologie ou l'Archéologie de la Mort. In O. Dutour, J.-J. and B. Vandermeersch (eds) *Objects et Méthodes en Paléoanthropologie*, 153–215. Paris, Comité des Travaux Historiques et Scientifiques.

Duday, H., Depierre, G. and Janin, T. (2000) Validation des paramètres de quantification, protocoles et stratégies dans l'étude anthropologique des sépultures secondaires à incinération. L'exemple des nécropoles protohistoriques du Midi de la France. In B. Dedet et al. (eds) *Archéologie de la Mort, Archéologie de la Tombe au Premier Âge du Fer*, 7–29. Lattes, Monographies d'Archéologie Méditerranéenne, no. 5.

Duday, H., Laubenheimer F. and Tillier A.-M. (1995) *Sallèles-d'Aude: nouveau-nés et nourrissons chez les potiers gallo-romains*. Besançon, Centre de recherches d'histoire ancienne, Université de Besançon.

Duday, H., Lambach, F. and Plouin, S. (1990) Contribution de l'anthropologie de terrain à l'interprétation architecturale d'un ensemble funéraire: la tombe 12 du tumulus 2A Nordhouse (Bas-Rhin). *Les Nouvelles de l'Archéologie* 40, 15–18.

Eleure, C., Drilhon, F., Duday, H. and Duval, A. R. (1989) L'or et l'argent de la tombe de Vix. *Bulletin de la Société Préhistorique Française* 86 (1), 10–32.

Guillon, M., Sellier, P., Pecqueur, L., Creveuil, S. and Durand, R. (2001) La mort antique, médiévale et moderne en Île-de-France. In M. Tabeaud, (ed.) *La mort en Île-de-France*, 84–100. Paris, Publications de la Sorbonne.

Kapandji, I. A. (1975) *Physiologie articulaire. Schémas commentés de mécanique humaine*. Vol. 3: *tronc et rachis*. Paris, Maloine.

Large, J.-M., Birocheau, P., Cros J.-P. and Duday, H. (2004) *Les Châtelliers du Vieil-Auzay: une archéologie d'un site exceptionnel de la préhistoire récente*. La Roche-sur-Yon, Groupe Vendéen d'Études Préhistoriques.

Leclerc, J. (1990) La notion de sépulture. *Bulletins et mémoires de la Société d'anthropologie de Paris*, n. s. 2 (3–4), 13–18.

Leclerc. J. and Tarrete, J. (1988) Sépulture. In A. Leroi-Gourhan (ed.) *Dictionaire del la Préhistoire*, 963–964. Paris, Presse Universitaires de France

Le Mort, F. and Duday, H. 1987. Traces de décharnement sur un humérus dysmorphique néolithique. *Bulletins et Mémoires de la Société d'Anthropologie de Paris* 4 (Series XIV.1), 17–24.

Saunders, S. R. (1978) *The Development and Distribution of Discontinuous Morphological Variation of the Human Infracranial Skeleton*. Archaeological Survey of Canada, 81. Ottawa, National Museums of Canada

Ubelaker, D. H. (1974) *Reconstruction of Demographic Profiles from Ossuary Skeletal Samples: A Case Study from the Tidewater Potomac*. Smithsonian Contributions to Anthropology no. 18, Smithsonian Institution Press.

Vigneron, E. (1985) *Recherches sur l'histoire des attitudes devant la mort en Polynésie Française*. Toulouse, Unpublished Ph.D. dissertation, École des Hautes Etudes en Sciénces Sociales.

Villena i Mota, N. (1997) *Hiérarchie et fiabilité des liasons ostéologiques (par symétrie et par contiguïté articulaire) dans l'étude des sépultures anciennes*. Unpublished Ph.D. Dissertation, University of Bordeaux 1.

Villena i Mota, N., Duday, H. and Houët, F. (1996) Hiérarchie et fiabilité des liasons ostéologiques par symétrie et contiguïté articulaire dan l'étude des sépultures anciennes. *Bulletins et Mémoires de la Société d'Anthropologie de Paris* 8 (3–4), 373–384.